Beyond RISC!

Reprinted by permission: Rich Tennant

B E Y O N D
RISC!

**An
Essential
Guide To
Hewlett-Packard
Precision Architecture.**

EDITOR   Wayne E. Holt

AUTHORS   Steven M. Cooper
                  Jason M. Goertz
                  Scott E. Levine
                  Joanna L. Mosher
                  Stanley R. Sieler, Jr.
                  Jacques Van Damme

Software Research Northwest, Inc.

First printing   January, 1988
Second printing March, 1988

This book was typeset in Century Schoolbook, Bauer Bodini, and Letter Gothic typefaces. Original pages were formatted using the LARC Laser Package and were printed on a LaserJet Series II operating on an HP 3000 Series 950 executing in Native Mode SPLash! under MPE XL. While the authors have endeavored to keep the information in this book accurate and up-to-date, the publisher and authors make NO WARRANTY, EXPRESS OR IMPLIED, ABOUT THE ACCURACY OF THIS INFORMATION AND THE PERFORMANCE OF ANY PRODUCT MENTIONED HEREIN. The publisher and authors are not liable for any loss of data, damage to databases or software, or for incidental or consequential damages in connection with the furnishing, performance, or use of this material.

ALLBASE, IMAGE, MPE V & MPE XL, TurboIMAGE, and VPLUS are all products of Hewlett-Packard
IBM is a registered trademark of International Business Machines Corporation
DECserver, PDP, and VAX are trademarks of Digital Equipment Corporation
UNIX is a trademark of A.T.&T. Bell Laboratories
SPLash! is a trademark of Software Research Northwest, Inc.

Software Research Northwest, Inc. 17710-100th Avenue SW, Vashon Island, WA 98070

iv

ACKNOWLEDGEMENTS

Cover Photography	Bruce Wilson Photography Seattle, WA
Epilogue	Gail Terzi
Editorial Assistance	Jane Sallis and Associates
Technical Review	Dennis Mitrzyk Donald Nagle
Additional Material	Joseph Brothers Gary Todoroff
Production Management	*Elgin Syferd:* Bob Frause Mary Gogulski Kristi Rowland Terri Small Melissa Stalsberg
Copy Editing & Proofreading	Phyllis Kaiden Kathy Kreps
Typesetting & Layout	Mark Wysoski Tony Krebs Nancy Bayer
Typesetting Software	LARC Laser Package Martin Gorfinkel LARC Computing, Los Altos, CA
Printing	R. R. Donnelley & Sons Company

In the beginning, it must be conceived. . .
even in the face of opposition and expert opinion.

And then it must be designed. . .

And then it must be built. . .

But if it is to succeed, it must also be *tested*.

It is to the men and women of
the Systems Engineering Lab of HP ITG,
and especially
to the folks in the SEA Reliability Project,
that this book is dedicated.

And, oh yes, to the true soldiers
of the RISC revolution:
Gozer, KeyMaster, GateKeeper, *et. al.*
who obligingly die a thousand deaths
so that we may learn.

Table of Contents

Figures

Introduction

In November, 1986 the Hewlett-Packard Company shipped its first product based on Reduced Instruction Set Computing, the HP 9000 800 Series computer. It was not the first RISC computer in the marketplace, but it was the largest. It was followed by an even larger HP 9000, and an MPE version called the HP 3000 900 Series. Above all else, Hewlett-Packard weighed the risks and boldly stepped forward into the future by making the largest commitment of any computer vendor to this new, relatively unproven computing methodology.

The pundits noted that while everything looked good in the wind tunnel, the move by HP was akin to jumping off the cliff with an untested glider. The rebuttal to the attitude of the industry is the evidence of the results -- the new architecture is out the door *and it works!*

Yet HP's new venture is more than just RISC. If the only strategy change involved reducing the size of the instruction set, it is clear that RISC would not have been successful. The real magic behind the new machines involves new hardware technologies, new software optimization algorithms, and a host of innovative changes in operating system principles that go beyond RISC. Taken together, this total new approach is called Hewlett-Packard Precision Architecture, or HPPA.

The purpose of this book is to provide you with a guide to all of the essentials necessary to understand the new architecture. As a guide, the book does not try to provide everything you need to know -- rather, we have attempted to create a balanced presentation of the issues and techniques that are essential to HPPA.

The purpose of this **Introduction** is to provide you with a guided tour of the book -- to call your attention to how it has been arranged and to warn you of a few pitfalls along the way.

The book was designed with more than one audience in mind. At a basic level, much of the material was aimed at the decision makers in an organization. Where possible, every chapter has non-technical descriptions of the subject being examined. It was expected that the book would also have a technical audience, and that certain subjects could not be discussed without a very technical approach. Many chapters are designed for systems programmers with a solid knowledge of how MPE V works. The book is thus an amalgam of simple explanations and technical detail, a combination which may cause some consternation among both audiences.

Section I covers important background material about Hewlett-Packard and the HP 3000. It is not technical, and is recommended for all readers. Chapter 1 gives a brief history of Hewlett-Packard, noting several important milestones in the development of the company. Chapter 2 discusses the history of the HP 3000 family, and the decision to continue the family under the new architecture -- HPPA.

Section II has four chapters that address the essentials of HPPA. A solid foundation is laid regarding the development of RISC, ranging from a discussion of the history of computing methods to a technical discussion of how HPPA is different from other approaches. Chapter 3 is really a short course in the history of computing methods. It is an appropriate review for all readers, and sets the stage for very technical discussions. It is followed by an examination of the 'Classic 3000', the MPE V-based HP 3000 computer, in Chapter 4.

In Chapter 5, RISC and HPPA are examined in technical detail. Many of the features of the architecture are covered, including data types, registers, addressing, pipelining, and mapped I/O. The discussion continues in Chapter 6 where software conventions are examined, along with the HPPA approach to compilers.

Section III is devoted to examining the implementation of HPPA. The components of the new computers are discussed, including the hardware (Chapter 7), the operating system (Chapter 8), and the data communications methods (Chapter 9). While some of the material is technical, the section has useful information for all readers.

Section IV begins the technical review of MPE XL. It has information about the file system of interest to the technician, and will be difficult for a non-technician to absorb. Chapter 10 examines the directory structures of both MPE V and MPE XL. Chapter 11 discusses the concept and application of "mapped files", a new file construct under HPPA. Chapter 12 closes the section with a brief, non-technical discussion of file access differences between MPE V and MPE XL.

Section V contains a non-technical review of HP data base systems, coupled with a detailed look at TurboIMAGE and HP SQL. Chapter 13 reviews the history of HP's data base structures, as well as the new generation of products. An example problem is illustrated and used for comparison in both Chapter 14 (for TurboIMAGE) and Chapter 15 (for HP SQL). While the initial portions of these two chapters are fairly general, the balance of the material is quite technical.

Section VI covers the HPPA approach to languages. While technical, it is appropriate reading for all audiences. Chapter 16 discusses compiler features and optimization. In addition, it examines the MPE V Segmenter and contrasts it with the MPE XL Linkedit process. Chapter 17 focuses on the languages themselves, with an emphasis on differences between MPE V and MPE XL.

Section VII discusses migration issues in both a technical and non-technical manner. Chapter 18 reviews the major differences between MPE V and MPE XL and examines the tools that are available to assist in migration. Chapter 19 explores language-related incompatibilites. Chapter 20 contains a step-by-step approach to migration from MPE V to to MPE XL. It also examines the special problems of migration from IBM or DEC to MPE XL.

Appendix A contains a summary of the new Instruction Set, while **Appendix B** discusses the native debug facility. Both are intended to supplement the material presented in the main body of the book.

It may seem unusual that this book is being published outside of Hewlett-Packard, particularly by a small software company located on an island in the middle of the Pacific Northwest's Puget Sound.

For quite a while, the only information available to the public about HPPA was sales literature. Few outside sources had the necessary background to provide the detailed information that the community wanted, and none had authorization to discuss subjects covered by non-disclosure agreements.

Three companies (Software Research Northwest of Vashon Island, Washington, Allegro Consultants of Redwood City, California, and Denkart N.V. of Kontich, Belgium) saw a need and decided to create this book. As consultants to Hewlett-Packard on the new architecture, engineers from SRN, Allegro, & Denkart were working with the new systems on a daily basis, and because of their 'outsiders' perspective, they were in an ideal position to comment on the architecture.

Authorization was obtained from Hewlett-Packard regarding non-disclosure, and the book was written in late 1986 for publication in early 1987.

And, inevitably, the delays crept in . . .

Important changes that rendered certain sections inaccurate occurred on a regular basis through mid-1987. In turn, we continued to rewrite those portions of the book to keep pace with these changes. The decision to publish was a difficult one -- at what point would the information be solid enough?

The answer, of course, is that the information in this book, or any book about any computer, will begin to decay as soon as it is printed! By late 1987, the rate of change of information about HPPA, and especially the MPE XL operating system, at last leveled off, thus encouraging the publication of this book. Of course, you will find that certain details written in the book may vary a bit from newer sources, but we believe that the essentials will continue to be accurate for some time to come.

Today, there *is* more information available from several sources. Hewlett-Packard has started distributing extensive documents about the new architecture, and many of the independent monthly publications within the HP community have begun printing articles from knowledgeable sources outside of HP. Now, little in the book will challenge non-disclosure rules.

Originally, we had planned to subtitle the book *The Comprehensive Guide to Hewlett-Packard Precision Architecture*, but the use of 'The' seemed a bit presumptuous. Having settled on *A Comprehensive Guide* ... as a reasonable substitute, we came to believe less and less that this book, or any book, could be truly comprehensive on the subject of HPPA.

Finally, we took a hard look at how *we* would use such a book. It seemed to embody all of the essentials that anyone would like to find in a single source *before* wading into all of the information that HP provides in a variety of forms -- handbooks, sales guides, manuals, and resource people. Thus, the subtitle became *An Essential Guide to Hewlett-Packard Precision Architecture*, reflecting the idea that the book contains the basic information in a single source.

Beyond RISC! is the product of seven authors, with one author serving as the editor of the book. It is *not* an anthology -- every author participated in the composition of almost every chapter, and several of the topics required the expertise of people outside of the authors' group.

It is our hope that this book is of assistance to you as you examine and evaluate the new architecture. The future is here, in HPPA, and we believe you will not be disappointed in what you find . . .

WEH
November, 1987
Vashon Island, Washington

I

The HP Environment

1

A Brief History
of Hewlett-Packard

Once upon a time, in a garage in Palo Alto ... Those of us who live in the Hewlett-Packard community have heard this story so many times that we could probably recite it from memory. But no book on a major contribution to computation methods could possibly be complete without at least a brief history of this company and how it came to make such an advance.

Bill Hewlett and Dave Packard met during their undergraduate days at Stanford University in the early 1930s. Upon their graduation, receiving their A.B. degrees in 1934, the two considered the idea of going into business for themselves. However, before diving headfirst into the business world, they ran their ideas by Frederick E. Terman, dean of Stanford's electrical engineering department. The dean recommended that they obtain some additional experience before tangling with the business world, and they agreed to do this.

Dave Packard went off to the Vacuum Tube Research Department of General Electric Co. in Schenectady, N.Y., and Bill Hewlett began graduate work at Stanford. Bill went on to the Massachusetts Institute of Technology, but the temperate climate of the San Francisco Bay Area became too much for either to resist. Bill returned to Stanford to begin research for his next degree, while Dave returned to the campus on a research fellowship.

During the next three years, their conviction grew that there was a real and immediate future for a new kind of company that specialized in electronic test instruments. So Dave Packard and his wife moved into a house in Palo Alto, and Bill Hewlett took up residence in the garden cottage behind it. They set up their first laboratory and factory in the small one-car garage located between them. Working in their spare time (both were still in school), they developed a diathermy machine and sold it to the Palo Alto Clinic. Their inventions continued to flow: an electronic device for tuning harmonicas, a foul-indicator for bowling alleys, and a reducing machine which worked by applying an electric shock to the appropriate areas.

As Bill was finishing his thesis on the resistance-tuned oscillator, it seemed to him that he had designed an instrument that was far more reliable and cheaper to manufacture than the oscillators currently on the market. So he and Dave built one and began talking about it at various electronics meetings.

The Instrumentation Era

The resistance-capacity audio oscillator (an electronic instrument used to test sound equipment) found a market. Among their first orders was one from Walt Disney Studios, which wanted eight oscillators (but with a different physical configuration and a different frequency range) to use in a unique sound system that Disney was building for a movie called *Fantasia*. Thus, the company's first product and first 'volume' order came to pass. With this undeniable success and initial capital of $538, they were in business. It was January 1939, and only one more decision needed to be made. One toss of the coin decided that it would be the Hewlett-Packard Company, instead of the Packard-Hewlett Company.

By 1940, they had outgrown the garage and had moved into a small building nearby. The first employees of the company were hired that same year, but it was not until 1942 that HP found it necessary to construct a building of its own.

By 1949, the Hewlett-Packard Company had grown to 150 employees, with annual sales of $2.25 million. The company continued as a one-plant operation until late in 1957, when with an employee base of 1500, the company went through the first of what would become frequent amoeba-like divisions. Four separate operations were formed along the R&D product lines: Audio-Video, Microwave, Time & Frequency, and Oscilloscopes.

As HP grew, space continued to be a problem. So in 1956, HP broke ground for a new engineering/manufacturing complex located in the nearby Stanford Industrial Park -- and the Silicon Valley was born. Despite increased numbers of employees and increased product lines, as late as October 1958, all HP buildings were still located in Palo Alto within a short walk of each other.

That situation ended abruptly in 1959 (the company's 20th year), when the company began to establish its presence abroad. By renovating an old knitting mill in Boeblingen, West Germany, HP began its first overseas manufacturing operation. A European marketing organization was also started in Geneva, Switzerland. By 1963, HP had acquired companies in Southern California, Massachusetts, and Pennsylvania; opened new operations in Colorado and the United Kingdom; and entered into a joint venture in Japan.

Until 1961, HP did little direct marketing of its products. In fact, back in 1939, when Bill and Dave were selling the audio oscillators to Walt Disney Studios, another person was present: Norm Neely. Norm had founded Neely Enterprises in 1933 to represent manufacturers who specialized in audio equipment for the movie and radio industries. A few weeks after the Disney deal, the three met again to shake hands over a verbal agreement that made Neely Enterprises HP's first sales representative.

But starting in late 1961, HP began to acquire the independent sales companies that had been doing most of its U.S. marketing -- including Neely Enterprises. Out of these firms developed the regional sales organization of today. (The Western U.S. sales region is still called the Neely Sales Region.)

In the mid-1950s, a semiconductor operation was established to produce special-purpose diodes. This opened the way for the research and development efforts in solid-state electronics that began in 1961. By 1966, however, HP's management realized that it was too costly for each operational division to individually carry on the R&D efforts that it felt were necessary to maintain its competitive position in the marketplace. Consequently, a central research facility, called HP Laboratories, was formed. Its charter was: *to carry on basic and applied research studies, to assist the operating divisions in finding solutions to their technical problems, and, if necessary, to develop prototype products in new and promising fields.* And that's exactly what it did. The HP Labs launched HP into the computer field and thus is responsible for the invention of the HP Precision Architecture and the Spectrum family of computers.

The Computer Era

The first HP product that could actually be called a computer, the HP2116A, was introduced in November 1966. But HP made it clear that it was in the instrument automation business -- not the computer business. As a result, it developed the environmental specs for this 'instrument-automator' to the same Class B specs used on its other products. This meant that purchasers could place the HP2116A right on the factory floor instead of having to build the special, hospital-type computer rooms needed for most other computers of the day. Consequently, the demand for the HP2116A quickly increased, as did HP's reputation for building reliable computers.

HP's next major computer breakthrough came in late 1971 when it began to market the HP-35, the first hand-held scientific electronic calculator. For the first time, HP was at the forefront of a new technology which would change the world. Projected sales for the first year were 10,000 units. Actual sales for the first year were 100,000 units -- and the slide rule was buried forever.

To keep up with its expanding data products business, HP built new plants in France, Singapore, Malaysia, Brazil, and within the U.S. in California, Colorado, Idaho, Oregon, and Washington.

By 1972, having sold over 15,000 desktop calculators and 4,500 digital computers, the company finally acknowledged that it was in the computer field. This was also the year that HP first ventured from its traditional areas of electronic test and measurement instruments into a new area: administrative and business computers. When HP announced its first general-purpose computer, the HP 3000, it entered that market in a strong way. The HP 3000 was a relatively inexpensive computer, capable of multi-tasking and supporting on-line, interactive, database-oriented application systems.

To get an idea of how fast things began to happen, consider some of the highlights of 1975:

☐ January: Data Products Division shipped its 10,000th minicomputer.

☐ February: Data Terminals Division shipped its first HP2640A terminal. The first HP-21 calculator was shipped. Price: US$ 125.

☐ July: An HP-65 calculator was used onboard the joint Apollo/Soyuz mission.

☐ November: Nine months after the first HP2640A terminal was shipped, the Data Terminals Division shipped its 2,000th HP2640A terminal.

The success of the HP 3000 has continued, making it one of the most popular super-minicomputers of all time. The company, of course, has continued to grow as well, with over 56 product divisions, over 82,000 employees in 78 countries throughout the world, and annual sales of over US$ 7.2 billion, ranking it 58th among U.S. corporations as of 1986, according to Fortune magazine. From the twelve products listed in its initial 1943 instrument catalog, the company has expanded to more than 4,000 products.

This book is focused on the latest of these products. In November 1986, Hewlett-Packard shipped the first of its next generation of computers, the so-called Spectrum family of computers, which is based on HP Precision Architecture (HPPA). 'Spectrum' is not an HP trademark or product name; in fact, another company owns the right to use that name. Spectrum is the internal code name for the project that developed HPPA, and the use of this code name within this book will be limited to discussions about RISC and HPPA, rather than to refer to actual products.

The HP Way

To better understand the company, it is necessary to examine its motivations and objectives. Years ago, Bill Hewlett and Dave Packard developed a set of management objectives for the company. With only slight modification, these became the corporate objectives of the Hewlett-Packard Company and were first published in 1957. These objectives give a clear idea as to how the company views itself and its position in society.

The *Hewlett-Packard Statement of Corporate Objectives* (September, 1983) lists these objectives:

- ☐ **Profit** - To achieve sufficient profit to finance our company growth and to provide the resources we need to achieve our other corporate objectives.

- ☐ **Customers** - To provide products and services of the highest quality and the greatest possible value to our customers, thereby gaining and holding their respect and loyalty.

- ☐ **Fields of Interest** - To build on our strengths in the company's traditional fields of interest and to enter new fields only when it is consistent with the basic purpose of our business and when we can assure ourselves of making a needed and profitable contribution to the field.

- ☐ **Growth** - To let our growth be limited only by our profits and our ability to develop and produce innovative products that satisfy real customer needs.

- ☐ **Our People** - To help HP people share in the company's success, which they make possible; to provide job security based on their performance; to ensure them a safe and pleasant work environment; to recognize their individual achievements; and to help them gain a sense of satisfaction and accomplishment from their work.

- ☐ **Management** - To foster initiative and creativity by allowing the individual great freedom of action in attaining well-defined objectives.

- ☐ **Citizenship** - To honor our obligations to society by being an economic, intellectual and social asset to each nation and each community in which we operate.

Besides leading to a hugely successful company, the pursuit of these objectives has brought HP wide recognition as a model for a US-based multinational company. HP is credited as being one of the first companies to implement the management technique known as MBWA, or 'Management By Wandering Around'. The company is a source of study in many leading business schools and is one of the firms featured in the best selling book, *In Search of Excellence*, by Thomas J. Peters and Robert H. Waterman, Jr..

Despite this strong foundation and consistent set of objectives, changes have taken place at HP. Gone are the morning doughnuts and Friday afternoon beer-busts that used to characterize HP, but more fundamental changes have also occurred. In the past, management usually worked its way up from the proverbial mail room, but from 1983 to 1986 (the Spectrum transitional years) much of HP's upper-middle management left the company and was replaced with others brought in from outside.

Some say this has had a profound effect on the company in several ways. One way is the cancelling of the next, bigger, HP 3000 project, code named Vision, for the more revolutionary Spectrum project. This is thought by many to be the result of the 'new blood' in HP Labs. Another effect is the shifting from a product focus to a market focus, but this may be just a logical step in the evolution of HP's organization.

In the 1960s, the company had a product line focus that was supported through the independent divisions. These divisions competed for resources within the company and occasionally even produced products that competed with each other.

In the 1970s, the company developed an integrated product focus supported through a product group structure. Price and performance became important factors. Divisions began to work more closely together within a given product group, but boundaries between groups began to blur. The calculator people were producing high-end 'calculators' that looked a lot like the low-end products of the technical computer people which in turn had similarities to the computers being produced by the business computer people. But, all were incompatible with each other.

The organizational structure in both the 1960s and 1970s was based on technology. In other words, the company would invest in new technologies, and when it thought it had hit upon something good, it would produce a product and *then* try to market it. The evolution of the organization is away from this technology-driven approach towards a market-driven approach. Such an approach drives the company to first find out what the market wants and then build it.

The computer industry has been a tough one from the beginning. The extensive list of defunct computer companies is proof enough of that. HP not only survived but flourished during the industry 'shakeout' of the 1980's. It is doing now what it must in order to continue growing in the short term, while positioning itself for a significant market role by the end of the century.

2

The HP 3000
Computer Family

Before beginning a detailed look into the newest HP 3000s, it is worthwhile to look at where they came from. After all, their ancestors stretch back nearly two decades (a long time in computer-years), and several members of the previous generation look like they will still be around for years to come.

As discussed in the last chapter, HP's first computer (actually an 'instrument-automator') was introduced in 1966. By 1969, a project was under way to develop a brand new, general purpose computer. Code-named the Omega-32, this machine was to be a 32-bit-per-word computer featuring up to 4 megabytes of memory, a complex instruction set, and a hardware stack. Unfortunately, the project never made it past the paper stage.

A year later the Alpha project was born, resurrected from the remains of Omega-32. This time, however, the design had been scaled down to a 16-bit-per-word, 128-kilobyte computer. Still remaining, however, were the complex instruction set and stack, which would be implemented in the firmware via microcode.

In the meantime, the HP software designers, many of them from a Burroughs background, set out to design the system's software. Burroughs' operating system, the MCP, was written in a high-level language called 'ESPOL', a special version of its

ALGOL language. In a similar manner, HP began to design POS (Primary Operating System) in another variant of ALGOL that they dubbed SPL, for Systems Programming Language.

The First Generation

Unlike the ill-fated Omega, the Alpha project survived. The hardware was given the product name HP 3000, and the POS operating system was called 'MPE', for Multi-Programming Executive. Aimed at the market for administrative and business computing, this computer was introduced in 1972.

These first years were rough ones for HP. Early on, the hardware and software were so plagued with reliability problems that it was difficult to get any work done on them. A few years later, when the machine began to settle down, users began to realize that 128 kilobytes was just not very much memory, considering the sophisticated operating system and the needs of multiple users.

Relief came in May 1976 with the introduction of the HP 3000 Series II. Through the addition of the concept of 'banks' of memory and bank registers, the machine was now capable of supporting 512 kilobytes of memory.

It was around this time that HP announced its objective to decrease the HP 3000's price/performance ratio by 30 percent per year. In other words, at any given time, you could assume that a year from now you would be able to buy either a computer comparable in performance to today's computer at a price 30 percent less than today's, or buy a computer 30 percent more powerful for the same price as today's.

1978 saw the release of two new models, the HP 3000 Series III and the HP 3000 Series 33. The Series III was much like the Series II but the bank concept was expanded to allow up to 2 megabytes of memory. The Series 33, on the other hand, was a departure from the HP 3000. This was a brand new processor, based on hardware technology known as SOS (Silicon-on-Sapphire). Though generally slower than the Series III in overall throughput, the Series 33 was the first HP 3000 to support terminal speeds in excess of 2400 baud.

In 1979, HP introduced the Series 30, a scaled-down version of the Series 33. While it had an identical SPU (System Processing Unit) to the Series 33, the Series 30 had lower limits in maximum memory and peripherals than its big brother.

The next year saw the announcement of the next significant SPU enhancement with the introduction of the HP 3000 Series 44. Supporting up to 4 megabytes of memory and built with the fastest SPU to date, this computer offered the highest throughput yet seen on an HP 3000, with terminal support up to 9600 baud.

In 1981, HP introduced two new models: The Series 40, using the same SPU as the Series 44, but with lower limits analogous to the Series 30, and a new machine at the high-performance end, the Series 64. The Series 64 offered several enhancements over all previous HP 3000s. For one, memory was increased to 8 megabytes; but much more important, you could order a Series 64 with not one, but two InterModule Buses (IMBs). By now, many sophisticated, database-oriented commercial applications had been written for the HP 3000, and the vast majority were I/O-bound. That is, the number of inputs and outputs to disc was the most limited resource; total system throughput was determined by the bottleneck in getting data to and from the disc. By adding an additional IMB, the I/O-to-disc rate was effectively doubled, assuming that multiple discs were spread over the two buses and that accesses to discs on both buses were required concurrently. Together with the faster SPU, the Series 64 brought the HP 3000 to a new level, by its ability to support as many as five times the number of users a Series II could -- with equal or improved performance.

The Series 64 also added something else to the HP 3000 family. Until this time, the firmware that contained the microcode was etched into ROMs (Read-Only Memories). ROMs, after all, had traditionally been faster than RAMs (Random Access Memories), which could not only be read but also written to. However, taking advantage of the new, faster RAMs that had recently been developed, the microcode of the Series 64 was put on RAM.

Typically, a new floppy disc arrives with each new release of MPE and the microinstructions are then loaded from the floppy into the RAMs. If it becomes necessary to change the firmware, say to fix a bug, add a new machine instruction, or speed up an existing instruction, the customer would merely get a new floppy. With ROM-based HP 3000s, however, a Customer Engineer would have to come and change chips inside the computer to accomplish the same upgrade.

Over the next few years, with the surge of technology brought on by the advances of large-scale integration techniques, the new models continued to be introduced at a rate approximating the calling of numbers at a bingo parlor. Here's a list of the HP 3000 models introduced between the years 1983 and 1986: Series 42, Series 39, Series 48, Series 68, Series 37, Series 70, Series 42XP, Series 52, Series 48XP, Series 58, Series 37XE, the Micro 3000, and the Micro 3000XE.

The Series 37, code-named 'Mighty Mouse', extended the HP 3000 family at the entry level. This computer, which is about the size of a small file cabinet, is designed to fit into the office environment. Unlike most computers of its power, it does not require a special 'computer room' environment with special air conditioning, humidity control, conditioned electrical power, and raised flooring. Typically, it is placed right in the office next to someone's desk, plugged into the wall, and immediately begins supporting five or ten users with excellent response time.

At the high end of the MPE V-based HP 3000 family is the Series 70. Through a number of enhancements, this computer averages about a 40 percent performance improvement over the Series 68. Memory is expandable up to 16 megabytes, a 144-fold increase over the original Series I. In addition, a 128 kilobyte memory cache is included. This memory cache holds both data and instructions. When a required word is available in this cache, it can be obtained in a single machine cycle. Additional improvements came from recoding certain frequently used operating system routines in microcode.

From a software point of view, an analogous history has also unfolded. Along with the hardware enhancements of the Series II came MPE II, a major new release of the operating system. Through the years, regular updates to MPE have been released, usually at the rate of between one and four per year. Every two or three years, a major release comes out. The most recent, MPE V, added (among other enhancements) disc caching. Remembering that most sites were, in fact, I/O-bound before the advent of disc caching, this turned out to be a major performance enhancer for many systems. By adding more memory and using spare CPU cycles that used to be wasted waiting for disc I/Os to complete, many sites are able to eliminate 50 or 60 percent of the physical I/Os to disc, satisfying the I/O request out of a cache domain. This technique has proved so successful that for the first time since the introduction of the HP 3000, many sites are finding that their machines have become CPU-bound and are no longer I/O-bound.

These releases of MPE are commonly called 'MITs' (Master Installation Tapes). The identification of the various MITs, however, is not an easy thing to understand or explain. Through the years, HP has tried several different naming methods to keep track of the various versions. None seems to have worked very well, and with each change in the naming method, the confusion grows greater. Certain names, such as 'MPE V/T-Delta 5' or 'MPE V/UB-Delta 1', are commonly known among users, but the actual software that these names correspond to use identifications such as 'G.A1.06' or 'G.02.B0'. Unfortunately, it is unlikely that a definitive naming system will be implemented soon. Perhaps the most impressive fact about all of these versions is that with very few exceptions, programs written and compiled years ago will run without modification on the current MIT.

The Second Generation

Today, HP produces new computers based on HP Precision Architecture (HPPA). Because there seems to be a lot of confusion over names, it is important to initially get a few definitions straight. Even though the new machines are quite different, from an internal perspective, than the HP 3000s described above, HP has chosen to call some of the new ones HP 3000s as well. This makes sense because from an external perspective they look quite similar. These machines run the next generation of the MPE operating system, called 'MPE XL'; they look like HP 3000s when you log on; and they run almost the same software as all other HP 3000s. To distinguish them from the HP 3000s described above, HP refers to the new machines as MPE XL-based HP 3000s, and to the others as MPE V-based HP 3000s.

As previously stated, some of the new HPPA machines are called HP 3000s, but what about the others? Well, although in some cases the hardware is nearly identical to the hardware of the MPE XL-based HP 3000s, these other machines use the HP-UX operating system, instead of MPE. These machines are known as HP 9000 Model 800s. Though full-fledged HPPA computers, they are not members of the HP 3000 family. These machines will be discussed in Chapters 7 and 8.

As will be seen in more detail later, the MPE XL-based HP 3000s will run virtually all of the software from the MPE V-based HP 3000s in an emulation mode known as Compatibility Mode (CM). The software that will not run tends to be Privileged Mode programs that rely on system tables or other hardware aspects of the MPE V-based machines that have no counterpart on the MPE XL-based machines. It is possible to write programs that better utilize the features of HPPA. Instead of running in the Compatibility Mode, these programs run in what is known as Native Mode (NM), and as such, will not always run on MPE V-based systems.

With the introduction of this new generation of HP 3000s, HP will continue to meet its price/performance and compatibility objectives through the end of the century. This new lease on life will undoubtedly make the HP 3000 one of the most successful and popular computers of all time. In June of 1987, HP celebrated '30K the 3000 Way'; 30,000 HP 3000s -- in banks, in lumber mills, on oil rigs, in drug stores, in colleges, and in almost every type of business environment imaginable.

II

HP Precision
Architecture

3

Evolution of
the Architecture

The introduction of Hewlett-Packard's RISC-based Precision Architecture (HPPA) to the commercial market represents a significant development in computing history. As the first major hardware vendor to base its product line on RISC, HP's commitment to HPPA certainly underscores its continuing focus on technological and engineering excellence.

A full understanding of HPPA's significance requires a brief review of computer architectures. Like all histories, it contains stories about brilliant people, common problems, and crushing disappointments.

Sticks and Stones ...

Man's first computers called for no manufacturing and enjoyed a worldwide market. Distribution was handled through natural forces and upgrades were immediately available -- depending upon what you could lift.

Plucked from the ground and stored in groups, small stones or pebbles served as handy counting devices for shepherds. Each represented an animal going to pasture in the morning, and as the herd returned each evening, one stone was removed for every member of the flock. If any stones remained, shepherds knew that stock was missing. In fact, the words calculate, calculus and calculator all derive from a common Latin root - *calculos*, which means 'small stone'.

This concept of pebbles or small objects as counting devices was formalized by the Babylonians in the abacus. Consisting of a wood frame with vertical rods and sliding beads, the abacus is still widely used in China. In the hands of a skilled operator, it is capable of rapidly performing very complex calculations.

The next major development is credited to John Napier (1550-1617) who invented logarithms. He devised a set of rods with multiple logarithmic markings. Called 'bones' because of their ivory material, Napier's rods could be placed side by side in a variety of combinations to solve relatively complex multiplication problems.

In 1654, Robert Bassaker used a similar principle in designing two sliding sticks, each marked with Napier's logarithms. When moved past one another, the rods depicted a variety of mathematical results. Bassaker's invention served as the basis for the modern slide rule.

Napier's and Bassaker's machines were different in more than physical appearance. Napier's bones utilized digits imprinted on ivory sticks and therefore operated on digital principles. Neither the location of individual digits on the sticks nor the size of the sticks mattered much, as long as the digits themselves lined up across corresponding sticks. Bassaker's slide rule, on the other hand, *depended* upon properly scaled numbers. For example, the logarithm of 4 *had to be* twice as far from zero as the logarithm of 2.

In short, Napier's bones were digital, while Bassaker's slide rule was analog. This same distinction still exists in modern pocket calculators (digital) and slide rules (analog).

The design of the first computing machine is credited to the 17th century mathematician and philosopher Blaise Pascal (1623-1662), for whom the computer language Pascal is named. Built in 1642, the Pascal 'adder' was a simple affair of knobs and dials. Each dial was notched with numbers ranging from 0 to 9, with a different dial for ones, tens, hundreds, etc. Each carryover was supposed to cause the next dial to click ahead one place. Unfortunately, the engineering was less than precise, and Pascal's adder suffered inaccuracies from imprecisions in its moving parts.

Devices like Pascal's adder are classified as mechanical addition machines. While not sophisticated, they are theoretically capable of additional arithmetic functions, especially if each is defined as a variant of addition. For example, subtraction is the inverse of addition, multiplication is repeated addition, and division is repeated subtraction.

Pascal never developed his adder, however, leaving the next theoretical advance to Charles Babbage (1792-1871), who designed a machine he called 'the Analytical Engine'. This device had the ability to perform arithmetic functions, but, more importantly it was programmable.

His design called for unique cards controlling the operation of the machine. One type of card defined variables, while another contained a definition of the operation that would be performed on the variables. Not wanting to stop with a single machine and function, Babbage envisioned several machines working independently -- but in harmony. He specified a 'mill' for arithmetic, a 'receiver' to take in information, a 'device' to transfer the information from one component to another, and a 'store' of information. Each of these design elements is found in every modern computer system.

Primarily a theoretician and philosopher, Babbage never saw his machine through to production. At one point he attempted a prototype, but government funding evaporated for lack of tangible results. Modern experts have concluded, however, that his ideas were sound, and small, working versions of machines based on his designs have been built.

Although Babbage broached the possibility of new technologies, refinements of the Pascal basic adder supported most arithmetic functions for the next 200 years. Hand-cranked adding machines and their descendants, electric adding machines, are nothing more than Pascal adders, with keys replacing the original dials.

Pursuing a line of inquiry similar to that which interested Babbage, Joseph Jacquard (1752-1834) experimented with pre-punched metal plates to control textile looms. Introduced in 1804, his punched-hole concept was further developed by an American, Herman Hollerith, for use during the national census of 1890. In order to speed the tedious and time-consuming task of counting census data, Hollerith developed a machine that counted punches made in cards. Various data was transferred to pre-defined holes in cards, and as the machine scanned each card, it tallied data. The 1890 census was tabulated in record time, and Hollerith established a company to manufacture his machines. Eventually, that small venture spawned International Business Machines (IBM).

Little changed in machine computing until the mid-1940s, when the dials and knobs of Pascal's adder were replaced by the much faster electronic switches made possible through the development of vacuum tubes. Their availability made the first digital computer a reality. Dubbed the Harvard Mark I in August 1944, its original name was the IBM Automatic Sequence-Controlled Calculator. The Harvard Mark I was electrically powered and employed a mix of mechanical and electrical parts (vacuum tubes). Data was entered via punched tape, a miniaturized version of Jacquard's metal plates and Hollerith's punched cards.

The first fully electronic machine came along in 1946 with the appearance of ENIAC (Electronic Numerical Integrator and Computer). Consisting of 18,000 vacuum tubes or diodes, this monster filled a huge basement at the University of Pennsylvania and generated so much heat that powerful air conditioners were needed to keep its tubes and machinery from melting into a viscous mess.

While ENIAC's tubes and diodes represented a new technological dimension, they necessitated the development of programming techniques much different from metal plates and punched cards. Focusing the potential power of ENIAC on a specific problem required 'programmers' who plugged wires into large patch panels. The electrical circuits formed by their ad hoc wiring determined the logic path for ENIAC's computations, much like the mechanical stops did on Babbage's Analytical Engine.

The disadvantages of this kind of structure soon became obvious. Machines like ENIAC were incredibly expensive to build and consumed enormous quantities of power. Programming changes were slow to accomplish, sometimes entailing weeks of work. And once a program was set, altering the machine's circuits for another task required an equally laborious process.

So it was back to the labs, where the transistor was born. Invented at Bell Laboratories by Drs. Brattain, Bardeen, and Shockley, the transistor made possible the continuing race to reduce size and power requirements while simultaneously enhancing speed and performance. Capable of the same functions as the vacuum tube (amplification and rectification), the transistor drew a fraction of the power of a comparable vacuum tube, and served as the technological basis for the smaller and more powerful machines to follow.

Although transistor-based models were still programmed mechanically, their small size allowed proportionate reductions in the size of programming panels. Instead of the giant plugboards and thick cables of the ENIAC, technicians now worked with panels of about 6 by 14 inches. These more manageable models allowed programmers to alter the machine's instructions much more quickly, thereby increasing both productivity and speed.

In addition to hardware advances, similar efforts in related research brought forth an entirely new field of scholarly endeavors, 'computer science'. This discipline focused on the study of the behavior and application of machine computations, as well as the ways in which such computations were performed and analyzed. Emphasizing the machine's internal processes as opposed to the design of its hardware components, computer science soon began increasing the speed at which computers operated.

One of the great computer scientists of the day was John Von Neumann. Working at Princeton University in the mid-1940s, he contributed many fundamental ideas to the field. Foremost among these is his model of computing called the 'Stored Program Machine'. Prior to Von Neumann's model, plugboard programming involved physically redirecting electrical current to various parts (registers) of the machine, which caused the electrical impulses representing output to be redirected accordingly. In a somewhat abstract sense, the wiring represented a binary numbering system imposed on the electrical circuits of the machine. A connection represented the number one, and *no* connection represented a zero. Von Neumann proposed that it should be possible to place these numbers, called 'instructions' or 'opcodes'(operational codes) in the memory storage of the machine, then sequentially retrieve (fetch) the instructions from this store, and have the hardware execute the corresponding operation. Thus, the same binary number coding scheme was employed for both the instructions and the data, freeing people forever from the drudgery of plugboards.

Commercially available computers paralleled the developments described above. The UNIVAC I became available around 1954. Needless to say, the power and site requirements of this machine limited the customers to government and colleges, the two areas with a great deal of money. With the advent of transistorized machines, the machines got smaller and the customer base increased. The IBM 1401 was probably the first popular commercial computer system to be bought by the business world.

The developments that occurred in technology from this point on can be summarized in a few words: smaller, faster, cheaper, and power-saving. The integrated circuit developed for the space program in the 1960s provided cost reductions and speed increases to the computer industry that are still accelerating at breakneck speed. The pocket calculator was made possible by the invention of the 'silicon chip', which miniaturized thousands of components (transistors, capacitors, diodes) onto a single, small piece of material. Semiconductor technology of the 1970s and 1980s saw incredible miniaturization, to the point where, in 1985, individual wires on the integrated circuit were only one micron apart -- a distance of 1 millionth of a meter.

Different methods of building integrated circuits are given different acronyms. Each successive order of magnitude increase in component density is given an ever better name to the point that almost no more superlatives can be employed. The first to be developed, now known as 'Small-Scale Integration' (SSI) allowed the integration of several hundred components on a chip. MSI (Medium-Scale Integration) allowed several thousand. The next step was LSI (Large-Scale Integration), which allowed for chip densities in the thousands on a single silicon wafer about one-half a centimeter square. Then came VLSI (Very Large Scale Integration), which permitted hundreds of thousands of components to be integrated.

Hewlett-Packard developed one of the first VLSI processes at its chip production facilities in Fort Collins, Colorado. The process, called 'NMOS III' (Negative Metal Oxide Semiconductor), produced a complete 32-bit computer on just 3 chips. This chip set, dubbed Focus, was the basis of the first HP 9000. The process gave HP a temporary advantage in developing very sophisticated chips for specialized purposes.

Machine Balance

Paralleling the development of enhanced hardware technologies was the concept of machine balance. Examining the factors surrounding this phenomenon is crucial to understanding the impact of RISC technologies.

All computer systems must contain two or more registers to store data, and it is upon these registers that the machine's logic circuits act. This manipulation is efficient only if both the logic circuits and the registers are implemented in technologies capable of the same level of performance.

For example, in the original UNIVAC machines, logic circuitry consisted of vacuum tubes. Accordingly, the registers were built with vacuum tubes as well. (Because they were so expensive to build, UNIVAC had only two such registers.) The primary reason for this decision was speed; it made no sense whatsoever to build expensive, fast logic and arithmetic circuitry if it sat idle while data was moved from a slower storage medium.

Expense also plays a major role in determining what fundamental operations the hardware can perform. Certain functions, such as adding two numbers, loading a register from memory, and shifting data left and right, should be built into the hardware design of the machine. The expense of early UNIVAC-style machines dictated a limit to the number of operations, or machine instructions, it could perform. Building such instructions into the machine meant designing the hardware by hand, then adding discrete components which implemented a given instruction. Because the components were large, power-hungry, and expensive, limitations were stringent and compromises resulted.

The machines were very simple indeed, and by today's standards had a reduced number of instructions. This design philosophy has no popularized name, but it might be called 'ERISC' (Early Reduced Instruction Set Computing). For instance, the first MARK I computer had only seven instructions. Because subtraction was just the addition of negative numbers, only addition needed to be built in. The different instructions were strung together by the machine language programs stored in memory that were fetched and executed. Each machine cycle resulted in a fetch, then an execution.

As technology progressed and transistors emerged, machines became smaller and less power-hungry. However, demand for computing power increased, mandating the need for more and more memory. It was not cost-effective to implement memory storage in the same expensive technology, so memory was implemented in slower technologies, such as ferrite core (and later, dynamic RAM). The result was a speed gap between the memory storage of the computer and the circuitry that performed the computer's real work. The logic and arithmetic circuitry (CPU) of the machine was idle too much of the time. A solution had to be found to increase the efficiency of this expensive hardware.

At the same time, computer scientists were seeking to reduce the enormous gulf between the conceptualization of the problems the computer was asked to solve and the language in which the problem was defined for the machine. The original machine language of UNIVAC and other machines consisted of ones and zeros being fed into the machine. This disparity of concept and realization was extremely difficult for humans to grasp and needed to be addressed if computers were to be more commonly used. From this need for simplification grew the use of assembler languages and high-level languages.

Assembler languages were built by assigning symbolic names to the various machine instructions, which was vastly simpler than coding programs in the tedious string of ones and zeros. High-level languages which allowed even more English-like access to the machine's facilities were also developed. The language FORTRAN (FORmula TRANslation) was developed at IBM in the late 1950s and was probably the first high-level language to run on any machine. A single FORTRAN statement might produce hundreds of machine instructions, freeing the programmer to think more about the problem and less about the limitations of the computer.

The development of high-level languages created a gap between the expression of the solution (via the computer language) and the execution of the solution (via the small machine instruction set). The problem was exacerbated by the speed disparity between the hardware and memory storage. Computer scientists in the early 1960s solved both problems with the same solution: 'microcode'.

Machines were created that had a store of small subroutines embedded in their native instruction sets. Each routine corresponded to a higher-level concept or instruction. This set of subroutines was (and still is) called 'microcode'. For example, multiplication may be performed by repeated addition. Rather than write a small multiply routine every time a programmer needed to multiply two numbers, a routine performing this operation is written once and stored as microcode. Since the microcode store was fast, the individual low-level machine instructions that made up this multiply operation could be fetched at close to logic circuit speeds, solving the speed gap.

Likewise, higher-level machine instructions could be devised that closely mapped the constructs present in the newer high-level languages. For example, FORTRAN supports an arithmetic operation called 'exponentiation', by which one number is raised to the power specified by another number. If it were desirable for the machine to perform this function a lot, the exponentiation microinstruction (a sequence of microcoded machine instructions) could be written and placed in control store (as microcode is often called today) and assigned a symbolic name, such as EXP.

Thus, the language disparity was solved. Beginning in the 1960s and continuing through the present, machines were developed that contained large numbers of these complex instructions. These CISC (Complex Instruction Set Computing) machines have as many as 300 instructions, each of which can have many options imbedded in the machine instruction format. Different memory address modes, parameters and other data may be encoded directly into the binary pattern, adding further nuances to the complexity of these instructions.

The performance gains from microcode were significant. Semiconductor ROM (Read Only Memory) was developed in the late 1960s, allowing almost full-speed access to this control store. The speed gap between memory and the CPU was now closing, as was the disparity between high-level languages and the native language of the machine. The CISC model was so well ingrained in the computer world that no longer were people concerned with the fundamental machine instructions in which microcode was written. Machine instructions, as far as humans were concerned, were those defined by the set of microcode subroutines. The lower-level hardware architecture was the concern only of the few micro-programmers working for the computer vendor itself. Higher-level concepts dominated the thinking of computer programmers.

The other advantage of microcode was economic. Memory was very expensive, and steps had to be taken to minimize the use of available memory. By using microcode, it was possible to remove a great deal of code from the program's code space and use the microcode in the control store.

How Microcode Works

It is useful to examine what happens at the machine level when a microcoded hardware scheme is implemented. (The terminology in the description below is borrowed from the HP 3000, but the concepts generally apply to all machines.) Note that additional hardware must be built into the computer to deal with the microcode. This hardware is built with the same technology as the logic and arithmetic parts of the computer and is thus relatively expensive. Refer to Figure 3.1 during the discussion.

The first part of the sequence is performed by the instruction fetch logic. This brings in the microinstruction binary pattern from memory. Because memory is much slower than the CPU hardware, you want to fetch as many instructions as possible so CPU waiting time is limited. A concept called 'pipelining' (to be discussed in Chapter 5) accomplishes this quite nicely.

Once the instruction is brought in, it is decoded to determine which instruction it is. In many machines, such as the IBM 360/370 series, the microcode is actually a small interpreter running at all times. Once an instruction is brought in and examined, execution branches to the proper microprogram, starting the sequence of microinstructions that correspond to the microprogram.

This process imposes a significant amount of overhead, as each microinstruction must be interpreted one at a time. The MPE V-based HP 3000 hardware performs this step not with a microprogram interpreter but by maintaining a table of starting addresses. The binary pattern of the instruction is encoded in a particular fashion (called 'Huffman coding'), which allows the binary number to index into a LUT (Look-Up Table). The LUT contains the starting address of the microprogram corresponding to the particular microinstruction, and the hardware branches to that point and starts execution of the microprogram.

When the microprogram starts execution, each microinstruction is fetched from the control store by hardware called the 'micro-stepper' and 'micro-fetcher'. Each microinstruction is fetched and executed directly by the hardware. When the microprogram is finished, control returns and the next microinstruction (already filled by the pipeline) is interpreted (or looked up) and executed.

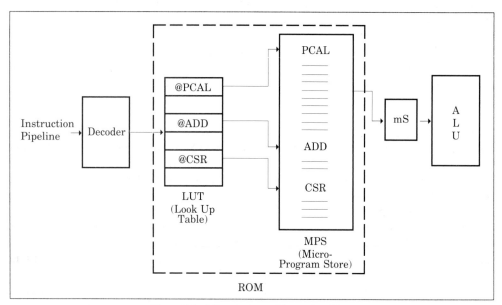

Figure 3.1 Microprogram Execution Flow

Microinstructions are written in such a way as to manipulate the hardware parts (registers, logic circuits, etc.) simultaneously. Each microinstruction executes in one clock cycle. Thus, each machine instruction executes in a variable number of clock cycles, depending upon the microcode path for that instruction. This point will be of interest later, when alternatives to microcode are discussed.

The important point to note is this: Like all other aspects of computer science, dealing with microcode involves a trade-off. While creating a microcoded machine *does* provide more speed in some respects, a noticeable overhead is imposed by the mechanism itself. The trade-off was felt to be more than justified by the computer scientists who devised the scheme, and this type of CISC machine is still the standard for building computers.

The advantage of microcode is that very, very complex instructions can be created, giving the machine enormous power.

Reduced Instruction Set Computing

The discussion of the history of computing and the design choices leading to modern CISC machines will now be put into perspective by discussing one of the newest concepts in computer science: Reduced Instruction Set Computing, or RISC, the basis of Hewlett-Packard Precision Architecture.

As CISC machines were built through the '60s, '70s, and '80s, scientists lost sight of the reasons behind the creation of microcoded machines. However, several accomplishments in the field caused re-examination of the complex instruction set machine concept.

First, memory technologies improved at an exponential rate. Almost daily, semiconductor (RAM) memories became cheaper and denser -- to the point that memory sizes are now measured in the tens of megabytes rather than in kilobytes, as was the standard in the '70s. In addition, new memory technologies caused computer scientists to augment previous CISC designs.

The standard memory technology in most large and small modern computers is called 'dynamic RAM'. Such memory consists of an array of microscopic capacitors, each holding an electrical charge. These charges are interpreted as binary ones and zeros. The word 'dynamic' refers to the fact that the memory must be periodically 'refreshed'. In other words, the RAM memory 'forgets', or loses the charge, unless an electrical current is reintroduced every few milliseconds. While this refresh cycle is occurring, no other part of the machine may access the memory chip. Thus, the CPU (or other parts of the machine requiring access to memory) must be delayed and coordinated around refresh cycles. The need to refresh the memory also means that additional hardware and logic must be designed into the machine. The additional cost for this hardware is more than compensated for by the lower cost of the RAM memory chips.

The newest technology of note is static RAM. Unlike dynamic RAM, static RAM does not require refresh cycles. Similarly, there is no need to delay the CPU when accessing memory. Because of this, static RAM is almost as fast as direct-register access. The trade-off on this type of memory, however, is that it is very expensive. Thus, computer designers have employed static RAM memory only to act as a CPU cache (a small, 'fast' area between the CPU and the slower dynamic RAM memory).

Other areas have improved steadily as well. The newer CAD/CAM software packages and techniques allow hardware designers to develop incredibly sophisticated designs with hundreds of thousands of components. Unlike the hardware designs of the early UNIVAC machines, a great deal of capability is bestowed directly upon the hardware. The design process for circuits of this complexity is now cost-effective, and the development of VLSI technologies allows the hardware designs to be implemented in a minimum chip space.

In the software realm, computer scientists had made steady progress in the systematic development of compilers and code generation system. Specifically, techniques had been developed that allowed the compiling systems to optimize the programs being compiled by modifying or eliminating code. Optimizations come in two flavors: those constructs that are created by the programmer (such as duplicate expressions close together) and those produced by the code generator (such as a sequence of three instructions that can be executed as one instruction. These so-called optimizing compilers allow reductions in code size and improve the performance of the generated code.

The second set of accomplishments which enabled the re-examination of CISC design parameters was the increasingly scientific measurement of the behavior of the computer systems themselves. Instrumentation on both hardware and software was refined in the late 1970s and early 1980s to the point where computer scientists did not have to theorize about what was occurring inside the computer. They could tell, for instance, precisely what areas of memory were being referenced, what machine instructions were being used, and what type of I/O traffic was occurring.

Machine instruction mixes were measured, and a very amazing fact was discovered: by far, the most used instructions were the simple ones. The lengthy, time-consuming, complex instructions were used only 20 percent of the time, and the simple instructions (add, subtract, branch, load, store) were used 80 percent of the time. Thus, a small amount of the microcode was used most of the time. This disproportionate use of the microcode resources occurs in current CISC machines.

Based upon these measurements, computer scientists re-evaluated CISC designs and proposed a new design philosophy that encompassed the following precepts:

□ Only a small number of fundamental instructions -- the ones executed most of the time -- would be included.

□ Complex operations would be accomplished by software that strings simple instructions together. The optimizing compilers could reduce the total number of instructions.

□ All instructions would be implemented directly in hardware; thus, each instruction would execute in one clock cycle.

Based upon these concepts, the principle of RISC was born. The first theoretical treatises on RISC proposed a computer with about 30 instructions (one-tenth the size of many CISC machines) and a fairly high number of registers. The engineers at Hewlett-Packard Laboratories took these concepts and expanded upon them. The result is known as 'Hewlett-Packard Precision Architecture', or HPPA.

HPPA -- RISC and Beyond

Hewlett-Packard Precision Architecture goes far beyond the fundamental precepts of RISC. HPPA encompasses aspects of the computer system other than the instruction set and operating philosophy.

HPPA is the result of one of the most exhaustive measurement projects ever undertaken by a computer manufacturer. Over *one billion* lines of program code acquired from end-users in the HP, IBM, and DEC communities were compiled, executed, and measured with innovative instrumentation and techniques. Numerous new concepts in operating system and compiler design have been incorporated into the MPE XL implementation on HPPA. These innovations are coupled with new hardware concepts that are also the result of the measurement project.

Advances such as these led to the establishment of the formal architecture known as HPPA. The main points of HPPA are described below. Those points that represent Hewlett-Packard extentions to RISC are denoted by the special symbol ∎:

☐ A reduced number of instructions (HPPA has 140, while the CISC-based HP 3000 has over 250), most of which execute in one clock cycle. Instructions fall into the general categories of load, store, branch, add, subtract, and control. Further, they are implemented in hardware in order to speed execution.

☐ Instructions have a fixed size, which simplifies the fetch mechanism.

☐ All memory access done via load and store instructions. All other instructions act solely upon registers.

☐ The design facilitates pipelining, which increases instruction throughput. HPPA uses a three-level pipeline approach.

∎ Virtual memory is very large, with a 64-bit addressing capability.

∎ Memory-mapped I/O, which make I/O drivers easier to write and enable the user to perform direct I/O functions.

- Separate high-performance cache memory for both data (D-cache) and code (I-cache).

- Optimizing compilers.

- Support for multiple coprocessors for increased performance.

By implementing these ideas, the engineers at Hewlett-Packard have created a computer architecture which meets many criteria:

- A single architecture, scalable from small desktop computers to large mainframes.

- Execution speeds limited only by the target IC technology and clock speeds.

- Capability of leveraging software development from different markets and HP divisions onto the entire product line.

- Lower support and maintenance costs, because support personnel can be trained across the product line.

The evolution of computer architectures has advanced greatly in the last few decades. Developments in hardware design, technologies, and software tools have made possible a simple yet powerful design that is capable of many varied applications. Hewlett-Packard Precision Architecture is the culmination of all of the developments and ideas, and it is the architecture that will carry HP's product line to the end of the century.

4

The HP 3000
Architecture

The HP 3000 family of computers has been and continues to be the foundation of Hewlett-Packard's commercial computer product line. So significant is the market recognition of the HP 3000 that the company chose to market the commercial version of Hewlett-Packard Precision Architecture (HPPA) machines under the HP 3000 name rather than as a new line of computers.

The existing HP 3000 product line, introduced in 1972, has therefore had tremendous influence on the look and feel of MPE XL, the HPPA version of MPE. To better understand the impact of this influence, this chapter will take a theoretical look at the hardware architecture of the traditional HP 3000s.

Complex Instruction Set Computing

There are several ways the HP 3000 satisfies the classic description of a CISC (Complex Instruction Set Computing) machine, as described in Chapter 3. First, the machine instruction set is large and depends heavily upon microcode. The instruction set is quite 'rich' and has many addressing modes, and it provides full functionality. Specific instructions have been added to the instruction set over the years to assist with COBOL, packed decimal instructions, and to speed up entire procedures within MPE. The HP 3000 Series 37, 5X, 6X, 7X, and the Micro 3000 have Writable Control Store to increase the usefulness and flexibility of the microcode.

Another hallmark of the HP 3000 is its use of a stack model in accessing data. The stack model of data storage can be illustrated by the stack of building blocks shown in Figure 4.1. Just as building blocks can be placed one on top of the other, the stack model in a computer system allows data to be placed on top of the stack -- and to be removed from the top.

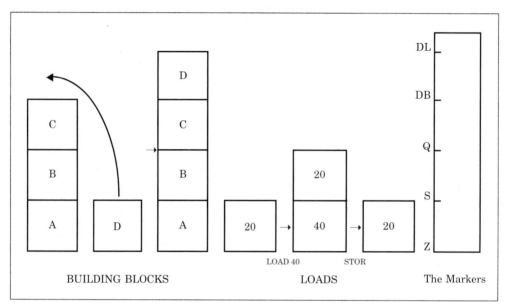

Figure 4.1 The MPE V Stack

This constitutes a data access queuing method called 'Last In First Out' (LIFO). Many elegant computer algorithms depend upon the simplicity of the stack and this LIFO queuing capability. When data is placed on the stack, it is said to be 'pushed' or 'loaded'. Removal from the stack is done by 'popping' or 'storing' the data. Figure 4.1 shows this loading and storing operation with numbers and the upside-down method in which a stack is usually drawn. This is done because it more closely models the top-to-bottom method used when writing program code.

The data stack concept has existed for many years. Most applications of stacks are done by software, usually on a small scale to provide a tool within a program for a specific task. Most CISC machines provide some sort of hardware-assisted stack. This applies even to the new generation of small-but-sophisticated microprocessors, such as the 8086/88 family from Intel and the 68000 family from Motorola.

But in very few cases has the stack model been used as the principle way of accessing data. Many Burroughs machines used the stack design, and because many HP 3000 designers came from Burroughs, so do the HP 3000s. In the HP 3000s, the stack model is used to the fullest, and depends heavily upon microcode.

Unlike the MPE V-based HP 3000s, RISC machines have no microcode, so the stack model is left to the software level. As shall be seen in Chapter 6, HPPA does make use of the stack structure, but not in the same way as the traditional HP 3000. (For the remainder of *this* chapter, the term HP 3000 will refer to those HP 3000s other than the Series 930 and 950, which are not based upon HPPA.)

Overall Hardware Structure

As with any computer system, the HP 3000 has two primary resources: memory and CPU. The registers that delimit various objects within memory are 16 bits wide. Consequently, no memory address can be larger than the quantity that can be contained in 16 bits, which is 65535 two-byte words. In the original HP 3000, this was the total amount of memory possible, measured in 16-bit words. Thus, 128K bytes of memory were possible, as a 16-bit word consisted of two bytes.

Even in 1972, this maximum memory size was a severe limitation. To get around the problem, another 16-bit register was added, and memory was divided into banks, each of which could contain 65535 two-byte words.

The memories of all computer systems contain two entities: code and data. Code consists of individual instructions that the computer must act upon in order to do useful work; data consists of bits of information upon which the code acts. Physically, data and code are just numbers stored in memory. Many machines built before and since the HP 3000 do not provide any type of explicit separation between code and data; code can locate and modify itself just as if it were data. This can lead to some interesting problems when done inadvertently -- and to comfortable job security for programmers who do it intentionally.

Code Segments and Data Segments

The HP 3000 divides and explicitly separates code and data into segments. Executable HP 3000 machine code resides in code segments, and modifiable data areas reside in data segments. These entities are known to both the microcode and software. Code is not modifiable by normal (non-privileged) means, and this protection is stringently enforced by the microcode. Data segments are modifiable, and the memory manager (in software) ensures that the copy in memory is swapped to disc when appropriate.

All stacks are contained within data segments. A stack data segment contains the main data areas built by the compiler when the program is compiled and prepared. Both code and data segments are tracked by the Code Segment Table (CST) and Data Segment Table (DST). These tables are known and modified by both the operating system software and the system microcode.

Registers

The HP 3000 has a variety of registers that perform different functions. (Registers are high-speed, relatively expensive data storage areas in the CPU.) The main registers delimit areas of the stack and are changed by the microcode and operating system as the program executes. There are three basic groups of registers: data registers, code registers, and miscellaneous registers.

All registers are 16 bits wide. The stack registers start with the S (Stack) Bank and DB (Database) Bank. Memory in the HP 3000 is divided into banks of 64K words. These Bank Registers contain the memory bank number that contains the stack and the current location of DB, respectively. The DB register acts as a 'zero point' for addressing a program's data. DL (Data Limit) points to the area of the stack that is the lowest addressable memory address available to the user. The Q Register provides a movable base (zero point) for a procedure's data area. The S Register points to a word called 'Top-Of-Stack' (TOS), where calculations are performed, and the Z Register delimits the top of the stack area in memory. In other words, the stack is shown as growing down on the page, and shrinking up on the page. Thus, higher memory addresses are listed lower on the page.

The PB (Program Base) Bank contains the memory bank number of the executing code segment. The PB Register delimits the beginning of the executing code, and the PL (Program Limit) marks the end of that segment. The P (Program) Register points to the currently executing machine instruction.

The STATUS Register contains many fields which describe the current state of the machine. The X (Index) Register is used by many of the various load and store instructions as an aid in indexed addressing. The CIR (Current Instruction Register) contains the actual value of the executing machine instruction. The other miscellaneous registers vary among the specific CPU models, and they are primarily of interest only to the microcode programmers and hardware support technicians.

The data registers have a very important role in the definition of HP 3000 architecture. The specific manipulation of these registers defines -- to a large extent -- the unique features of the HP 3000. The area between DL and DB has no specific purpose defined by the hardware or software architecture. It is capable of being expanded and contracted at will by software and is thus accessed as a dynamic data buffer.

A good example of the use of the DL area can be seen by the utility program FCOPY, which is used to perform various file copy and dump functions. FCOPY must be able to handle a file with an arbitrary record length, as long as the record size does not exceed the maximum allowed for the system. Thus, FCOPY's data buffer must be able to handle up to this maximum record size. While this may seem simple, it is actually somewhat tricky.

The simplest technique to overcome this problem is to define a buffer in the program as large as the largest data record allowable. This would work, but FCOPY would then have a very large stack, which would impose a large memory requirement (and overhead) on the system. In practice, very few files have this large a record size. Thus the memory allocated to this large data area would be unused and therefore wasted most of the time.

A much more efficient and elegant approach is to use the DL-DB area. When FCOPY is given file names of the source and destination files, it uses the file system to interrogate the files and determine their record sizes. It then expands the DL area to the largest record size and proceeds by using the DL-DB area as a buffer. When the copy is done, FCOPY shrinks the DL-DB area back to the minimum, thus returning memory to the system.

VPLUS/3000, Hewlett-Packard's Form Management System, also uses this area to store data buffers for an arbitrarily large screen definition. When VPLUS/3000 opens a form file, it determines the largest data buffer of any form in the file and allocates a DL-DB area that size. Additional storage is retained in this area for other data structures required by VPLUS/3000.

Another subsystem on the HP 3000 that avails itself of this useful area is Pascal/V. The Pascal language embodies a concept known as a 'heap'. Philosophically, a heap is much like a stack. Data can be placed on the heap, accessed, and deleted. The implementation of Pascal on the HP 3000 uses this DL area for its heap storage. Because the heap expands and contracts, the DL-DB area allows for a very efficient implementation of this concept.

The DB-Q area is accessible by all parts of a program. This is the area where the main data used by the program is stored, and it also houses those data areas declared in the main part of the program, such as working storage in a main COBOL program. Other languages make use of this area in slightly different ways, depending upon the requirements of the compiler and language constructs. Of particular interest is the way in which SPL (Systems Programming Language) accesses this area.

Spl and Data Addressing

The language SPL was developed by Hewlett-Packard at the same time as the HP 3000 and MPE -- and by the same people. Although the trend was to use some sort of assembler as the prime language for constructing the operating system and utilities, this small group opted instead for a high-level systems language.

Foremost among this group were Burroughs engineers and others familiar with Burroughs equipment. The Burroughs development language was a version of ALGOL with some extension. Likewise, SPL is an ALGOL-like language with extensions that allowed the programmer to access some of the hardware/ architectural features of the machine.

SPL was conceived as a language whose statements mapped closely into the instruction set of the HP 3000. SPL represented an easily understood software manifestation of these instructions. For example, the SPL grammar includes a statement called 'MOVE', which allowed a data array of arbitrary length to be moved from one area of the stack to another. Moves can be done for word (16-bit) data and byte (8-bit) data. The machine instruction set provides the MOVE instruction (move words) and the MVB (move bytes) instruction, which the SPL MOVE statement directly generates. The MOVE statement allows certain types of stack manipulation which directly map into the MOVE and MVB instruction parameters.

Another example is the SCAN instruction. SPL defines a SCAN WHILE statement and SCAN UNTIL statement, which correspond to the SCW and SCU instructions. Again, stack manipulations provided by the machine instructions are made visible to the SPL programmer through the language grammar.

Given SPL's philosophy of representing a high level interface to the machine hardware, note how SPL accesses the DB-Q area, as this most naturally maps into the various address modes and data access instructions provided by the instruction set. SPL divides the area into two areas: the primary DB and the secondary DB, as shown in Figure 4.2.

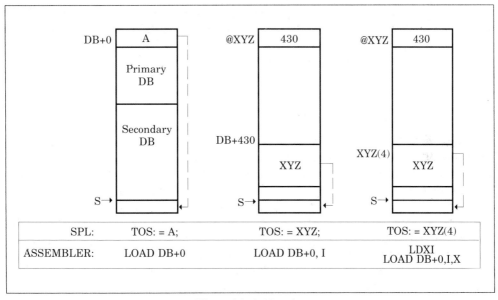

Figure 4.2 Addressing

The primary DB area is used to contain primary, simple variables, such as 16- and 32-bit integers (type INTEGER and DOUBLE), 16-bit unsigned quantities (LOGICAL), and 32- and 64-bit real numbers (REAL and LONG). The machine instruction format for data loading and storing (LOAD and STOR instructions) allows 8 bits for a DB-relative address; thus, 256 words of data storage can be accessed directly by the LOAD and STOR instructions. Direct access to data is one address mode provided by the instruction set. If the instruction LOAD DB+24 is executed, the HP 3000 will access the 16-bit memory word pointed to by the DB Register plus 24. This word is loaded onto TOS, the top of the stack. The SPL statement for this would be:

```
INTEGER I;       << Assume I at DB+24 >>
     .
     .
TOS := I;        << generates a LOAD DB+24>>
```

The secondary DB area of SPL contains data defined in arrays. The arrays are accessed by another address mode called 'indirect addressing' (see Figure 4.2). In this mode, a 16-bit word is addressed via the instruction using direct addressing, and this word is interpreted to be a 16-bit address of the beginning of the data array. Thus, the array is accessed indirectly through a DB-relative word.

In Figure 4.2, the array XYZ is accessed through DB+0. An instruction to load the first word of this array onto TOS would be LOAD DB+0,I, where I stands for indirect. The SPL statement that corresponds to this instruction would be:

```
ARRAY XYZ(0:10);
        .
        .
        .
TOS := XYZ;       << generates a LOAD DB+0,I>>
```

One other address mode is provided: indexed addressing. In this mode, the load or store operation uses the Index (X) Register as an additional level of indirection. In Figure 4.2 you can see an example of this type of addressing. The fourth word of array XYZ is to be loaded. It is assumed the X Register has been loaded with the number 4 at some point before this. The SPL compiler will normally perform this function. When the LOAD DB+0,I,X instruction executes, the HP 3000 uses the 16-bit word at DB+0 as a 16-bit, DB-relative address, then adds the contents of the Index Register to access DB+434. This type of addressing allows for indexed addressing of arrays. The SPL statement for this would be:

```
ARRAY XYZ(0:10);
        .
.TOS := XYZ(4);    << generates LDXI 4;LOAD DB+0,I,X>>
```

The next area of the stack is the area between the Q and S registers. This area is used by procedures to contain local data areas. A procedure is a special type of code module on the HP 3000 and deserves some special attention.

The way in which the stack is manipulated during the call to a procedure is by far the most elegant example of the power of the stack model and its use on the HP 3000. A procedure is entered via the PCAL (Procedure CALl) machine instruction. This instruction locates the proper area of memory where the target code resides. It sets the PB and PL Registers to delimit this area, and it sets the P Register to the proper starting point. In addition, it places a special data structure called a 'stack marker' on the stack at the current location of the S Register. Refer to Figure 4.3 for diagrams of the stack before and after the procedure call.

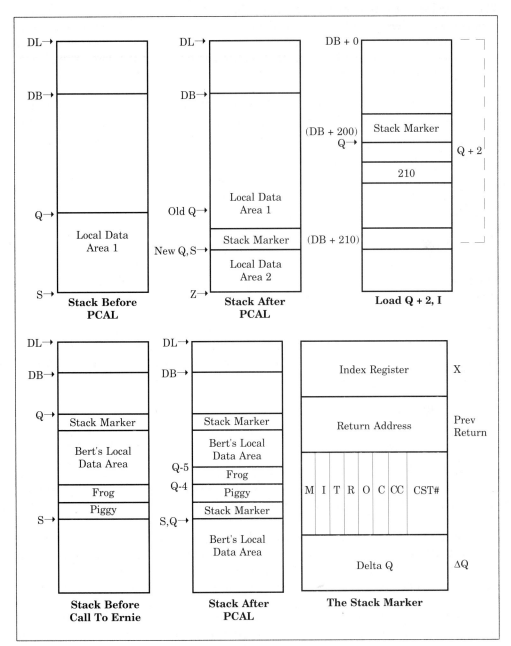

Figure 4.3 Views of the Stack

Just as Hansel and Gretel left bread crumbs in the forest, the stack marker helps the HP 3000 to find its way from one procedure to another. When the called procedure ends, it returns to the calling procedure via the EXIT instruction, which uses the stack marker to reset the machine to its state before the call. The PCAL/EXIT instruction pair thus provide the means to utilize the power of stack data storage paradigm to its fullest.

At the start of the procedure, the needed amount of Q-S area is allocated on the stack. This is the responsibility of the called procedure and is done simply by incrementing the S Register the desired number of words.

The Q-S area acts as a data storage area for that procedure. Like the DB area, this area is also divided into primary and secondary areas. The data access machine instructions can access the Q+ and Q- areas via direct access, and they can use both of these address modes for indirect and/or indexed addressing as well. In addition, the DB area also is available to the procedure, just as before. Note that when accessing data via indirect addressing, the address contained within the word being accessed is interpreted by the machine instructions as being DB-relative, even though the data word may be accessed Q+ or Q- relative.

An example of this is shown in Figure 4.3, described as follows: A LOAD Q+2,I is executed. This tells the machine to take the current value of Q (200 in this case) and add 2 to it, then find a 16-bit word at this location and interpret the number it contains as a DB-relative address. Likewise, the Q+ area can be used to contain simple type INTEGER and DOUBLE variables. In this way, each time the procedure is called, the local data area is freshly created, and there is no need to clear the data area. The advantages of this use of the stack include being able to call an individual procedure from any other procedure without regard to where its data will be stored, and allowing the procedure to call itself (a so-called 'recursive procedure').

The Q- area is used to address the stack marker and the parameter area. Philosophically, a procedure can be thought of as a 'pre-packaged' chunk of code available to do a particular task. In mathematical terms, this is known as a 'function'. When the procedure is called, data known as 'parameters' are passed to it that are unique for that invocation of the procedure. On the HP 3000, the stack is used both to pass the parameters and to store data. Refer to Figure 4.3 for a more complete view of the stack.

In this example, the procedure BERT is calling the procedure ERNIE and is passing two integer parameters, FROG and PIGGY. The parameters are loaded onto the stack just before the PCAL. The Q+ area is available for local storage, and the parameters are addressed via references to Q-5 and Q-4. Notice that the stack marker can also be referenced via Q- addressing. This is often done in order to pass data (such as condition codes) back to the calling procedure.

When the procedure has finished executing its designed task, it returns via the EXIT instruction, as previously mentioned. This instruction is essentially the opposite of the PCAL instruction. It, too, must set the stack and code registers to the proper positions, but does so primarily via the stack marker. Refer to the stack marker diagram in Figure 4.3.

The first word, called 'Delta-Q', is used to decrement the Q Register back to the point of the last stack marker. The second word is the hardware status register and contains the code segment number of the calling procedure. The stack marker also contains the condition code, information on whether the machine is running in Privileged Mode, etc. The third word contains the location within the code segment to set the P Register upon return. The fourth word is the value of the Index Register, which may be needed to complete a pending operation in the calling procedure.

In addition to restoring the state of the machine via the status register, the EXIT instruction decrements the S Register to the current value of Q (before subtracting the value of Delta Q), effectively peeling off the area of the stack used by the current procedure. Thus, when the procedure exits, the local data area used is effectively destroyed -- although this area is not explicitly cleared. Again, this technique illustrates the stack's versatility.

The area between the S and Z Registers has two distinct uses. As described above, it is used as an area for stack expansion when a procedure is called. During a procedure call operation, the Q Register is set equal to the S Register, and the S-Z is used to contain the procedure's local data area. It is also used as a dynamic calculation area. One class of machine instructions exists called the 'stack operations' (stackops). This set of instructions acts upon the top few words of the stack, with these stack words being implicit operands.

An example of this type of operations is the machine instruction ADD. The ADD instruction is designed to take the top two 16-bit words of the stack and add them. The two operands are then popped from the stack, and the result is pushed back onto the stack. Figure 4.4 shows the various operations involved in this, including the two LOAD instructions that would be necessary to initialize the two top stack words, and the STOR instruction that would be executed to place the result in the proper storage location.

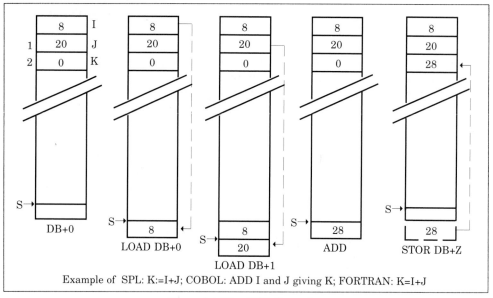

8	I
20	J
0	K

Example of SPL: K:=I+J; COBOL: ADD I and J giving K; FORTRAN: K=I+J

Figure 4.4 The ADD Operation

Typically, a machine instruction will include a number representing an address to be acted upon. For example, the LOAD instruction includes 8 bits for a DB-, Q- or S-relative address that is to be loaded onto TOS. Stack operations are the exception to this rule. Since the operands of the instructions are defined to be some number of words on the stack, no room in the instruction format need be reserved for operands. Because of this, the machine instruction itself occupies less space, and two stack operations can be packed into a single 16-bit machine instruction word. From this we see another benefit of the stack architecture: increased code density.

Code Registers

There are three code segment registers: the PB (Program Base), PL (Program Limit), and P (current Program instruction) Registers. These delimit the top and bottom of the executing code segment and point to the location of the instruction that is executing at that given instant. When one instruction executes, the P Register is incremented and the next instruction fetched.

All computer systems have registers, and what really differentiates the architectures of most computers is the number, width, and function of the registers. On the HP 3000, a key architectural limitation is that the registers are all 16 bits wide.

When the HP 3000 was introduced in 1972, it could only address 128 kilobytes of memory. The ramifications of this very fundamental limitation affect virtually every aspect of the HP 3000 architecture.

This is indeed the case with the HP 3000. No single segment (code *or* data) can be larger than 64K words. In fact, the maximum size is smaller for several reasons. For code segments, the size is limited by the fact that the code segment table allows only for a size of 14 bits, resulting in a maximum code segment size of 16K words. The stack is limited to 32K words because the DL area is addressed negatively, relative to DB. (The instruction set does not allow DL relative addressing). This negative addressing dictates the use of a sign bit, lowering the number of available address bits to 15.

Add to this that the machine must be able to address on byte boundaries, and a situation is created that limits the address space to 64K bytes (32K words). A factor which further limits a segment to less than 64K words is the data overhead which must be maintained in the memory bank for MPE's use.

All of these registers (except those containing bank numbers) store values relative to the beginning of a bank. The full location of the beginning of a code segment is indicated by the PB Bank Register and the PB Register. Similarly, the DB Bank Register tells the machine in which bank of memory to look for the stack. Notice, however, that there is not a PL Bank Register or a Z Bank Register. The implication of this is that no segment can span a bank boundary, which is another factor that limits the size of a segment.

The specific function of the registers is determined by microcode. When a particular machine instruction is executed, the microcode manipulates the various registers in a particular fashion dictated by that instruction. For example, when a LOAD instruction is encountered, the microcode determines the memory address to access, and that word is loaded at the memory location currently pointed to by the S Register. When this is done, the microcode increments S, increments P, and fetches the next instruction to be executed.

The microprogram breathes life into the registers. Without this control by the microcode, the registers have no real meaning. On the HP 3000, the registers are really defined by a software entity (microcode) and not necessarily by any inherent hardware design.

Another very important use of microcode is low-level error checking. For example, the microcode for the LOAD instruction checks the value of the newly incremented S

Register to see if it is equal to the Z Register. If it is, a condition called 'stack overflow' has been created, and a trap call to an interrupt procedure to handle stack overflows is generated. All machine instructions that explicitly or implicitly move the S Register up in memory check for this condition. There are many such traps, including stack underflow, integer overflow, and execution mode (privileged vs. user) traps. The access to these interrupt routines in software is done via hard-coded calls, called 'ININ' (INternal INterrupt), to specific routines in a specific code segment. Again, the microcode is a very large and complex part of the implementation of the system architecture.

Virtual Memory

Another important subject in this discussion is 'virtual memory'. On MPE V-based HP 3000 machines, virtual memory is a specific area of the disc used to store data segments when there is no room in real memory. A given data segment is assigned a specific disc address, which is used by the memory manager whenever the segment is swapped out. The hardware (in reality the microcode) knows very little about virtual memory. It knows only how to determine whether or not a segment is in memory and how to interrupt the system when someone tries to access a segment that is not in memory. Software takes over from there.

Software Conventions

We have discussed several conventions which collectively constitute the architecture of the HP 3000. These can be thought of as hardware conventions, although many of them are built into the microcode. But before leaving this discussion of the HP 3000, it is important to discuss software conventions as well.

Essentially, the HP 3000 architecture *per se* does not impose any conventions upon the software. The closest it comes to software-regulated architecture is the way in which SPL accesses the machine, and in those conventions that make use of the stack architecture.

One of those conventions is the use of the Q-S area for procedure parameters and local variables. Some languages have features which dictate a modified use of this area. For example, COBOL embodies a concept called a 'non-dynamic subroutine'. Put in terms of the HP 3000 architecture, this would be a procedure in which the data area does not get reinitialized every time it is called. To accomplish this, COBOL must do its data addressing in a manner different than SPL.

Typically, Q+1 is set to point to an area in memory that contains the data area necessary for the particular code module executing. All addressing of data is done directly relative to Q+1, with the byte addresses of the data being loaded directly from code. Thus, COBOL does not maintain primary and secondary DB areas, but addresses all data directly, as SPL does with primary DB.

One convention strictly adhered to by all compilers is parameter passing. Because there are not explicit registers that can be used for parameter passing, this is really the only avenue left for the compilers. The only way this convention could be averted is if the compiler reserved space in a specified area for parameters. Because the stack model is so elegant for this use, such reserved space is not seen on any compiler that runs on the HP 3000. It is therefore possible for a procedure to call or be called from a procedure in any other language.

5

RISC and
HP Precision Architecture

This chapter examines several facets of Hewlett-Packard Precision Architecture (HPPA) and the origins of Reduced Instruction Set Computing (RISC).

Webster's New Collegiate Dictionary defines the term 'architecture' as:

> 1. the art or science of building; specifically the art or practice of designing and building structures and especially habitable ones, 2. formation or construction as or as if as the result of conscious act, 3. architectural product or work, and 4. a method or style of building.

In regard to computers, the term can be applied to the underlying formation or construction of a system. This doesn't mean the hardware boards and backplanes, but the models and ideas behind how the computer accesses memory, adds numbers, and so forth. For example, Chapter 4 describes how segments are used by the HP 3000 to separate code and data. The 'segment' concept is part of the overall architecture. That code and data are kept separate and that code is not modifiable are also parts of the HP 3000 architecture.

Because of HP's desire to unify all computer product lines under a single architecture, the definition of the machine became as important as the machine itself. In fact, in the minds of everyone at HP, the architecture became an entity unto itself. It was designed and argued about, tested and verified, and finally given life. For the first time in HP's history, the design of the computer system was largely disembodied from the realization of the design.

To understand why this kind of emphasis is placed on the architectural aspects of a new line of computers, it is necessary to examine the history of the design and take a look at the motivations behind its development.

Hppa and RISC

The idea that computers should be made simpler -- not more complex -- was all that was needed to initiate the development of HPPA. (See the Reduced Instruction Set Computing design precepts listed in Chapter 3.) This set of precepts did not represent a specific computer as much as an idea about the way computers should work -- an idea in direct conflict with the prevailing CISC (Complex Instruction Set Computing) philosophy of building machines with microcode and many complex instructions.

One computer scientist who worked on developing this concept of simpler computers was Dr. Joel Birnbaum at IBM's Thomas Watson Research Facility. His work was to develop RISC concepts and create working models of computer systems. After much research and development effort was expended by Birnbaum and his associates (most notably, William Worley), IBM decided not to develop RISC into actual products at that time. It was not until Dr. Birnbaum became head of HP Laboratories that he was able to realize his ambition to build a RISC-based computer. With corporate support for his ideas, he started what is now known as 'the Spectrum Program'.

Development of HPPA

A development team was created within HP Labs to analyze the requirements of a RISC-based computer architecture. The team consisted of computer hardware experts, of course, but because the early research into RISC showed that a heavy involvement by software would be necessary to make the architecture viable, the design team also included software experts (compiler writers, specialists in system performance, and specialists in computer simulations). This mix of disciplines was unique within HP. Typically, a computer system is designed by the hardware group, then once the fundamental architecture is completed, the documentation is given to the software group so they can design the operating system. Thus, most fundamental decisions are made by the time the software group gets involved. (A very good example of this is chronicled in Tracy Kidder's Pulitzer Prize-winning book *The Soul of a New Machine*.)

One of the assumptions made by the original RISC proponents was that most of the work done by the computer system was done by a very small subset of the instruction set. But because no large-scale scientific measurement had been done on commercial systems running actual customer workloads, the first task given to the performance analysis experts was to gather specific data on exactly what machine instructions *were* executed in these environments. To do this, various data collection and measuring tools were gathered and/or developed and used at HP customer sites. Traces of billions of instruction sequences were analyzed. After a year or so of data collection, some very good and accurate assessments were made about the type of instructions and work mixes used by real computers doing real work for real people.

Armed with this data, the design team began to make detailed decisions about which machine instructions should be included in the HPPA instruction set. Because the compilers played a key part in the architecture, the software experts provided input as to what instructions should be included and debated the relative difficulty of implementing particular functionality in the hardware versus the software and the compilers. Likewise, the hardware experts made sure no instructions would make the hardware unduly difficult to design or implement. Hundreds of these design trade-offs were made, and finally an instruction set was agreed upon which provided the best mix of hardware and software functionality.

One of the results of this development effort was a set of documents called *The Architecture Control Documents* (ACDs). This set was the 'Bible' for everyone within the Spectrum Program, and collectively these documents constitute *the* definition of Hewlett-Packard Precision Architecture.

Another result of this development effort was a computer simulator program which ran on the HP 9000 series of computers under an HP-UX environment. Along with this, a test suite of programs were developed which could be run on a processor to verify whether that computer adhered to the architecture as defined in the ACDs. These Architecture Verification Programs (AVPs) would become necessary later when different processors were designed using very different semiconductor technologies. The simulator provided some modeling capabilities which were very important to the software people who were to do the initial algorithm and performance development and testing.

The important distinction to make here is that the architecture was *on paper only*, with some simulations in software written on a Motorola 68000-based microcomputer.

At Hewlett-Packard, none of the major computer architectures (HP 3000 and HP 1000) had ever been conceived apart from the environment within which they would operate. The HP 3000 had been conceived as a commercial computer that would be used for payroll, personnel, and related applications. The HP 1000 line had always been intended for use within a technical process control and real-time computing environment. However, commercial and real-time environments require very different capabilities for the computer systems used within them.

While there are some commercial applications written for the HP 1000 and some real-time applications written for the HP 3000, these do not represent the best fit of application to hardware. The microcoded environment of the HP 3000 does not provide facilities for handling interrupts in any prioritized manner and provides no guarantees as to the timing possible for response. Thus, the very architecture that has made the HP 3000 such a good business machine precluded its use in a real-time environment. Likewise, the HP 1000 did not (until recently) have virtual memory. It was conceived as a page- and partition-based architecture to guarantee real-time response when necessary. Consequently, the HP 1000 was not designed with some of the features required of a good commercial machine.

The most important goal of the Spectrum Program was to produce computers that could operate in virtually any environment (real-time, commercial, multi-processor, fault-tolerant) and be scalable from small to large systems. Only by conceiving of the architecture as separate from any one of these environments could HP build computer systems that could perform all the functions. HP has done this in HP Precision Architecture. Philosophically, the computer systems resulting from HPPA could be described as blank pieces of paper upon which a software environment that fulfills the requirements of a particular market can be imposed. This software layer takes the place of the microcode layer in CISC machines. Obviously, multiple processor environments must be conceived along with the hardware architecture, but this can be separate from such facets of an architecture as addressing modes, instruction sets, and procedure-calling conventions.

Technical Aspects of HPPA

Hewlett-Packard Precision Architecture has been called the first viable commercial implementation of the RISC model, but it is unfair to describe it in these RISC terms only. It is probably more accurate to say that HPPA is a RISC-like implementation, since the main attributes of HPPA (as outlined in Chapter 3) do at times deviate from the original RISC concept. The specific features of this architecture were determined by the careful measurement studies performed by the HP Laboratories. The following sections detail the features and describe how they can be utilized to provide computing power to HP's diverse markets. Finally, HPPA will be contrasted with the traditional HP 3000 architecture.

Data Types

Hewlett-Packard Precision Architecture supports the most commonly used data types. All the HPPA registers are 32 bits wide, the most common and natural format for the machine. This type is defined as type integer in Pascal/XL. Integers that are 16 bits wide (and thus provide compatibility to MPE V-based HP 3000s) are called 'half-words' and are defined as type SHORTINT in Pascal/XL. Bytes are 8-bit quantities and can be defined as type CHAR in Pascal/XL.

Real (floating-point) numbers are stored in formats that correspond to the proposed Institute for Electrical and Electronic Engineers (IEEE) standard for floating point. This standard was created with the goal of increasing compatibility and transportability of code written on different computers. The significand and exponent are stored in a normal form, which means that the numbers are adjusted such that an implicit binary 1 is inserted before the binary point. In addition, a constant is added to the exponent, which is biased. This is done to make comparison of real numbers possible via a simple byte comparison.

No hardware instructions defined by HPPA directly manipulate these real numbers. All that is defined is that the real formats adhere to the IEEE standard. (Note: This is not the real number standard used in MPE V-based HP 3000s.) Floating point calculations are performed either in hardware by the floating point co-processor or by software routines if a co-processor is not installed on the system.

In addition to the hardware data types listed above, you can use software to declare other data types. The Pascal language (and thus HP Pascal/XL) allows the definition of user-definable types called 'enumerated types'. Using these, programmers can define symbolic names for data properties, such as defining sex and marital status as types for employee records. The data abstraction defined by the record is thus closer to the way people think of the data.

For example, an employee is male or female, and these words can actually be used in an enumerated type. In other languages, the data item containing the sex will contain a number and each value will be made equivalent to a sex. Thus, male might be stored as the value 0, and female as the value 1. In reality, Pascal will translate the enumerated type into a number corresponding to its position in the definition. For example, consider the following definition:

```
TYPE
    sex     = (male,female);
```

Type male will be assigned a zero by the compiler and type female will be assigned a one. The programmer need never know this and need think of the sex only in terms of male or female, not in terms of zeros or ones. It is important to realize that the hardware of an HPPA machine deals with this type of data only in an integer form, and thus these data types are strictly defined by software.

Registers

The first major difference between HPPA and MPE V-based HP 3000 is the presence of numerous general-purpose registers. In the notation of HPPA, these are called 'General Registers' (GR0 through GR31). In assembly language, these are R0 through R31. As discussed in Chapter 4, the MPE V-based HP 3000 has quite a few registers which have special names, such as DB and Q, and are defined by the microcode. They also have special purposes and are manipulated by the microcode in special ways. In general, a programmer does not have or need explicit control over these registers. Operations are performed by loading data on the stack, then executing some sort of instruction that acts using the data just loaded.

Here is a sample of SPL (Systems Programming Language) code performing simple addition.

```
BEGIN
INTEGER A,B,C;

  A := B + C; << SPL statement >>

END.
```

The following sequence of HP 3000 machine instructions could be generated:

```
ASSEMBLE(LOAD B; LOAD C;  ADD; STOR A); <<ASSEMBLER statement>>
```

The Top-Of-Stack (TOS) region for the above code is shown in Figure 5.1. The first two loads take data from some memory location assigned to B and C and place the values at those locations on top of the stack. As each datum is loaded, the S Register is incremented by the microcode so it points to the word just loaded. The ADD instruction microcode knows to take the two words on the top of stack and add them, pop both words off the stack, and push the result back on the stack. (This operation was described in Chapter 4.)

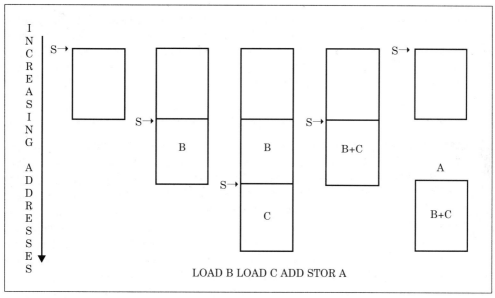

Figure 5.1 MPE V-based HP 3000 Stack Operation

It could be assumed from this example that the machine instructions act upon memory locations. The picture presented of the MPE V-based HP 3000 is that the TOS location is in memory, located at the bank and offset of memory pointed to by the S-Bank and S Registers. But in reality, the top data words on the stack (pointed to by the S Register) are *not* in memory. They are CPU registers.

The first four TOS words are referred to as the A, B, C, and D registers. Different MPE V-based HP 3000 models have different numbers of TOS registers. The Series II/III have four, while the Series 70 has eight. The original instruction set was optimized for four registers, but the packed decimal and COBOL II instructions demanded more than four. Thus, for performance reasons, the later machines were given a more generous supply of these very fast, very useful registers.

You cannot, however, access these registers explicitly. For instance, there are no 'LOAD into Register B' or 'Add using C and A as operands' instructions. You can load and store to and from these registers, but the instruction set does this *implicitly*, not explicitly. The programmer knows *only* that the machine is loading and storing to and from the stack. The original HP 3000 designers felt that the microcode and SPL would manipulate these registers, leaving less work and worry for the programmer.

Compiler design and newer languages (such as Pascal) have also greatly simplified the programmer's task. On an HP 3000 Series 930, for example, the Pascal/XL compiler statements and assembly code would look like this:

```
PROGRAM MAIN;
VAR

    i,j,k: integer;

BEGIN

  i := j + k; {Note similarity of this code to SPL}

END.
```

The code generated could look like:

```
LDW 84(0,27),5        ;assume j at DP+84
LDW 88(0,27),6        ;assume k at DP+88
ADD 5,6,7
STW 7,80(0,27)        ;assume i at DP+80
```

A diagram of the above sequence and the corresponding register manipulation and data flow are shown in Figure 5.2.

HP Precision Architecture, in contrast to the MPE V-based HP 3000 philosophy, has opened up these registers for explicit manipulation. All HPPA machines have 32 general-purpose registers that are 32 bits wide, all accessible from the instruction set. One of the many controversies that has raged in the academic community regarding implementation of a RISC machine concerned registers. It was believed that hundreds would be needed to make RISC viable. The measurements and modeling done by HP Labs in the investigation stages of the Spectrum Program showed, however, that this was not the case. After extensive experimentation, 32 registers were found to provide the optimal performance.

These registers, like all CPU registers, are implemented in very fast electronics within the CPU itself. Only GR0, GR1, and GR31 have been given specific uses by the hardware architects. A load from Register GR0 will always load a zero, and when stored to, will cause the stored data to be discarded. Register GR1 is used as the target of the ADDIL (ADD Immediate Left) instruction, and GR31 receives the branch target address when executing the BLE (Branch and Link External) instruction. This facilitates very fast initialization of registers, and allows for a NOP-type instruction, as one does not exist in the HPPA instruction set. Many of the other registers have uses by software and compiler convention, and these will be discussed in Chapter 6.

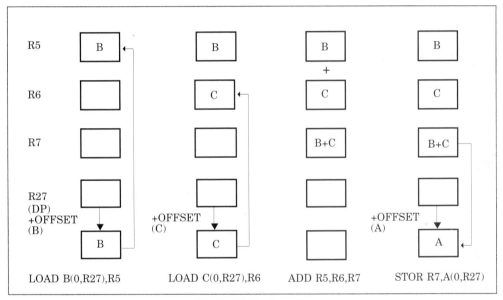

Figure 5.2 HPPA Register Operation

Other registers exist as well, most of which are controlled by the hardware and not explicitly by the programmer. All are 32 bits long. The IA (Instruction Address) Register is analogous to the P Register of the MPE V-based HP 3000 and keeps track of the address of the executing instruction. The IA Register tracks the space number of the currently executing code, and is, in fact, the offset into the instruction code space.

There are eight general-purpose space registers, numbered SR0 through SR7, which keep track of various space numbers, and some can be loaded and stored by code at various privilege levels. There is the Processor Status Word (PSW), which is similar to the status register of the MPE V-based HP 3000. In HP Precision Architecture, however, the status register contains only status-oriented information and does not include such things as the code segment number. There are 25 control registers, most of which are inaccessible by unprivileged software but are necessary for the operation of the machine. These are referred to as CR0 and CR8-32, denoting Control Register n.

Addressing

Discussion of the registers flows naturally into discussion of how addressing is done on HPPA. There exist two address modes: real and virtual. Real addressing is used to address actual semiconductor memory on the machine. This is a 32-bit address space, and thus HPPA can theoretically support 2^{32} bytes of real memory, or four gigabytes. In reality, the real memory supported is less, because the I/O is mapped into part of this address space. The addressing mode more commonly used is virtual addressing. To understand virtual addressing, the concept of an address space must first be examined.

Essentially, address space can be thought of as an area of virtual memory that can be 2^{32} bytes long. The closest analogy in the MPE V-based HP 3000 architecture is the data segment. Just as data segments are assigned numbers, so too are spaces. The analogy breaks down quite rapidly, however, because a data segment is limited to 32K words, while the address space is four gigabytes. Also, the data segment has to be manipulated as a unit and can be brought into and out of memory only in its entirety.

The address space, however, is allocated in units of 2048 bytes, called 'pages'. When a space is created, as few as zero pages can be allocated. Each page can contain either code or data, the code and data pages can be contiguous within the same space, and each page is manipulated independently by the hardware and the (software) memory manager. This is in sharp contrast to the MPE V-based HP 3000, which segregates code and data into separate code and data segments. Pages are allocated whenever an area of the space is referenced that has not been previously allocated.

Thus a complete virtual address is created by combining the contents of a space register (different ones are used at different times) and an offset register which points to a specific byte within the space. This creates a total of 64 bits for addressing. Theoretically, you can address 2^{32} address spaces of 2^{32} bytes each, for a total of 2^{64} bytes. This provides an address space that is 2^{32}, or 4.3 billion, times larger than typical 32-bit computers.

One of the main goals of HPPA was to provide for scalable computers. Towards this goal, HP Precision Architecture calls for three levels of addressing. Level-zero systems have only real addressing and thus have a total address space of only four gigabytes. Level-one systems can support 2^{16} virtual spaces. In other words, the space number is limited to 16 bits. The HP 3000 Series 930 and the HP 9000 Series 840 are level-one systems and can thus support 65535 address spaces, for a total of 281 trillion bytes of address space. The final level, level-two, provides full 32-bit space addressing.

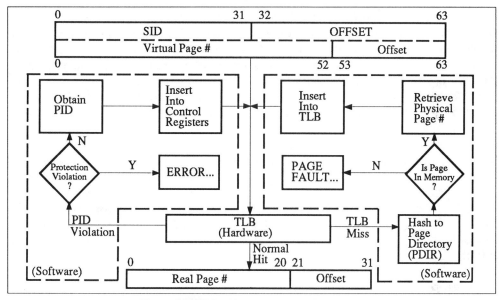

Figure 5.3 HPPA Virtual Address Translation

The 'magic' of calculating the real address that corresponds to the 64-bit virtual address is done by a special hardware/memory structure called the 'Translation Lookaside Buffer', or TLB (see Figure 5.3). For simplicity, this example assumes a level-two system with a full 32-bit space register. Since a page is always 2048 bytes, the 64-bit address can be thought of as a 53-bit page number, followed by an 11-bit offset within the page. The TLB hardware maintains a list of page numbers in extremely fast static RAM memory. The 53-bit virtual page is then found in this buffer, and a 21-bit real page number is produced. This is concatenated with the 11-bit page offset, and a 32-bit real address is produced. This sounds like it would impose a lot of overhead, but in fact the whole process takes less than a single clock cycle. Additional checking is done by the TLB, as shown in Figure 5.3.

A very important aspect of memory addressing in HPPA systems is cache memory, not to be confused with disc caching, as implemented in MPE V. Cache memory is a layer of memory that sits between the CPU and main memory, and is used by the CPU as a buffer to address memory. CPU cache is a set of small, very fast static RAM memory that can be accessed more quickly than regular RAM memory. (The concept behind static RAM and its significance to HPPA was discussed in Chapter 3.)

The philosophy behind cache memory is that most memory accesses are very close to or the same as previous memory accesses. This property is called 'address access locality'. Cache memory hardware actually fetches more words of memory than is being requested by the CPU. If the scheme works correctly, the requested word of memory will almost always be already in cache, and the machine will hardly ever have to make the CPU wait for a relatively slow fetch from main memory. When presented with an address to fetch, the cache memory hardware searches its internal tables, finds the data corresponding to the requested address, and delivers it to the CPU. Indeed, the cache 'hit' rate on the HP 3000 Series 930 is 90 to 98 percent, according to measurements done by HP's hardware labs.

The hardware mapping has to be very fast to support the benefit of this fast memory. In fact, the address translation done by the TLB and the cache memory are almost identical, and this results in hardware that is virtually identical for the two subsystems. When memory is accessed, both cache and TLB are concurrently searched. The combination of the results dictates whether the TLB or cache needs to be updated. If the address resides in TLB but not in cache, a cache 'miss' results, and the cache is updated from the proper area of memory. If the cache contains the data but the TLB does not contain information on the page, the TLB is updated by software.

Cache memory has been recently implemented on some MPE V-based HP 3000 systems. The Series 6X has always been equipped with cache memory. The Series 70 has a significantly increased portion of cache memory over the Series 68, accounting for much of its performance gain over the Series 68. In addition, the Series 5X and Series 42XP have cache memory. Thus, this newer memory technology has found its way into many of the current HP 3000 models -- not just the machines based upon HPPA.

All but perhaps the smallest HPPA systems have, and will have, hardware TLB and cache. The HP 3000 Series 930 has separate data and instruction caches, referred to as a D-cache and I-cache, respectively. An interesting facet of the architecture is that both caches, as well as the TLB, can be explicitly manipulated by software. This is different from MPE V-based systems, where the CPU caching scheme is transparent to the software, and system performance must rely on optimal performance by the cache memory hardware. In HPPA, the software kernel can decide what it wants in cache and TLB to enhance its algorithms for memory management.

The benefits of this 64-bit addressing scheme are tremendous. Not only is the stack limitation of the MPE V-based HP 3000 systems removed, but huge amounts of data can also now be accessed. An exciting ramification of this addressing scheme can be seen in a new feature of the MPE XL file system called 'mapped files'. This feature, which allows a file to be treated as a very large data array, is examined in detail in Chapter 11.

At the hardware level, there are really two different ways to generate virtual addresses. The method described above uses a 64-bit pointer, called a 'long pointer' in HPPA terminology. Use of long pointers allows a program to access the entire four gigabytes of an address space. Its use requires that the compiler generate more code than just a simple access to the memory location. Because 32 bits of the 64 contain a space number, the compiler must load this value into a space register using the Move To Space Register instruction (MTSR), then generate the proper sequence to reference that register. An example of this type of addressing is shown below. The first part is the Pascal XL source code that defines the extended pointer, the second part shows a subset of the corresponding assembler code generated.

```
PROGRAM MAIN;
VAR
   int_extended_pointer  :  ^$EXTNADDR$ ARRAY [0..1000] of integer;
   j                     :  integer;

BEGIN
   { code here to set int_extended_pointer to a mapped
     file or other address space}

   j := int_extended_pointer^[100]; {load 100th word
                                     from pointer}

END.
```

The assembler for this:

```
LDW  88(0,27),10    ; Load space portion   R27+88 to R10
MTSR  10,3          ; Move R10 to space reg 3
```

```
LDW   92(0,27),11     ; Load offset portion   R27+92 to R11
ADDI  100,11,12       ; Add 100 to the offset portion->R12
LDW   0(3,12),13      ; Load using SR3 as base with offset of
                      ; R12 into R13
STW   13,84(0,27)     ; Store R13 into j (R27+84)
```

As can be seen, the space register is loaded for each access. This adds code (and thus time) to each access of the long pointer. This sequence is initially generated by the compiler, but can -- under some circumstances -- be removed by the optimizer. (More information will be presented on the compilers and optimizer in Chapter 6.)

Another type of pointer defined by HPPA is more efficient, but does not allow full access to an address space. These pointers are 32 bits long and are called 'short pointers' (see Figure 5.4). When the short pointer is initialized, the high-order 2 bits are loaded with a number from zero to three. When accessed, the hardware adds this number to four, and that space register is used. For example, if the high-order 2 bits contains a one, then SR5 is used as the space register, as five equals one plus four. An interesting facet of this scheme is that the high-order 2 bits are also included in the address calculation. This simplifies the hardware, and allows access to a one-fourth of an address space, or a quadrant. Thus, SR4 can address only the first quadrant (hexidecimal values $00000000 to $3fffffff), SR5 the second quadrant ($40000000 to $7fffffff), SR6 the third quadrant ($80000000 to $bfffffff) and SR7 the fourth quadrant ($c0000000 to $ffffffff). This type of pointer is used by MPE XL to access system tables. Most table pointers are stored as short pointers and reside in quadrant four of space A. Thus, SR7 is more or less permanently loaded with the value A, and the operating system can access this one-gigabyte quadrant in the most efficient manner. It is important to note that the remaining three gigabytes are not wasted or even allocated. These three quadrants represent virtual addresses which may be accessed through other space registers -- or not at all.

Both long and short pointer access can be seen in the example of long pointer access above. When the space portion of the long pointer is loaded into Register 10, it is done via the instruction LDW 88(0,27),10. The (0,27) portion of the instruction represents a short pointer access via Register 27. As will be discussed in detail in Chapter 6, Register 27 contains a short pointer to the global data area of the program, analogous to the DB Register on MPE V-based HP 3000s. The zero in front of the 27 tells the hardware to interpret GR27 as a short pointer and use the first 2 bits in choosing a space register.

Later, when the long pointer is used to access data, the instruction LDW 0(3,12),13 is used. The (3,12) portion of the instruction tells the hardware to use Space Register 3 and General Register 12 for the space and offset portions of the address. The only allowable values for the space register of the address portion in the instruction set are zero through three.

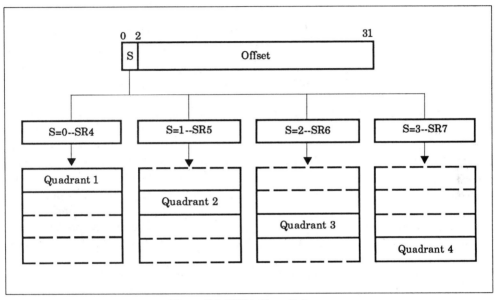

Figure 5.4 HPPA Short Pointers

Pipelining

Before discussing the instruction set, it is important to understand how HP Precision Architecture implements the instruction pipeline. Pipelining is a concept that has been used on some machines for over 15 years. Even microprocessors implement some sort of pipeline. The concept is simple: In hardware, you can have several components operating simultaneously, all driven by the same digital clock 'heartbeat'. While part of the CPU is executing an instruction, another part of the hardware is bringing the next instruction (or instructions) into a register 'buffer' of sorts. When the execution of one instruction is complete, the next is ready and waiting. Moreover, one instruction can be finishing execution concurrent with the initiation of another. Coupled with the instruction-cache mechanism, this becomes an incredibly fast and efficient process.

The problem with pipelining arises when the executing instruction is a branch. The 'next' instruction is not the next sequential memory location after the branch. If two more instructions have been pipelined in, they must be thrown away, the new code address calculated, and the pipes started up again at the new location. This wastes several clock cycles.

HP Precision Architecture mitigates this problem with a very interesting scheme. When executing a branch instruction, the instruction after the branch instruction (residing in the delay slot) is executed before the branch is actually taken. The instruction which physically resides after the branch in the code is the one that, logically, should be executed first. A branch instruction takes two clock cycles to complete, since the address of the branch must be calculated and the instruction at the target fetched. The hardware is designed such that the target fetch can happen while the next instruction is executing. When the branch is actually taken, the pipeline is already being filled at the new location (the branch address), and no clock cycles are wasted.

Figure 5.5 shows this scheme as well as the effect of pipelining. At time T1, the address of the branch is calculated. At T2, the branch actually occurs, the LDW instruction finishes and the code at the target address begins execution. Since one instruction begins execution each cycle, in effect (through not in actuality) every instruction executes in one cycle. Thus in Figure 5.5, the three instructions execute in three cycles, even though two of the instructions require two cycles to complete.

The one exception to this compaction scheme comes when the instruction following a load needs the register which is the target of that load. This condition is called a 'register interlock' and it causes the loss of a usable clock cycle in the instruction stream. In Figure 5.5, the LDW instruction specifies R8 as its target. If the next instruction starting at time T3 were STW R8, 12(0,R30), a register interlock would occur since R8 is not actually available until time T4. Thus, the STW instruction could not begin until time T4, causing a partially wasted cycle. The optimizer does its best to avoid this condition.

	T1	T2	T3	T4
BL R2	CALC ADDR (Execute)	Fetch Target		
LDW -14(0,R27), R8		CALC ADDR (Execute)	Load Data	
Code @ Target			EXECUTE	

Figure 5.5 Branch Execution Sequence

This branch scheme points out an interesting and absolutely critical aspect of the HP Precision Architecture: the compilers are as important to the machine as the hardware. The optimizer goes to great lengths to find an appropriate instruction from the code paths to move into the delay slot. As mentioned earlier, many of the general registers had no purpose dictated by the architecture definition, but they were specified by software conventions. Well, the implementation of these conventions is done entirely by the compilers.

The HPPA Instruction Set

The following discussion regards the instruction set as a whole. A complete listing of the instructions and a summary discussion of each one are in Appendix A.

All HPPA instructions are a fixed length of 32 bits. This large size provides room for a great amount of information and offers a rich set of capabilities which can be exploited by the software. The instruction set is divided into several groups. The add instructions are used to add registers and constants to registers. The branch instructions perform a variety of transfer of control functions, and some allow the return address (the next instruction) to be loaded into a register for the return. These are the 'Branch and Link' (BL) instructions.

The compare instructions are also branch instructions, but allow for branching to be performed *only* if a particular condition is true or false. The load and store are by far the largest groups of instructions. You can access a full word (32 bits) as well as half-words and bytes. A large number of shift instructions are implemented, with special instructions to facilitate certain operations such as multiplication, because there is no multiplication instruction in the standard HPPA instruction set. There are a number of deposit and extract instructions, plus a large set of instructions to allow manipulation of the TLB, I-cache, and D-cache.

Conditional branch instructions can nullify the next instruction execution by setting a bit called 'Nullify On Condition' (NOC), done for many of the branching conditions that occur in looping situations. NOC allows the instruction following the branch to be executed most of the time, but not when a condition is true. Typically this will be at the end of a loop. As an example, consider the following pseudo-Pascal code:

```
i := 0;
DO BEGIN
   ...
   i := i + 1
   END UNTIL  i = 100;
```

The pseudo-assembly code for this construction could look like this:

```
        LDO 0(0),10          ; Load 0 to R10 (i).
        FIRST_INST           ; First instruction of the loop
L$0:                         ; label 0

        ...
        ADDI 1,10,10         ; Add 1 to i in R10;
        LDO  100(0),11       ; Loads 100 into R11
        COMBF,=,N 10,11,L$0   ; Compare and branch if false
                             ; Compare 10 to 11. If R10 not equal
                             ; to 11, then branch to L$0. If R10
                             ; equal to R11, then nullify the next
                             ; instruction, and drop through.
        FIRST_INST           ; First instruction is repeated.
                             ; Executed as slot instruction of COMBF
                             ; Execute until loop condition is met
```

Nullification of the next instruction is not a new concept. It is commonly used in microcode. The type of construct above is probably one of the first times it has been explicitly used at the machine-instruction level.

With HPPA, Hewlett-Packard has gone far beyond the original academic descriptions of RISC in defining this instruction set. At 140 instructions, it is large and rich in the functions it provides, compared to the RISC machines implemented in academia.

Hardware Security

No discussion of a machine architecture would be complete without a discussion of security. In this case, protection of memory is discussed, rather than much higher-level security implemented within the operating system.

As mentioned earlier, anyone on the system can access any address space. At first glance, it would appear there is no security. In reality, a very excellent security system is implemented at the page level. The system defines four privilege levels, numbered from zero to three. The higher the number, the lower the privilege level. All code has a particular privilege level associated with it, and code running at a given privilege level can access anything that code at lesser levels can access. This type of security system is referred to as ring security.

Actual privilege access checking is performed by the TLB mechanism at the page level. The TLB contains several pieces of data about that page, such as what privilege level can access a page in a particular fashion. For example, the system can establish a page used to store data and can specify that only the most privileged processes (those running at level zero) can modify (write to) it, but that any level process can read it. In theory, certain system tables could be placed in read-only pages, and could be accessed by any user mode program, or a program running at a specified privilege level.

Another hardware security mechanism is 'Protection Identifiers' (PIDs). These are 15-bit numbers that can be assigned to a page and carried in the TLB along with the access levels. A PID of zero indicates to the hardware that no checking is to be done. The PID mechanism involves loading the PIDs of the current process into four control registers. When a page is accessed, the hardware ensures that the PID in the TLB matches one in the control registers (See Figure 5.3). If the PIDs do not match, the hardware 'traps' to an appropriate software handler and access to the page is denied.

An example of the use of PIDs can be seen in the MPE XL file system. This system maps all files into an address space and accesses the space via long pointers. Because of this, every 2K-byte segment of the file becomes a page. File locking is done down to the page level. You can lock a single page or range of pages. To accomplish this, you assign a PID to the page(s) when the lock is placed, and the process or processes involved in the lock are made aware of the PID. The file system ensures that the PID is properly loaded before access until the lock is released. Any process not involved in the lock that attempts to access the page(s) will trap to the file system's lock handler. When the lock is removed, so is the PID.

Access-level checking takes precedence over PID checks. Thus, a process may have the proper PIDs loaded in the control registers, but if it is not running at the proper privilege level, access to the page will be denied by the hardware.

The I/O Subsystem

The I/O architecture is very elegant. Part of the four gigabyte real memory space is reserved for the I/O system, thereby logically dividing real memory into a memory section and an I/O section. The hardware boards are designed to be dynamically configured by the system at startup to respond to addressing within a two-page range. Each hardware module is assigned two pages of memory space, and certain I/O control registers are at certain locations. Thus, the I/O drivers merely do loads and stores to specific memory locations to facilitate I/O initiation and completion. This facility is known as memory-mapped I/O. It is different than the channel I/O on the MPE V-based HP 3000, which demands the I/O drivers build channel programs and not only be familiar with the hardware device (such as the disc drive) but intimately know how the particular interface card works. HP Precision Architecture I/O is more consistent among the different I/O interfaces.

The ease with which I/O drivers can be written is key to HP Precision Architecture's ability to exist in the technical marketplace, an area that the HP 1000 has dominated for years. Many real-time applications in this world rely upon explicit control over the hardware devices being driven by the system. Many times, if the system is driving some sort of measurement system, the system has to be able to collect the data and act upon it quickly, sometimes in milli- or microseconds. RTE, the HP 1000's operating system, has extensive facilities for such real-time programming. Indeed, RTE stands for Real-Time Executive.

Sometimes, the best way to accomplish these programming tasks is to write an I/O driver. The HP 1000 system has supported user-written drivers for years. This task is made much easier by the I/O system described by HPPA.

6

General
Software Aspects

A tenet of the RISC paradigm and therefore of HP Precision Architecture is that only the most basic of instructions be implemented in the machine, and that complex operations be created by stringing together these simple instructions. In this chapter, this fundamental principle of HPPA -- and how the software and compiler architects at HP have built upon this idea -- will be examined.

When microcode was discussed in Chapter 3, it was mentioned that increasing program complexity and slower RAM speeds necessitated going to the faster ROM control store program . With this methodology, very complex instructions could be implemented relatively easily. The problem mentioned was that simple instructions pay a penalty for using the microcode mechanism. This can be likened to everyone's insurance rates going up because a few people get a lot of speeding tickets and have a lot of accidents.

The whole idea of HP Precision Architecture is to implement all instructions in hardware. The complex operations are implemented by the compilers generating a sequence of simple instructions. This concept can best be illustrated by a discussion of an MPE V instruction pair that was presented in an earlier chapter.

When calling another procedure, you must provide a local data storage area for that procedure, as well as provide a way to restore the environment of the machine when the procedure is finished. This is assuming the called procedure will change the machine environment, which is normally a safe assumption. As mentioned in Chapter 4, the instruction pair on MPE V-based HP 3000s that saves and restores the state of the machine is PCAL/EXIT. These instructions affect both code and data segment registers, as well as the stack.

When a PCAL is executed, a four-word stack marker is pushed onto the stack at the current location of S. The microcode calculates the difference between the current Q pointer and S+4, the value S will be when the marker is pushed. This value, called 'Delta Q', is placed on the stack, along with the current status register value, the value of P+1, and the current value of the X Register.

The PCAL instruction has imbedded within it an index into the Segment Transfer Table (STT). This table lies at the end of each code segment. Each word of the STT table is a pointer to either a location within the current code segment (as would be referenced by an internal or intrasegment PCAL) or is a pointer to an STT entry within another segment (as would be referenced by an intersegment PCAL). The formats of these two types of STT entries are internal and external PLABELS. The STT is built in stages by the compiler, the segmenter, and the loader when the program is first loaded. The compiler is the entity that assigns the proper STT index to correspond to an external procedure. Thus, the compiler knows at compile time what index to generate in the PCAL instruction.

The microcode takes the current value of PL, subtracts the index in the PCAL and goes to that memory location. The microcode inspects the STT entry there and determines whether it is external or internal. If internal, it sets the P Register to the address in the STT entry and continues execution. If external, the microcode takes the segment number in the STT, uses it to index into the Code Segment Table (CST), which tracks each code segment's location in disc or memory. Assuming the segment is in memory, the microcode uses the CST number to determine where in memory the segment is, then sets PB and PL to that segment. In addition to the CST number, the calling STT entry contains the STT index of the desired procedure within the called segment. The microcode goes to the PL-STT# entry of the target segment, where it finds an internal PLABEL. P is set to this number plus the value of PB, and execution resumes.

When the called procedure has completed its task, it executes an EXIT instruction to return to the calling procedure. The EXIT instruction essentially reverses the above PCAL steps. The Stack Marker at the current Q is examined. The rightmost 8 bits of the Status Register at Q-1 are extracted and used to index into the code segment table. The microcode uses this table to locate the calling code segment in memory and sets the PB and PL registers. The P relative return at Q-2 is used to set the P Register, and the system's Index Register is reset from the value at Q-3. Finally, the Q Register is reset by subtracting the Delta-Q value at Q-0. S is set to the old value of Q-4 minus the number of words used for parameters. This last value is encoded into the EXIT instruction itself, just as the STT value is encoded in the PCAL instruction at compile time.

The main point of this discussion is that PCAL and EXIT are extremely complex instructions requiring a great deal of microcode. It would be incredibly difficult to implement this sequence of events in hardware alone, although this has been done on some machines. Even if it were done, changing it in the future would require a total redesign of the hardware. The recent expansion of the CST and removal of certain key tables from memory bank 0 in MPE V/E relied upon the fact that the PCAL mechanism, as well as other microcoded instructions, could be changed relatively easily. This is possible on the MPE V-based HP 3000 because of microcode, which is relatively easy to modify, compared to the cost of modifying hardware. This is one advantage that offsets the overhead of microcode.

Software Conventions

Hewlett-Packard Precision Architecture does not define any instruction pair analogous to PCAL/EXIT. However, it is still necessary to provide the ability to call procedures and exit from them. Rather than provide hardcoded functionality in the hardware (and thus create expensive and difficult-to-build designs), this is accomplished by establishing standards in the way the registers and data spaces are manipulated by software.

Like the instruction set and other facets of HPPA dealt with in Chapter 5, some of these standards are considered part of the architecture because of the extensive interaction between the PCAL and EXIT instructions and the MPE V-based HP 3000 data stack and code segments. And just like the hardware, some of these standards also have Architecture Control Documents written to guide their actions.

Actually, the standards are stringently enforced conventions which are implemented by the compilers. Just as PCAL and EXIT deal with both the code and data portions of the machine, so too do the software conventions deal with code and data. The data stack in the user's data space is the center for a large number of conventions. Additionally, the code segments have certain formats and standards which must be adhered to and are enforced by software modules.

Software Register Conventions

Before discussing the specific hardware and software conventions, the use of the machine's registers must be examined. Certain of the general registers, referred to as Rn (where n is a number from zero to 31) have specific purposes and names associated with them. Some of the more important ones will be discussed here. In all cases, unless otherwise noted, the registers contain short pointers and thus depend upon a space register being pre-loaded by the system. Typically, this will be SR5 for registers delimiting user data areas.

Register R2 is referred to as the Return Pointer, or RP. This is the address to which the IA Register must be set when returning from the procedure call, and is analogous to the P-relative return value in the stack marker on the MPE V-based HP 3000. This return address is formed by the 'link' portion of a branching instruction with a link function. An example of this is:

```
BL    L$0              ;Branch to L$0, place the
                       ;return location in R2
NOP                    ;slot instruction
NEXT_INSTRUCTION       ;<-Address loaded into R2
```

The Branch-and-Link (BL) instruction is used only for branching within the same code space. Thus, the return address represents only the offset within the current space. Although the instruction set allows any register to be used as the object of a BL instruction, the software conventions of HPPA dictate that R2 be used. If the procedure being called does not call any other procedure, then the return address loaded by the BL instruction is untouched and used for the return. If the procedure does call others, R2 is saved and restored as necessary. The entire procedure-calling mechanism will be examined later.

Other registers are used as pointers to the various data areas. Register R27 is called the 'DP' and serves as a base address for global data. The equivalent on the MPE V-based HP 3000 is the DB Register. Using DP as an address to access data can be illustrated by the following Pascal/XL addition statement:

```
PROGRAM MAIN;
VAR
   i,j      : integer; {assume i at DP+80,j at DP+84}
BEGIN
   i := i + j;
END.
```

The assembly language for this construct could be:

```
LDW     80(0,27),10     ;Load DP+80 into R10
LDW     84(0,27),11     ;Load DP+84 into R11
ADDT    10,11,12        ;Add R10 and R11, trap if overflow
STW     12,80(0,27)     ;Store the result to DP+80
```

Register R30 is called the 'Stack Pointer', or SP. It is roughly equivalent to the S Register in the MPE V-based HP 3000, and is used to delimit the top of the current stack. The prime difference between the stack used in HPPA and that on MPE V-based HP 3000's is that, as we have seen, calculations are not performed on the stack, but directly in the registers. The stack in HPPA is used primarily as a parameter and state-saving mechanism. This will be illustrated fully when the procedure-calling convention is discussed.

Philosophically, these registers are like their MPE V-based HP 3000 counterparts. They are given meaning by a series of fundamental instructions that execute in one or two clock cycles. The only difference is that these instructions reside in RAM (both main memory and cache), not in ROM, as is the case with microcode. Access to the RAM in this case is as fast as the ROM used in most CISC machines because of the intervention of CPU I-cache memory. Indeed, the Writable Control Store (WCS) on the Series 68/70 uses this type of static RAM memory. The main difference between the CISC microcode and HPPA machine code is that the microcode tends to be thought of as part of the hardware. In HPPA, philosophically speaking, the microcode is now visible to the programmer.

Other registers serve a variety of purposes at different times. Four registers that are defined as argument registers are GR23-GR26 (sometimes referred to as ARG0-ARG3). These are used to store the first four parameters when calling a procedure. RET0 and RET1 (GR27 and 28) are used to contain the functional return value from a procedure. There are areas within the stack frame to accommodate these values; the registers serve as an optimization method because if the registers already contain the correct data, the values do not have to be moved to and from memory.

Spectrum Object Modules (SOMs)

A very interesting entity described by the software standards in HPPA is the format of the files that contain object code. The format itself is not that fascinating, but an examination of the format along with the definitions for some of the fields *does* provide some interesting concepts about code and externals resolution.

Before examining this format, however, it would be beneficial to review the process by which executable programs are created. In general, a source program is written in some language and compiled by the compiler for that language into an object format. Sometimes this object file can be directly run by the target computer. More often, the object format is designed so that the code can be moved, or relocated, to other forms. (The code can be moved to several object formats or can be combined with other relocatable code for executable modules.)

In the MPE V operating environment, the relocatable file is called a 'User Subroutine Library' (USL) file. This file is manipulated by the segmenter to the other forms. By using the :PREP command (from the MPE command level) or the -PREPARE command (within the segmenter), the USL file can be transformed into a program (PROG) file. After the program file is produced, a :RUN command is entered, and the loader within MPE brings the program into memory and starts its execution.

The scheme described above for MPE V has been brought forward in MPE XL for compatibility. The Compatibility Mode compilers still produce the same object code as under MPE V, and the segmenter is used to prepare the code for execution. For Native Mode, however, a different set of compilers exist which produce HP Precision Architecture instructions. The concept and capabilities of the segmenter have been expanded in a new program called the 'linker'. The linker allows manipulations analogous to those done by the segmenter but has more capability because the linker allows the linkages among modules to be edited (thus it is sometimes called the 'link editor'). The linker also lists the various symbols contained within the files. In the same vein, a loader for Native Mode programs exists in MPE XL.

The Native Mode object file produced and subsequently used by the linker and the loader is called a 'Spectrum Object Module' (SOM) file. The linker is similar in function to the segmenter on MPE V but has far more capabilities. The closest analogy in the MPE V-based HP 3000 world is the USL (User Subroutine Library) file that is subsequently used by the segmenter. Its function is analogous as well. The SOM file contains both relocatable and executable object code. Relocatable code is defined as that which can be moved to some other form. For example, if you want to place a subroutine in an external library to be loaded at load time (an SL in MPE V), the code is said to be relocated to this library. Similarly, code can be relocated to a program file to be run or can have other routines compiled into it before being prepared for execution.

The header record serves as a pointer to other records in the file. It contains such information as the 'magic number,' used to validate the file by the linker, and SOM file format version numbers. The main function of the header record is to point to other records in the file and to serve as a starting point for the linker. Some of the more important records will be described below.

The symbol header points to a set of records that describe the symbols in the file. A symbol is a name assigned to some entity in the file, such as the name of a procedure that has been called by some other procedure, or one that is capable of being called by another procedure. The symbol entries provide a method whereby procedure location resolution can be performed by the linker at a later stage.

The space and subspace records are used to define portions of the address space in which the program will eventually run. They correspond to the address space defined by HPPA. The subspace records specifically divide the space up into constituent parts. For example, one subspace is typically reserved for code and one for data, and others reserved for functions such as stack unwinding and symbolic debugging. The subspace records contain other information, such as in which quadrant in the space the subspace should be placed.

The fixup records are placed there to instruct the linker how to perform certain binding and address resolutions at link time. This resolution can only be done if the symbol is present in a file being linked. For example, consider the following linker command:

```
:LINK FROM=FILEA,FILEB,FILEC;TO=PROGA
```

This command draws relocatable object code from FILEA, FILEB, and FILEC and links them together into a single program file, PROGA. This is essentially the same as the :PREP command in the MPE V segmenter, except the :PREP command allows only one USL file, whereas the :LINK command allows many files. Assume FILEA calls the routine XYZ contained in FILEB. When the code in FILEA is compiled, the compiler does not know where XYZ is located. In this case, the compiler will leave the target address of the generated branch instruction blank and generate a fixup record in the SOM. This record contains the location in FILEA of the branch instruction, along with various codes that instruct the linker to what symbol (procedure name) the branch is, and the fact that the fixup pertains to a branch instruction. When the :LINK command is executed, the linker searches all the other SOM files for that symbol, then 'patches' (fixes up) the branch instruction in PROGA so that the branch transfers to the appropriate place. Because the three files are all linked together into a single program file, the address placed in the branch instruction reflects the linked program version, not the address in the SOM file.

Some other nomenclature should be discussed at this point. When a symbol name is used, it can be for one of two purposes. A symbol name that is defined in a file (such as XYZ is in FILEB above) is exported by the compiler. Essentially, this causes the compiler to create a symbol record that can then be accessed by the link operation, as shown above. The other use for a symbol is to be defined as an external, as is done with the symbol XYZ in FILEA, above. Such a symbol is said to be 'imported', because it is being brought in to the program from another location. Again, this causes the compiler to build a symbol entry. In both cases, the symbols are given a scope that defines under what circumstances that symbol name can be used. Symbols that are exported are given a scope of UNIVERSAL, which means the symbol can be used for local (intraSOM) access or by an external reference in another module (interSOM access). Other scope possibilities are EXTERNAL, LOCAL, and UNSAT. Symbols with an EXTERNAL scope can be imported by another module. Symbols with a LOCAL scope can be resolved only to references within the same SOM. Symbols with an UNSAT scope indicate that they were imported but not satisfied by the :LINK operation.

In the :LINK command example above, if the procedure name symbol is not found, it is assumed by the linker that the procedure will be bound (at load time by the loader and the appropriate structures created in PROGA to facilitate the loader's resolution of the procedure. This structure is called a 'stub', and it introduces a *crucial* concept in the HP Precision Architecture world.

A stub is any small piece of code that sits between two others. Typically, a stub is required if you want to isolate certain aspects of the environment from either or both pieces of code. In fact, the frequent use of stubs is to alter the environment from that of the calling code to that of the called code. For example, stubs are used during a call to a procedure which resides in another code space. To accomplish this operation, an interspace branch must be performed. To simplify the calling code, a stub is inserted in the space of the calling code that actually performs the interspace branch. The stub is then accessed by the calling code via an intraspace branch. In this way, the compiler need only generate intraspace branches which are simpler than interspace branches. This whole concept will be treated more fully later in this chapter.

Another structure generated by the cooperation of the linker and the loader is called the 'cross-reference table', abbreviated as XRT. This table, imbedded in the program file, provides the capability of locating external references that are not resolved at link time. The table contains the space identifier (ID) and the location of a specific procedure. The linker generates a calling stub which accesses this table, loads a space register with the space ID, and performs an intraspace branch. The XRT is analogous to the segment transfer table present at the end of code segments on the MPE V-based HP 3000s.

The XRT illustrates how the different pieces of software cooperate to produce a system with full functionality. Without this software cooperation and the knowledge of each module's contributions by the others, HPPA would not be a viable way to build a computer system.

This chapter started with a description of how the MPE V-based HP 3000 performs a procedure call, which was presented as an illustration of the complexity of microcoded machine instructions. What follows is a description of the same function in Hewlett-Packard Precision Architecture.

The Procedure Calling Sequence

The actual calling sequence alluded to earlier in this chapter is relatively sophisticated. As with the PCAL and EXIT instructions, the sequence has distinct events which occur within the code, and events which occur within the data area on the stack. The data stack convention will be discussed first, then the code.

The techniques illustrated below are not new. Many machines in the past did not have a microcoded calling sequence, such as PCAL/EXIT. In fact, at the time of its inception, the HP 3000 was considered quite revolutionary because of this procedure-calling capability.

For purposes of the discussion, the code (procedure) performing the call will be referred to as the caller, and the procedure being called as the callee. The sequence has four parts: steps performed by the caller on exit, those performed by the callee on entrance, those performed by the callee on exit, and those performed by the caller on re-entry. The first two are roughly equivalent to the PCAL instruction, and the last two to the EXIT instruction.

The first task of the caller is to preserve any registers that it has used and will use again, which are not being saved by the callee. (See Figure 6.1 for a diagram of the stack). This is done by loading the registers into the stack in the call save area. Since the compiler knows what registers it uses for certain operations, it has only to save these registers. Upon branching to the callee, the caller must not only pass parameters to the callee, but must also save the state of the machine. If the callee has four parameters or less, they are loaded into R23-R26. These are referred to as ARG0-ARG3. If any more are required, the caller loads the remaining parameters into the argument list area. The caller then sets RP (R2) and branches to the callee.

Upon entry, the callee first allocates the area of the stack that it will need. This area is reserved simply by incrementing R30, the Stack Pointer (SP). (As can be seen in

Figure 6.1, when FOO was called, it incremented SP to the point labeled PSP. When FOO called BAR, BAR incremented SP to the point labeled SP. FOO's SP then became the Previous Stack Pointer, or PSP.)

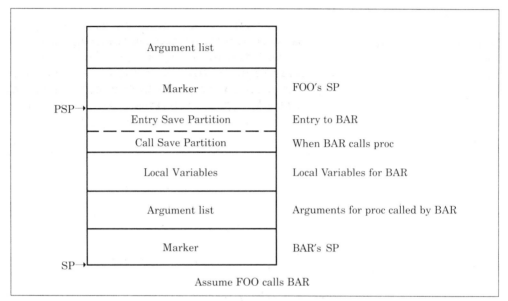

Figure 6.1 Native Mode Stack

After SP is incremented, the callee saves the entry-save registers in the entry-save area of the stack. If any local variables are to be accessed within a nested procedure, the value of SP at entry is saved at SP-4. The value of RP is saved at SP-20 if this procedure calls any others.

Upon exit, the callee must return the stack to the state that existed before the call. The callee restores the registers it saved in the entry-save partition and sets the functional return (if any) in R28 and R29 (RET0 and RET1). It then resets the SP to the value at entry.

The caller, upon re-entry, restores the call-save registers. This completes the data stack portion of the calling convention. The two different save and restore operations (caller and callee) are separated to optimize the overhead of the entire calling operations. Each entity saves and restores only those registers that are necessary. This is possible because the compiler knows at compile time what registers are necessary and what other procedures are called (thus, how many words of parameters are needed).

Beyond RISC!

The code execution path is a very interesting one. First, it must be emphasized again that the only transfer of control instructions defined by HP Precision Architecture are branch instructions. Therefore, any transfer that is done must be within the scope of these branch instructions. The code path taken between the caller and callee differs depending upon whether the callee resides within the same space or a different one. An intraspace call would be performed within the same program or between two procedures that were bound at link time. If the called procedure resides in a different space, as is the case when calling an 'intrinsic,' then an interspace branch is done. The convention is designed such that the branch instruction generated at the call point is always an intraspace branch, as is the branch executed for the return.

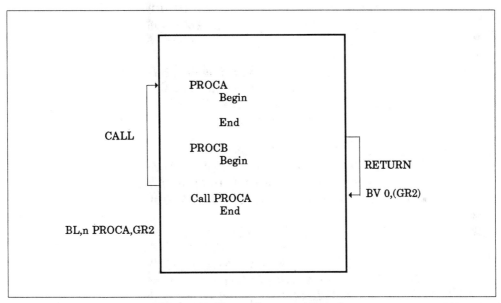

Figure 6.2 Flow of Intraspace Branch

In this case, the compiler generates a BL (Branch-and-Link) instruction to an address within the space. (See Figure 6.2 for a diagram of an intraspace call). The 'link' part of the BL instruction causes the return address (the next instruction after the 'slot' instruction) to be loaded into R2. Upon return, the callee loads R2 and performs a BV (Branch Vectored) instruction, which uses the value in RP as its target address.

As previously mentioned, branch address resolution for interspace calls between the caller and callee is accomplished by a stub. (See Figure 6.3 for a flow of the interspace call). In this case, the external stub performs the linkage of the caller and callee. There is one stub each for the caller and the callee, the calling stub and called stub. When calling, the caller actually performs an intraspace branch to its calling stub. The code contained in the stub acquires the address of the callee from the XRT, initialized at load time by the loader. The XRT contains the SID and address of the called stub for the callee. The calling stub loads a space register with the SID, then executes a Branch External (BE) instruction, which facilitates the switching of code spaces. The stub is logically divided into an entry part and an exit part. After the caller executes the BE instruction, the machine enters the entry portion of the called stub. The entry portion of the called stub executes a BL instruction to transfer to the actual entry point of the called procedure and store the return address in R2. Note that this is an intraspace branch. When the called procedure is finished, it must return to the caller. To accomplish this, the called procedure executes a BV instruction which transfer the return address stored in R2 by the BL instruction, to the exit portion of the called stub, which performs another BE instruction. The target for the BE is the return point of caller, which continues its execution.

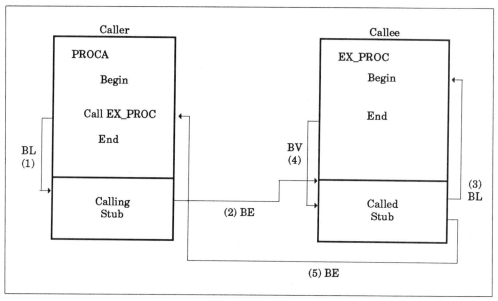

Figure 6.3 Flow of Interspace Branch

The code in the body of the procedures themselves perform only intraspace branches. Only the stubs perform interspace branches. This greatly simplifies the code required and isolates the more complicated BE instruction sequences external to the mainline of the code.

The above sequence can be made more complex out of necessity. For example, the Pascal language supports nested procedures (procedures defined within another procedure). The nested procedures are known only to the outer procedure, and all nested procedures can access data defined locally in a procedure of a higher level. To accomplish the addressing of data within a higher procedure, the PSP must be saved in the stack marker. This adds another step to the callee entry procedure. When the data is accessed, an indirect reference is created by the compiler by loading the appropriate SP from the stack marker and calculating the address of the data relative to that SP. This adds a bit of overhead for data access but is still faster than a typical indirect access on a CISC machine.

At first, all of this must sound as complex as the MPE V-based HP 3000 PCAL instruction described above. And although it *is* somewhat complex, it is also quite consistent. Many of the detractors of the RISC paradigm point to this type of gyration as being actually less efficient than microcode. It generates more code, they say, and causes some thrashing. They add that the compiler has to work harder to generate all of this code, plus it's more complex.

These are good points, but these arguments ignore the fundamental goal of the RISC philosophy, which is to make a faster machine. The real key here is how much time it takes to do the equivalent function on the different machines. It is true the compilers must be more sophisticated. However, our knowledge of how to write compilers, and software technology in general, has advanced a great deal in the past decade, and there is far less magic involved than there used to be. Actually, the amount of code generated to do the entire calling sequence is a few instructions. The code that saves the state of the data stack varies depending upon how many registers are used and what other types of procedures are to be called. Some actual examples of calls show that the instructions needed to perform the code portion of the calling sequence number about 15, including accessing the XRT. This amounts to no more than 30 clock cycles, as most of the instructions are branches, loads, and stores which take two cycles each. These numbers include both the data portion (saving registers) and the code portion (performing branches) of the calling sequence. This generally represents a smaller number of clock cycles than the equivalent microcoded procedure call mechanism.

The data state sequence optimizations mentioned are possible because the compiler knows a great deal about the environment of the program being compiled. It can dynamically determine if registers need to be saved, thus eliminating unnecessary instructions. In essence, the calling sequence can be longer or shorter if need be. With a microcoded machine, the same microcode sequence is performed every time, and the microcode has to determine certain things dynamically. For example, the HP 3000 PCAL instruction has to determine whether or not an external or internal PLABEL is being called, then go to another level of indirection if external. In HP Precision Architecture this is performed at compile and link time, when the proper exit and entrance stubs are generated, thus hardcoding the decision. XRT lookup is not hardcoded, but this is an extremely simple sequence of only eight instructions. The PCAL must make many slow memory accesses to calculate the address of the object code segment (if external). In fact, the actual time taken by the PCAL microcode is much longer on a Series 70.

Again, it is apparent that the different software pieces must work together. The linker must generate the stubs, and the loader generate the XRT. One component of the software puzzle that has not yet been well addressed is the compilers, which clearly have the most complex part of the calling convention above.

A Short Course in Compilers

The compilers used in HP Precision Architecture machines exhibit the most integration of any software component developed in the Spectrum Program. All the compilers are maintained by the same lab within HP, and all versions of a given language (i.e., MPE XL and HP-UX) are produced by the same project groups within the language lab. The compilers reflect this organizational structure and thus display a high level of integration.

This integration is crucial for any RISC architecture to succeed. A great deal of what makes a RISC-based computer system really work must come from the compiler. Additionally, much of the technological progress of the past few years makes RISC a viable computing alternative. To understand the ramifications of this, it will be helpful to examine compilers in general and the HPPA compilers specifically.

How compilers work has been the object of much computer science research in the past 25 years. When the first FORTRAN compiler was produced at IBM in the mid-1950s, the state of the art was assemblers. At that time, writing a compiler was almost an art. Little if any systematic study had been done on languages, and the FORTRAN that was produced was crude by today's standards. Starting about 1960, many of the eminent computer scientists began investigations of the many phases of computer languages and created a subfield that was much more a science than was the case with the first FORTRAN. What follows is a description of the various parts of the compilation process.

The purpose of a compiler is simple: translation. Symbols corresponding to a (hopefully) well-defined language are fed in, and the compiler produces output that conforms to a different language. In the compilers most people deal with, the input language takes the form of words that exist in human languages and symbols drawn from mathematics. Different computer languages draw different amounts from the human and mathematical sides of the fence. The language COBOL, for example, was patterned purposely after English. The statements all begin with a verb, have objects, and end with a period. The statement 'MOVE TRASH TO GARBAGE-CAN.' is a valid COBOL statement. Mathematical formulae take on a much lesser role in COBOL, as the language was designed to handle applications which do not require a great deal of mathematical manipulation. The FORTRAN language, on the other hand, was designed for engineering and scientific applications which deal heavily with formulae. FORTRAN just uses a few English words, such as WRITE, READ, and IF, but really shines when arithmetic expressions are needed. Other language elements can be used as well. Special characters such as parentheses, semicolons, etc., are used heavily by some languages. The language LISP, for example, makes heavy use of parentheses, and C uses the left and right braces ({}) to delimit compound statements.

A computer language is defined by specifying a series of formats that constitute valid statements in the language. These formats are called 'productions', and together, the set of productions forms a grammar. English defines a correct sentence as having a subject (which is a noun) followed by a verb. Whether or not it also has an object is optional. Thus, the sentence 'Jane sews' is a valid english sentence, as is the sentence 'Jane sews the blouse.' Several notational schemes have been devised to rigorously define grammars. By far the most common notational method is called 'Backus-Naur Form', or BNF. The symbol '::=' signifies a definition. The symbol to the left is called a 'non-terminal' and is defined by the symbols to the right of the definition symbol, which can either be another non-terminal or a terminal. Non-terminals are usually enclosed in inequality symbols (< >). In English, the first part of the sentence, the subject and the verb, can be defined as the words 'Jane' and 'sews', respectively. They can also be defined as 'Joe' and 'drives' or any other sequence of nouns and verbs. The object is optional and can thus be either an object or null. From this verbal description, the BNF for a basic English sentence would be:

```
<sentence>      ::=  <first_part><second_part>;
<first_part>    ::=  <subject><verb>;
<subject>       ::=  Jane|Joe;
<verb>          ::=  sews|drives;
<second_part>   ::=  the <object>|(null);
<object>        ::=  blouse|car;
```

The symbol '|' indicates an OR state, so the subject can be 'Jane' OR 'Joe'. The (null) indicates that the second part can be omitted. Thus, the sentence 'Joe drives' is valid according to this grammar, and the sentence 'Joe drives the car' is valid. Notice, however, that the sentence 'Joe drives the blouse' and 'Jane sews the car' are also valid sentences. We have not violated any of the rules of how to construct sentences, so the syntax of our English subset has been obeyed. What has been violated is the semantics of the language. The sentence 'Jane drives the blouse' has all of the nouns, verbs and objects in the correct places, the words are from the allowed combinations, and the spelling is correct, but our minds tell us the sentence is meaningless. Semantics of a language translate to the meaning or intent of the language. The following Pascal is valid syntactically, but semantically incorrect:

```
VAR
    R1, R2 : REAL;
    I1     : INTEGER;

BEGIN
    I1 := R1 * R2 * 100.433;

END;
```

The assignment statement is a valid Pascal statement, as it conforms to the syntactic rules for assignment statements. However, the result produced on the right side of the assignment operator is not compatible with the integer on the left. Another rule, external to the grammar, must be specified to remove this ambiguity. Three solutions are possible: the result can be rounded and stored into I1; the result can be truncated and stored; or an error can be generated. Most implementations of Pascal will do the last.

The output language is also well-defined. In this case, the term 'language' might be somewhat confusing to a human user. In most cases, the output language of the compiler is the machine language instructions of the computer the program is to run on, which compiler writers refer to as the target machine. This language is defined by the hardware designers and must be adhered to rigidly if the computer is to do useful work.

The compiler goes through numerous steps to perform this translation. Do not try to correlate the logical steps with what the compiler actually does. The physical processes that occur within the compiler often combine several of the logical steps in a single procedure or operation. (See Figure 6.4 for an overall flow of the compilation process).

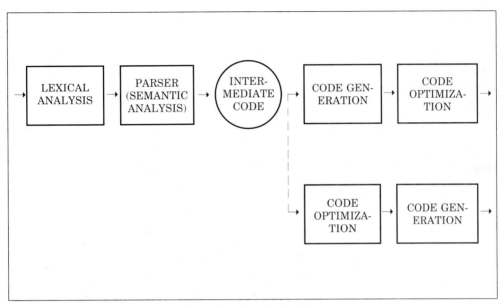

Figure 6.4 Compilation Flow

The first step performed by the compiler is called 'lexical analysis' or 'scanning'. Conceptually, this step is the simplest, but in practice it can be among the most complicated. Scanning is the process by which the 'words' of the input string, called 'tokens', are separated. Scanners usually examine the input text one character at a time and determine the start and stop of the token. This token is then available to other parts of the compiler when necessary. For example, in the COBOL statement:

```
MOVE ADB-ACCOUNT-NO TO OUTPUT-ACCOUNT-NO.
```

the tokens are MOVE, ADB-ACCOUNT-NO, TO, and OUTPUT-ACCOUNT-NO. In this example, the tokens are easy to discern by the scanner, because they are all delimited by either spaces or a period. A more difficult example is in the SPL statement below:

```
WHILE xxyy(a, b:=4, IF a THEN 1 ELSE 2*43, aaa(i*3+4))
    DO a := 3 + j;
```

For clarity, the reserved words are upshifted. Since SPL is not case-sensitive (unlike C), the compiler upshifts the input string. In this example, the symbol xxyy represents a logical procedure, and the scanner must determine its end by seeing the left parenthesis. In the assignment of b:=4, the symbol b is delimited by the colon, and the colon equals (:=) must be deciphered as an assignment statement. The symbol aaa is again delimited by a left parenthesis, and by inspection we cannot tell if this is an array and i*3+4 is the index, or aaa is a procedure with one integer parameter, passed by value. It is sometimes the job of the lexical analyzer to determine what the token is, and sometimes just to figure out where they are. In the latter case, determination of the symbol type is done by the parser.

There are many algorithms for parsing. Essentially, parsing is performed in order to figure out how the different tokens are to be treated. It is usually in this step that semantic analysis is done. For example, the statement:

```
i1 := aaa(i*3+4);
```

could be semantically correct or incorrect, depending upon the type of symbol aaa. If aaa is an integer array, or an integer procedure with one integer parameter passed by value, then the statement is syntactically correct. If aaa is an untyped procedure, then the statement is semantically incorrect.

Another very important part of the parsing process is deciding how to deal correctly with algebraic expressions. The different algebraic operators must be given their proper precedence for the computation to be correct. For example, to handle I := 4+8*3 correctly, the 8 should first be multiplied by the 3, then 4 added to the product, and the resultant 28 stored in I.

If the parser just performed the calculation from left to right, the result would be 36, which is incorrect. Typically, the output of the parsing step is to generate an intermediate code structure which will be used by the next step.

One additional step that is implicit in the lexical analysis/parsing phase is symbol table management. The symbol table is a data structure used to store data about the different variables, labels, and procedures that are encountered. The table can then be used to look up the symbol later. Such items as the variable data type, the address in memory, and initial value can be contained in the symbol table.

After parsing, the compiler performs code generation. This step is where the target machine code (or whatever output language is desired) is produced. Figure 6.4 shows the last part of the compilation process in two ways: with optimizations done before the code generation, and with optimizations done after the code generation. The difference here is whether the code optimization algorithms use the intermediate form, optimize it, and then generate code, or whether the optimizations are done on the object code itself. Code generation is perhaps the most difficult approach, as a great deal of knowledge about the target machine is necessary to generate good code. It is not enough to just generate code; the code generated must be good code, and ideally it should be the best code possible. 'Best' here usually translates as 'fastest.' Nowhere is this more necessary than in a RISC environment such as HPPA. Because there is a tendency to need many machine instructions to perform even simple tasks, it is critical that the compiler generates as few instructions as possible. This is where optimization comes into play.

The term optimization is perhaps a misnomer, because it is not always possible to know the optimal code sequence. A better name for this part of the compiler would be code reducer. The optimizer is such an important part of the compilers for HPPA that optimization and the optimizer will be discussed separately, after the overall design philosophy of HP Precision Architecture is examined.

Compiler Structure

As mentioned earlier, the compilers produced for the Spectrum Program show a high degree of integration and leveraging of other parts of the program. The compilation process consists of a set of distinct steps. The first three steps (lexical analysis, parsing, and intermediate code generation) are usually called the 'front end' of the compiler. The code generation and optimization steps are called the 'back end'. Because the steps are conceptually distinct, you can make them physically distinct as well. This is exactly what has been done in the language lab at HP.

The front end consists of the scanner, parser and UCODE generators for each language. Given the profound differences in language grammars and philosophies, the front ends of the different languages will vary a great deal in the way they handle the input string and in the way symbol table management is done. For example, because COBOL supports multi-level data items, the symbol table management must be significantly different from FORTRAN's, which does not support record structures.

Another example of the types of differences dictating different front ends is the language philosophy. FORTRAN statements are positional in nature. In addition, FORTRAN ignores all intermediate blanks, and allows reserved words to be used as variables. For example, the symbols 'DO 100 I = 1,200' and 'DO100I = 1,200' are equivalent. The scanner of most FORTRAN compilers must scan ahead and determine from the context whether the symbols are reserved words or variables. Pascal, on the other hand, does not allow redefinition of reserved words and has a somewhat unambiguous grammar. The Pascal compiler's scanner and parser are therefore very different from FORTRAN's.

Most of the front ends (except C) generate a common intermediate code called 'UCODE'. UCODE is a language that represents a 'generic' 32-bit stack-based machine. UCODE operators resemble assembler language but are not real assemblers for a real machine. This UCODE interface represents a clean common language that all compilers can generate.

The UCODE package then generates a very low-level intermediate language called 'Spectrum Low-Level Intermediate Code' (SLLIC, pronounced like slick). While UCODE consists of the assembler for a mythical 32-bit machine, SLLIC represents an interface to describe the individual HPPA instructions in a consistent manner and in a form that can be subsequently used by the optimizer. SLLIC is the package that actually builds the SOM object file and manipulates the various header records in the file.

It is also possible for a compiler to generate SLLIC directly, bypassing the higher-level UCODE phase. This is done, for example, by the HP C/XL compiler. In this case, the compiler is responsible for the optimization steps that are performed by the UCODE package for the compilers that do generate UCODE.

The output of the SLLIC package is a SOM file, which was described earlier. It must be emphasized that, although the descriptions of the compiler components represent them as being totally separate, the presentation to the user of all of these pieces is via a single program file, the compiler in PUB.SYS. The different components are written and maintained by different people within the language lab, but when the compilers are actually produced, the different modules are brought together to create a single program file. Thus, the Pascal front end, UCODE, SLLIC and optimizer modules are all combined to produce the HP Pascal/XL compiler.

After the SOM file is produced, the linker is used to create an executable program file. As mentioned earlier, the linker can be used to bind routines from relocatable libraries which become part of the compiled program. After the executable program file is produced, the loader of the specific operating system (MPE XL or HP-UX) is invoked, and the program is run. On the MPE XL operating system, external libraries can be bound at run time. This is typically done for operating system routines, such as intrinsics.

One additional step that also uses the program file is debugging. Part of the SLLIC package allows symbols collected from the front end to be placed in the program file for use by the symbolic debugger. The MPE XL system debugger can use some of the symbol information, specifically the parts that are placed in the program file regarding procedure names. Debugging then becomes much easier, as the program can be debugged by statement number, and the specific variables can be accessed.

Code Optimization

A great deal of the viability of RISC and HPPA stems from the fact that the compilers can now be made to optimize the code output from the code generator. This section will examine some of the philosophies and available techniques, as well as discuss how the HPPA optimizer works.

Essentially, the optimizer works by examining the code that is generated, performing different types of flow analysis, and then deciding which code can be eliminated, changed, or rearranged in the code flow for faster performance.

Before looking at specific cases, however, a small example will be presented. The statements are SPL, and the assembler code is that of the MPE V-based HP 3000.

Consider the following code:

```
PROCEDURE ADDEM(M);
    INTEGER M;

BEGIN

    INTEGER J,K,L;

    J := 4;
    K := J + 3;
    L := K + 10;
    M := L + 22;

END;
```

This sequence of SPL statements would generate the following MPE V-based HP 3000 pseudo-instructions:

```
LDI 4;  << LOAD 4 ONTO STACK >>
STOR J; << STOR INTO J       >>
LOAD J; << LOAD THE 4        >>
ADDI 3; << ADD 3 TO J        >>
```

```
STOR K; << STORE INTO K      >>
LOAD K; << RELOAD K          >>
ADDI 10;<< ADD 10 TO K       >>
STOR L; << STORE INTO L      >>
LOAD L; << RELOAD L          >>
ADDI 22;<< ADD 22            >>
STOR M; << STOR INTO M       >>
```

Assuming that M is the only variable used, we can treat J, K and L as temporaries that will never be reused. An optimizer uses data flow analysis to determine this property within a program. The declaration and usage of each variable is charted throughout the program, and it is determined where a variable must be saved and where it is no longer needed. In the above example, note that there are several sequences where a number is stored -- only to be reloaded in the next instruction. If we eliminate these sequences (and leave the result on the stack) we can eliminate a number of instructions:

```
LDI 4;
ADDI 3;
ADDI 10;
ADDI 22;
STOR M;
```

The ADDI instructions can further be combined into one:

```
LDI 4;
ADDI 35;
STOR M;
```

Finally, the LDI and ADDI both deal with constants, so they could be combined into:

```
LDI 39;
STOR M;
```

The code optimizations just performed could be shown at the source level as:

```
M := 39;
```

A good organic code optimizer (human programmer) would program the last statement.

This very simple example was purposely made that way to show how optimizations can be done -- and why. There are two kinds of situations which require optimizations: those with inefficient programing by humans, and those with code generation schemes which may be easy to implement, but are not as simple as they could be. The above example shows both of these. The whole source sequence could be considered bad programming. Then, when run through the SPL compiler, the code is generated by looking at each statement without regard to others. This is a common and straightforward way to generate code. A code optimizer takes the more difficult approach and looks at the code sequence in a holistic manner; it considers the whole block.

Code Optimization Algorithms

The HPPA code optimizer performs numerous types of optimizations. All of the compilers have options to specify three levels of optimizations: none, Level 1 or Level 2. Level 1 optimizations are very minor, and can be done with some change of the object code. Level 2 optimizations go all out, and code can be eliminated or moved at will. The length of the compilation is increased accordingly. Level 2 optimization adds some time to the compiler; the larger the program, the more time is added. Optimizations are generally applied just before code is placed in production.

Two types of analysis are performed by the optimizer on the SLLIC generated by the UCODE module. The first is data flow analysis, which was alluded to earlier. In this, the optimizer charts the declaration and usage of each variable. This data can be used to determine when a variable is no longer needed and how it is subsequently used at any point in the program.

The other type of analysis is called 'control flow analysis'. This charts out different code sequences and places them in a hierarchy. At the top is the program, followed by procedures, then loops and if-then-else constructs, then basic blocks, which are defined as sequences of code with no branches. From this analysis, the optimizer can then examine the code for many types of code sequences and modify or remove them if necessary.

Code optimization can change a program dramatically. Statements are changed or eliminated totally from the code. Data that is stored into variables may not be there when the optimized program actually executes. All of these together create an object program which can have little correlation -- at the machine code level -- to the source program. This has grave implications when the program is to be debugged with a symbolic debugger. Statements that show up in the source code may simply not exist in any form in the final program.

To illustrate this point, take a look at the function in the following example:

```
FUNCTION y(x:integer):integer;
VAR
 a,b,c:integer;
BEGIN
    a := 3;          { Statement 1 }
    b := 8;          { Statement 2 }
    c := x * b;      { Statement 3 }
    y := c;          { Statement 4 }
END;
```

When all Level 1 and Level 2 optimizations are applied, the above procedure becomes:

```
FUNCTION y(x:integer):integer;
BEGIN
  y := x * 8;
END;
```

Further, if function y is never used, then the code is eliminated as dead code.

Statements 1-4 become y := x*8 in the final output. If the user wanted to debug this code with a symbolic debugger and set a breakpoint at statement 1, he or she could not do it, because statement 1 (and 2 and 3) no longer exists in the object code. Another type of anomaly that optimizations cause is the inability to examine data locations. If a breakpoint were set at statement 1 of the optimized version (statement y := x*8), and the user wished to examine a, b, or c, this also would be impossible because these variables were not even allocated -- nor do they contain any data.

This whole situation points out one of the biggest problems with code optimization. Debugging code that is optimized is very difficult, although far from impossible. Symbolic debugging is out of the question, and even system level debugging is extremely difficult. (The person doing the debugging must be a virtual expert on the code sequences generated by the compiler and optimizer.)

In fact, this area is one of the 'hottest' areas of research in computer science today. About the only literature on the subject is a few doctoral dissertations. The projects that have been done thus far have had limited success. The reigning methodology is to build a debugger that is honest. If a variable is not defined and the user wants it displayed, then it warns that the variable does not exist.

The finest minds in the computer science field do not have a complete and final answer to this problem, and neither do the engineers at Hewlett-Packard's language laboratory, although they are currently researching the subject.

Because the Operating System and other code must be optimized to take full advantage of HPPA, leaving the code unoptimized is not an option. Because debugging optimized versions of the Operating System is difficult, it is important that code be made as clean and bug-free as possible, then optimization turned on before the software is released. In this way, the code will probably be much cleaner and more reliable than has historically been the case, and a much better product will be delivered to the user.

Software is an extremely important part of Hewlett-Packard Precision Architecture. Parts of the system that have traditionally been done in hardware or by microcode are now done in the software. Because of the nature of the RISC instruction set, the technique of code optimization becomes crucial to realizing the full performance benefits of the hardware. It is by the careful co-design of the hardware and software performed by Hewlett-Packard that this union comes to fruition in the Spectrum Program.

III

Implementation
of HPPA

7

The New Families

A discussion of Hewlett-Packard Precision Architecture is not a discussion about a computer, but rather about a set of documents that describe a potential family of computers. To transform these documents into a powerful machine that will run your payroll or control your nuclear power plant, you must determine the answer to several questions.

First, the hardware questions: How many central processing units (CPUs) will be used in parallel? How many and what kind of special-purpose coprocessors will be used? How much memory and what other hardware units will the CPUs have access to? Which semiconductor technology will be used? How fast will the clock go?

Next, the all-important software question: Which operating system will be used to control the computer? Once you've resolved these issues, you can use the HPPA documents to produce an actual computer.

The HP 3000 900 Series Family

Two families of HPPA computers are available today: HP 3000 900 Series computers (MPE XL-based) and HP 9000 800 Series computers (HP-UX-based). The HP 3000 Series 930 consists of a single central processor comprised of five circuit boards using high-speed Schottky TTL (transistor-transistor logic). It's configured with 32 megabytes of memory and is expandable in eight- or 32-megabyte increments up to a maximum 96 megabytes of memory using one-megabit, nibble-mode, dynamic RAMs. This memory is backed-up by a battery that retains the contents of memory over a power failure of at least 15 minutes.

The processor utilizes 128 kilobytes of high-speed cache divided into an instruction cache (I-cache) and a data cache (D-cache), each 64 kilobytes. These caches are further organized into 4,096 cache lines, each of 16 bytes. Because code is considered non-modifiable, the I-cache is read-only. The content of the D-cache, on the other hand, is written out to main memory only when it has been modified and the cache location is needed for other data, or upon a power fail.

These caches, operating in parallel, add to the efficiency of the processor, since the data or instruction needed is usually in cache. In practice, the desired instruction is in the I-cache more than 97% of the time. When it is not (known as an 'instruction-cache fault'), the instruction will take between 500 and 875 nanoseconds extra to complete. The D-cache contains the desired data more than 96% of the time. Data-cache faults add somewhere between 125 and 1875 nanoseconds to the time needed to complete the current instruction.

In order to speed up the translation of virtual addresses to physical addresses in memory, Transaction Lookaside Buffers (TLBs) are used. There is room in the TLBs to map 2048 entries for instruction pages and another 2048 entries for data pages. In practice, when the system needs to convert a 48-bit virtual address into a 28-bit address in real memory, the requested page's addresses will be found in a TLB more than 99% of the time. When it is not (known as a 'TLB miss'), the instruction takes an additional 8125 nanoseconds to complete.

This 28-bit real memory address is actually a 32-bit value. The high-order 4 bits indicate which logical section of memory the address refers to: "0000" indicates the memory section; "1111" indicates the I/O section.

The Series 930 utilizes a two-tier bus structure. The higher-level bus is the Central Bus (CTB). This bus provides the communication path between the System Processing Unit (SPU), the main memory modules, and the channel I/O adapters. It provides a 32-bit-wide data path, runs synchronously with an 8MHz clock, and supports a sustained data transfer rate of 20 megabytes per second. The CTB actually consists of 56 lines: 36 time-multiplexed, bidirectional lines used for addresses, data, and parity, one clock line, and 19 lines used for status and control information.

The lower tier is filled by the Channel I/O Buses (CIBs) of which up to three are supported. These CIBs provide for the connection of Hewlett-Packard Interface Bus (HP-IB) Channels and Local Area Networks (LANs). Each CIB provides a 16-bit-wide, bidirectional data path which runs synchronously with a 250-nanosecond clock and supports a sustained data transfer rate of 5 megabytes per second, in two- to 32-byte-long bursts. A CIB actually consists of 40 lines: 16 data lines, four channel-address lines, and 20 lines for status and control information.

Channel I/O adapters allow for the connection of the CIBs to the CTB. Each adapter serves as a channel multiplexer to provide direct memory access (DMA) for the HP-IB and LAN channels. It also synchronizes the differing speeds and bandwidths of the buses. This DMA allows large blocks of data to be transferred into and out of main memory with minimal SPU intervention and overhead.

Disc drives, tape drives, and printers are connected to the Series 930 via the Hewlett-Packard Interface Bus (HP-IB), an implementation of the IEEE 488-1975 standard. Up to six devices can be connected to each HP-IB channel. HP-IB is an eight-bit-wide, asynchronous bus made up of eight data lines and eight control lines. It can support data transfer rates up to one megabyte per second.

Terminals, personal computers, and serial printers are connected to the Series 930 via an IEEE 802.3 LAN. Communications are supported for asynchronous data transfer rates up to 19200 baud. The LAN itself has a maximum data transfer rate of 10 megabits per second.

A Floating-Point Coprocessor (FPC) is standard on the Series 930. This extra board performs single- and double-precision, floating-point calculations while the central processor continues in parallel. Recognizing 40 instructions, this coprocessor uses the ANSI/IEEE 754-1985 floating-point format.

As has been the case with all HP 3000s, the Series 930 has a rechargeable battery that aids in power-fail recovery. The battery is capable of maintaining the contents of memory and registers for at least 15 minutes in the event of power interruption. When power returns, the system resumes operation automatically. All jobs and sessions continue and all I/Os that were in progress are restarted, providing the associated Distributed Terminal Controllers do not lose power. If a DTC loses power, it will logoff all (up to 48) sessions originating from that DTC.

With a clock speed of 125 nanoseconds, the central processor performs most of its 140 instructions in one clock cycle (125 ns) and the rest of its instructions in two clock cycles (250 ns). Taking into account the effects of TLB misses, cache faults, nullified instructions, and interlocks, the average instruction time comes to 220 nanoseconds.

Keep in mind, though, that this number is meaningful only when compared with other machines that execute the same instructions for a given program. To compare with different computers, in addition to MIPS, you'd also need to know the number of instructions needed (known as the 'path length') to get a specific job done.

Think of the MIPS of a computer as analogous to the tachometer reading of a car (engine revolutions per second). A Yugo may be able to rev at 6,000 rpm, and a Ferrari may be capable of 8,000 rpm, but it is not realistic to claim that the Yugo has three quarters the performance power of a Ferrari. With MIPS, it is appropriate to compare the MIPS of the HP 3000 Series 930 to that of the HP 3000 Series 950 but not to that of another vendor's computer. To do the latter without additional information is to compare apples to oranges or Yugos to Ferraris.

Unfortunately, it's common to see ads that compare the MIPS of one machine to the MIPS of another. In an attempt to deal with this problem, some standard benchmarks have been developed. For example, common tests for floating-point calculation speed are known as the 'Whetstone benchmarks'. Developed by the National Physical Laboratory in England, these FORTRAN programs resulted from an analysis of a thousand ALGOL 60 programs, attempting to simulate an average program mix.

Included in the tests are floating point and integer calculations, transcendental functions, array manipulation, and conditional jumps. The single-precision version is referred to as the B1 benchmark, while the double-precision version is the B1D benchmark. Measurement is usually expressed in terms of Whetstone Instructions Per Second (WIPS). One pass through the loop in the program represents 1000 WIPS (or 1 KWIPS). With the inclusion of the FPC, the Series 930 performed 2795 B1 KWIPS and 1927 B1D KWIPS.

The first commercial computer to be offered in the HPPA family, the HP 3000 Series 930 offers a migration path for users of MPE V-based HP 3000 models. Using the MPE XL operating system (see Chapter 8), programs from these other models will run without modification using an HP 3000 emulation technique known as Compatibility Mode. By using one of the Native Mode language compilers, it is possible to get faster performance and access to the newer features of the HPPA.

Like the HP 3000 Series 930, the Series 950 is another commercial MPE XL computer. However, it uses a faster hardware technology, NMOS III VLSI. In fact, the entire CPU is implemented on a single chip, about 8.3mm square, the equivalent of five boards worth of chips in the Series 930, or about eleven boards in a Series 70. That's about 144,000 transistors on a single chip!

The entire Series 950 processor is contained on a single board. There are eight other NMOS III VLSI chips in addition to the CPU chip on this board: a Translation Lookaside Buffer Control Unit (TCU), two Cache Control Units (CCUs), a System Interface Unit (SIU), and four chips that make up the FPC: a Math Interface Unit (MIU), an ADD/SUB math chip, a MUL math chip, and a DIV math chip. This board does the job of 11 boards in the Series 70, with less than half the parts.

Memory on the Series 950 also starts with a standard 32 megabytes but is expandable to 128 megabytes in 16-megabyte increments. The 73-nanosecond clock cycle gives the Series 950 a rating of seven MIPS, about 50% faster than its little sibling, the Series 930.

The Series 950 has a three-tier bus structure, unlike the Series 930's two-tier bus structure. On a Series 950, the processor communicates with main memory via the System Main Bus (SMB). This very high-speed bus provides a 64-bit-wide data path and supports sustained transfer rates up to 100 megabytes per second. The SMB then connects with two CTBs, analogous to the CTB in the Series 930.

The HP 9000 800 Series Family

The HP 9000 800 Series Model 840 deserves to be called number one, as it was the first HPPA computer to be shipped to customers, back in November 1986. Using almost identical hardware to the HP 3000 Series 930, this model is intended as an extension to the HP 9000 and HP 1000 product lines, rather than to the HP 3000 line. Many of the 800 Series specifications are identical to those described above for the HP 3000 Series 930.

A few exceptions do exist, though. The system can be configured with eight, 16, or 24 megabytes of memory and comes standard with the FPC. Three types of interface boards may be ordered, to which other devices may be connected:

☐ The HP-IB interface supports connection of peripherals and instruments that connect to the standard Hewlett-Packard Interface Bus. This includes discs, printers, plotters, magnetic tape drives, and many instruments. In high-speed mode, the interface supports speeds of up to 980K bytes per second. In standard-speed mode, rates up to 500K bytes per second are supported.

□ The Asynchronous Six-Channel Multiplexer allows for the connection of RS-232-C- and CCITT V.28-compatible devices such as terminals, modems, printers, and plotters. This Z80B-based board supports full-duplex operation of its six ports at speeds between 50 and 19200 baud. The application software that is downloaded to the board by the CPU has been optimized for the single-character I/O nature of the HP-UX operating system. Ten-wire modem control is provided to meet European license requirements.

□ The Parallel Asynchronous FIFO Interface is used to connect to external devices that require eight- or 16-bit, parallel, half-duplex communications. For data transfers less than 66 words using differential signaling, the theoretical maximum data rate for this interface is three megabytes at 50 meters (maximum distance) or five megabytes at three meters.

This is the first technical/real-time computer offering in the HPPA family, and thus becomes an alternative to the other HP 9000 systems and, with a bit more difficulty, HP 1000 systems. The Model 840 processor with the FPC performs at the rate of 2.8 million B1 Whetstones per second and 1.9 million B1D Whetstones per second. The HP 9000 Series 500 Model 550 performs at .7 million B1s and .5 million B1Ds, or at about one quarter the speed. The HP 1000 A900 performs at 1.6 million B1s and .9 million B1Ds, or at roughly half the speed.

Like the other HP 9000s, the Model 840 uses HP-UX, Hewlett-Packard's version of UNIX for its operating system (see Chapter 8).

The HP 9000 800 Series Model 840S is an enhanced version of the Model 840. It has a rating of 4.5 MIPS, producing performance levels of 3.1 million single-precision Whetstones or 2.1 million double-precision Whetstones. Memory in this model also begins with the standard eight megabytes but is expandable to 96 megabytes.

The HP 9000 800 Series Model 850S is the technical offering, with hardware similar to the HP 3000 Series 950. As the current top-of-the-line of the HP 9000s, this machine has a MIPS rating of 7.2, producing 4.2 million single-precision Whetstones or 2.9 million double-precision Whetstones. Memory size can range from the standard 16 megabytes up to 128 megabytes.

The HP 9000 800 Series Model 825SRX is a superworkstation. It produces performance levels of 2.5 million Whetstone instructions per second (B1D). One of two HP 9000s based on this smaller SPU, this model compares quite favorably to other such superworkstations in the marketplace today.

The HP 9000 800 Series Model 825S is the second machine based on this SPU, and it bridges the gap between workstations and larger computers. With a MIPS rating of 3.1, this incredible little box performs 3.5 million single-precision or 2.4 million double-precision Whetstones. Memory starts with the standard eight megabytes and is expandable to 96 megabytes.

The Future

Although it is always risky business to predict what a vendor's future products will be, one can make an educated guess in terms of Hewlett-Packard and stand a good chance of being correct. HP's history has indicated its strong commitment to the trends of compatibility and price/performance. Hence, it seems clear that the future will bring a steady flow of computers, compatible with today's, that will either offer today's performance at a reduced price or increased performance at today's prices. Having met these goals consistently since 1976, and having reiterated its commitments, HP should follow these patterns for many years to come.

HP Precision Architecture is the foundation upon which these goals and objectives can be met well into the 1990s. The architecture is extensible, permitting it to be implemented on faster, smaller technologies such as Gallium Arsenide or on technologies yet to be invented. The trend, after all, is towards higher levels of integration, greater circuit density, larger chip size, faster clock speeds, and cheaper production costs. These trends will undoubtedly yield desktop computers and mainframes faster than today's fastest, all of which will be compatible, down to the object code level.

The Architecture Control Documents also spell out other techniques that will be used to increase the price/performance ratio. Multiple parallel processors, as well as other specialized coprocessors, could be used in the future. Today, the only coprocessor that's been built to enhance the performance when doing real number arithmetic is the FPC. The coprocessor technique can be used, however, whenever a specialized function, relatively expensive for the SPU to perform, is performed frequently. With HP's open-architecture intentions, one can probably expect third-party coprocessors to begin springing up, meeting specific performance needs of some users.

On the I/O front, it's reasonable to expect a replacement for the HP-IB interface in the not-to-distant future. The faster CPUs will soon be demanding higher I/O channel throughput to keep pace. Also, the networking trend will probably put pressure on HP to develop an interface that would provide shared peripherals (tapes, printers, maybe even discs). The tried-and-true HP-IB interface may prove too restrictive to support these growing demands. If so, HP will be certain to have a new solution at hand.

8

Operating Systems

Back in the old days, before computers had real operating systems, the computer was completely in the hands of the programmer. Once your computer card deck was ready to go, you rebooted the machine and read in your cards that loaded the assembler or a compiler and produced another deck of cards -- your program in machine-instruction form. Another reboot and your program was loaded. The machine was completely consumed doing what you told it to do, and other programmers had to wait for their turn. If your program went into an infinite loop, so did the computer, and only another reboot would allow the next program to run.

Operating systems were invented to bring order to this chaos. An operating system is software designed to control system flow, providing simplified access to and increased use of the hardware. Typically, when a modern computer is rebooted, its operating system is automatically invoked. All access to the computer is then done with the permission of, and through the capabilities offered by, the operating system.

As mentioned earlier, the HP 3000 900 Series and the HP 9000 800 Series are all HP Precision Architecture computers; their hardware is very similar and almost interchangeable. What makes, say, a Series 930 appear completely different than a Series 840 is its operating system. The HP 3000 900 Series uses an MPE XL operating system, whereas the HP 9000 uses an HP-UX.

The MPE XL Operating System

The very first HP 3000 used an operating system called 'Multi-Programming Executive' (MPE). Versions of this original operating system continue to be the only operating system available for the HP 3000. Through the years, as each new major version of the operating system was released, a suffix was added to indicate the version (e.g., MPE II, MPE III). Today, two versions are currently supported: MPE V is the operating system for the pre-HPPA computers -- the MICRO 3000 through the HP 3000 Series 70. A superset of MPE V, designed to take advantage of HP Precision Architecture, runs on the HP 3000 900 Series. This version is called 'MPE XL', for Multi-Programming Executive with eXtended Large addressing.

MPE XL is a disc-based operating system that manages all system resources and coordinates the execution of all programs running on the system. Designed for the commercial marketplace, it offers the capabilities and performance needed for transaction-oriented, I/O-intensive applications. It supports multiple users, multi-tasking, and virtual memory to allow for the simultaneous processing of multiple interactive sessions and batch jobs.

MULTI-PROGRAMMING. MPE XL supports the concurrent execution of multiple programs. Each user on the system is able to run as if each were the only user on the system. When the process currently being run by the SPU pauses for input, for example, the process with the highest priority that is waiting to run will be dispatched to the SPU. What the various users are actually doing is of no concern to the system. Hence, application transaction processing, program development, data communications, batch processing, and games can all be going on concurrently.

Code-sharing is an integral aspect of MPE XL. All code, regardless of its original language, is both re-entrant and reusable. In other words, if ten users all are running the same application program, only one copy of that program's code is actually in the system. Each user will, however, have her or his own data space. MPE XL provides complete protection against one user's program interfering with another's.

VIRTUAL MEMORY. By utilizing the 64-bit address space permitted by the HP Precision Architecture, the virtual address space can be thought of as 65,536 spaces of four billion bytes, or over 200 trillion (200,000,000,000,000) bytes. This address space is used not only for programs and data, but also for files, through a facility known as 'mapped files'. Hence, the operating system can reference directly all types of information it needs to access. This eliminates much of the overhead associated with other operating system designs.

Mapped files can be thought of as an extension to the disc-caching capabilities offered in MPE V. Every byte of every opened file on the system has a unique virtual address. There is no buffering; instead, a file is considered nothing more than a group of pages, just like programs and data areas. When a user accesses a page of a file not yet in real memory, the operating system transparently performs the I/O and brings that page, and often times those around it, into real memory.

This demand-paged virtual memory technique applies to all of memory, so the need for program segmentation is also eliminated; the system merely brings into memory just the pages of program code files that are needed or that the system anticipates will be needed shortly. Pages that are accessed most frequently remain in main memory. Seldom-accessed pages are overlayed when the system needs to bring in new pages being accessed.

COMMANDS. MPE XL is made up of more than 175 commands processed by a program called the 'Command Interpreter' (CI). These same commands can be used interactively in session mode, in a batch job, or programmatically (invoked by a user program). Therefore, no special job-control language is necessary for batch processing.

Users add their own commands via two mechanisms. Catalogues of User Defined Commands (UDCs) can be built, just as they existed in MPE V. Or, more simply, in MPE XL, command files can be built. These files are a list of other commands to be executed when the command filename is typed. Parameter substitution and default values for parameters make this a powerful feature.

DUAL MODES. MPE XL supports two run-time environments. When asked to run a program compiled with an MPE V-based compiler, whether actually compiled on an MPE V-based HP 3000 or a MPE XL-based HP 3000, the system will run this program in Compatibility Mode (CM), emulating the environment of an MPE V-based HP 3000, including code, stack structures, and MPE V system intrinsics. This mode provides complete object-code compatibility with the MPE V-based HP 3000s. That is, a program from, say a Series 37, along with its datafiles and databases, can be stored (:STORE) to tape and restored (:RESTORE) onto a Series 930, and the program will run as it did on the Series 37, without modification and without special action by the user.

The other run-time environment, Native Mode (NM), allows access to the higher performance and huge address space of HP Precision Architecture. Programs don't need to run solely in one environment or the other. Rather, the system will switch modes transparently, coordinating the two run-time environments, when calls are made to system functions that operate in a different mode than the calling procedure. A switch subsystem is also provided to allow user application programs to switch modes within a given program. This allows new programs to be written in a Native Mode language while still calling common routines used by older applications not yet converted from Compatibility Mode.

An Object Code Translator (OCT) is also available that will translate a Compatibility Mode program into a hybrid Compatibility/Native Mode program. Though at first glance the translated program appears to be a Compatibility Mode program, the Compatibility Mode emulator will detect that the code has already been translated, and will run much of the program with the Native Mode code. This provides a simple way to increase the performance of Compatibility Mode programs without the need to convert them or rewrite them in a Native Mode language.

DEBUG. MPE XL includes two different debugging tools. DEBUG, which has been enhanced beyond its MPE V version, is fully cognizant of both Native Mode and Compatibility Mode. With powerful window and macro capabilities, this facility allows users to set breakpoints or single-step through the execution of a program, and to examine or modify the values of variables at any point along the way. If the program under debugging switches environments (CM to NM, or vice versa) during its execution, DEBUG will also switch to the appropriate mode, showing the appropriate instructions and registers in the appropriate radix (by default, octal for CM and hexadecimal for NM).

XDB is a symbolic debugger. When compiled with the proper options, symbolic debugging information is included in the program file, so that XDB can show not only what is occurring at the machine code level but what is occurring vis-a-vis the original source code as well.

Both of these debuggers expect to work on non-optimized program files. Debugging should be performed before the code is subjected to optimization, because it is difficult and often impossible to trace program flow in the source when executing code that has been optimized. Remember that optimizers often shuffle the order of code execution and eliminate variables and subexpressions when it feels it can do that safely. What then should a debugger tell you if you ask for the value of a variable that doesn't exist anymore?

Additional information on these debugging tools can be found in Appendix B.

PRIVILEGE LEVELS. Whereas MPE V-based machines have just two privilege levels of execution, user mode and Privileged Mode, the MPE XL-based machines have four, numbered from 3 to 0, in increasing order of capability. User programs normally run at Exec Level 3, the equivalent of MPE V's user mode. Most system processes run at Exec Level 0.

Callable system intrinsics have two numbers associated with them: the Call Level and the Exec Level. If an intrinsic is defined to have a Call Level of 3 and and Exec Level of 1, then anybody calling from a process running at 3 or better can call it. Once called, it will run at Exec Level 1, providing access to certain features and files that require that level of privileged access. If an intrinsic is defined to have a Call Level of 0 and an Exec Level of 0, only those programs or procedures already at Exec Level 0 will be able to call this procedure. Once called, this procedure will continue running at Exec Level 0.

MPE XL ENHANCEMENTS. For those already intimately familiar with MPE V, here is a short description of some of the enhancements and additions made to the CI in MPE XL:

□ Command History Stack -- Under MPE V, the user was limited to a REDO of only the most recent command. Under MPE XL, a redo stack is maintained. Besides a greatly enhanced :REDO command, a :LISTREDO and a :DO command were added. While in the edit mode of a :REDO command, several additional edit directives are available.

□ Implied :RUN -- When a command is entered, the CI first checks to see if this command is a UDC. If it is not, the CI checks the MPE XL command dictionary to see if it is a built-in command. If still not found, the CI begins looking for a file by that name in one of the groups and accounts specified in the HPPATH variable. By default, this variable has the value of '!hpgroup, pub, pub.sys'; that is, the CI will look for a file first in the user's logon group, then in the PUB group of the logon account, and lastly in the PUB group of the SYS account. If a file is found, its type is examined. If the file is a program file (either CM or NM) then the program is run. If the file is not a program file, then it is treated as a command file. If no file is found, then the UNKNOWN COMMAND NAME error message is issued. Tokens specified after the command name itself are treated as parameters in the case of command files or as the info string and parm value in the case of program files.

□ Variables -- The concept of Job Control Words (JCWs) in MPE V has been greatly enhanced by session variables. Variables can have integer or string values. A large set of predefined variables exist. Some, such as HPHGROUP for the user's home group or HPDAY for the day of the week, are read-only variables. Others, such as HPPATH for the command search path or HPPROMPT for the user's current prompt string, may be examined or changed by the user. Users may also define their own local variables. Variables can be used in the :CALC, :IF, :INPUT, and :WHILE commands, as well as the commands added for the purpose of variable manipulations: :SETVAR, :SHOWVAR, and :DELETEVAR. They may also be used in UDCs, command files, and job streams.

☐ Command Files -- These files are a list of other commands to be executed when the command file name is typed. Parameter substitution and default values for parameters make this a powerful feature.

☐ :CHGROUP Command -- If users wish to change their current group without logging off and logging on again, they can use the :CHGROUP command. If users are prompted for the group password at logon time, they will be prompted for it here.

☐ New :LISTF Modes -- Two new modes have been added that will replace the LISTDIR5 program on MPE V-based systems. :LISTF,3 results in a listing similar to LISTDIR5's :LISTF command. :LISTF,4 results in a listing similar to LISTDIR5's :LISTSEC command.

☐ :CALC Command -- This command gives the user access to a desktop calculator directly from the CI. Logical, boolean, and arithmetic operators are supported, as well as bit shifts and some string functions. All results are formatted to $STDLIST in decimal, octal, and hexadecimal notations. A predefined variable, HPRESULT, is also set to the most recent :CALC command result.

Here is a list of some of the changes made to the operator and system manager interfaces between MPE V and MPE XL:

☐ The system configuration functions handled by :SYSDUMP under MPE V are handled by a new program called 'SYSGEN'. This program allows multiple configurations on disc at one time. Then, at boot time, the operator can decide which configuration should be used in bringing up the system.

- [ ] The disc volume management program, VINIT, has been replaced with VOLUTIL. Among many new and changed features, this program will allow users to format and place on line a new system disc volume without bringing the system down.

- [ ] The entire rebooting process has been redesigned. One of the nicer features is the addition of a clock that remembers the date and time, even over a system failure.

- [ ] A hardware serial number that can be accessed by software was added. This is a feature that third-party software suppliers have requested for years. It will allow them to check the serial number in software to prevent using the program on a system other than the one for which it was licensed.

The HP-UX Operating System

In 1969, according to legend, Ken Thompson of Bell Telephone Laboratories found a discarded DEC PDP-7 and wrote a real-time operating system for it in a few weeks. This was the birth of UNIX.

Operating systems are usually developed by a vendor for a particular hardware unit. UNIX, originally developed for the PDP-7 and later the PDP-11, stands apart from these vendor-specific operating systems (i.e., MPE, VMS, DOS/370) because it has been adapted to run on many different vendors' systems. In 1983, HP joined the growing list of computer manufacturers to put UNIX on one of its machines when it developed the HP 9000 Series 200 Model 16.

UNIX was developed by Thompson and another Bell Labs engineer, Dennis Richie, as a simple, powerful, and easily extensible operating system for software development. Over the years it has been enhanced a great deal. Much of the power of the current versions of UNIX rests in the large body of utilities written within Bell Labs, UC Berkeley and other institutions with heavy interest in UNIX. A large part of UNIX's appeal is the ease with which these user-written utility programs can be integrated into the UNIX environment and actually become part of the operating system.

HP's version of UNIX is called 'HP-UX'. It retains all of the standard features of UNIX, such as:

☐ Multi-programming, multi-user access with virtual memory support. UNIX allows each user to log on and initiate multiple processes for that session. Each process can be placed either in the foreground (comparable to MPE's session mode) or in the background. Background processes run at a lower priority, and other foreground processes can be initiated and run while background processes execute. The user has the ability to switch processes from one priority to the other at will.

☐ Multi-tiered directory structure. UNIX provides facilities for true tree-structure directories. Within a directory of files, another directory can be declared which can also contain files and directories. This structure can be continued almost indefinitely and provides the user with cataloging capabilities suitable for any purpose.

☐ The UNIX command interpreter, commonly called the 'Shell'. This, along with the Shell script language, affords the UNIX programmer an extremely powerful environment in which to develop programs and the ability to make those programs part of the operating system, if desired.

☐ Shell script language. This is essentially a free-form language that allows the programmer to execute operating system commands in a program-like form. Full transfer of control and looping constructs are provided. Conceptually similar to a batch job under MPE, this facility is executed like a program and runs either in the foreground or background.

☐ I/O redirection. UNIX provides very simple methods for redirecting the input and output of programs. Redirection is to and from UNIX files, which are viewed by UNIX as nothing more than a continuous stream of bytes.

☐ Pipes and filters. An extension of I/O redirection, pipes and filters provide the programmer with the ability to "string together" several programs by directing the output of one program to the input of another. This can be carried as far as desired. Much of UNIX's power stems from piping the output of one general utility to the input of another. In this way, complex new "applications" can be created by using existing utilities.

In addition to these standard UNIX features, HP has added many extensions of its own to HP-UX, especially for the HP 9000 Series 800. These enhancements include:

☐ Real-time features. This was necessary to accommodate the applications normally supported by HP 1000 systems, such as factory automation. These features include the ability to assign real-time priorities to processes, time-based scheduling to one-microsecond resolution, user control of buffering, software signals to allow asynchronous interprocess communication, and file-locking.

☐ Real-time performance enhancements. These include the ability to queue disc I/O's in priority order so lower-priority foreground and background processes do not interfere with higher-priority, real-time processes, as well as the tuning of HP-UX on the 800 Series to reduce process-dispatch latency to a fraction of what is normal for UNIX systems.

☐ Graphics, database management, and networking. These enhancements leverage on HP's strengths in these areas and allow the HP-UX system to further approach the functionality needed for commercial data processing systems.

☐ Native-language support. This facility, similar to the one available under MPE, allows for applications to be easily localized for different languages. This makes the system more marketable worldwide and allows software vendors the ability to widen the markets of their software packages.

The code for 800 Series HP-UX machines is source-code compatible with existing HP 9000 Series 200, 300, and 500 systems running their respective versions of HP-UX. In most cases, a recompilation and relink of the software is all that is needed to port the application to HP Precision Architecture. If, however, non-standard language, operating system, or hardware features are used in the software, a more extensive migration effort will be required.

Hewlett-Packard has announced its interest in maintaining and expanding its base of HP-UX systems. In fact, HP management has publicly stated its wishes to move HP-UX aggressively into the commercial arena. Using HP-UX, the user community can be assured of a highly compatible line of machines that can support commercial applications, general time-share and program-development environments, and real-time applications.

9

Data Communication Methodologies

From the beginning, the HP 3000 minicomputers were designed to be timesharing systems. Therefore, users needed a way to communicate directly with the operating system without relying on punch cards, paper tape, or magnetic tape. HP decided to use asynchronous devices and developed the Asynchronous Terminal Controller, better known as the 'ATC'.

This first data communication device was only the beginning. As the data communications industry grew during the 1980s, HP introduced more and more advanced technologies. This chapter presents a summary of the 'classic' MPE approach, a summary of the MPE XL approach, and a discussion of the most important differences between the two.

The Classic MPE Approach

The ATC was used by the HP 3000 Series I, II, and III, and allowed speeds of up to 2400 baud. It allowed direct-connect devices and modems and was capable of speed-sensing. Parity was determined by the initial carriage return and was restricted to odd or even. The parity-checking was done by the hardware, and the parity bit was always set to zero before being sent to the data buffer.

When the next generation of the HP 3000 was released, the Asynchronous Data Communications Controller (ADCC) was the new interfacing hardware. The Series 30/33 and 39/40/42/44/48/58 use the ADCC, which allows speeds of up to 9600 baud. It has all of the features of the ATC, but parity is handled differently.

Parity is sensed on the initial carriage return, but the ADCC allows only even or no parity. If a one is in the parity bit on the initial carriage return, even parity is selected. The parity bit is still set to zero before being passed to the data buffer. If a zero is seen on the initial return, the ADCC passes the parity through to the data buffer, requiring that it be dealt with by the application program. This is called 'pass-through parity'.

When the last generation of MPE V-based HP 3000 machines were released, HP's concept of the ultimate asynchronous interface was ready. The Advanced Terminal Processor (ATP) is found on the Series 37 and 64/68/70 and optionally on the Series 42/44/48/58. The ATP supports speeds of up to 19200 baud but does not allow speed-specified input devices, that is, it always speed senses. It handles parity the same as the ADCC.

Hewlett-Packard, unlike some other vendors, realized that other manufacturers build terminals. The ATC, ADCC, and ATP allow for this with a termtype parameter. HP developed termtypes for the GE Terminet, Datapoint and Hazeltine terminals, and dumb CRTs in general. Termtypes also exist for other vendor hardcopy devices and provide delays after carriage returns and form feeds.

When MPE V was released, HP included termtypes for serial printers connected over asynchronous lines. These termtypes allow for extensive status-checking so output does not end up in the 'bit bucket' if the line to the printer goes down. HP has also developed a product, the Workstation Configurator, that allows users to create termtypes for 'foreign' (that is, non-HP) hardware.

The ATC, ADCC, and ATP use two methods of output flow control between a host and a device: ENQ/ACK and XON/XOFF. ENQ/ACK, which is used to keep the terminal from overflowing, is controlled by the HP 3000. Every 80 characters, the HP 3000 sends out an ENQ. The device is supposed to respond with an ACK. For some termtypes, if the ACK is not received, data transmission is resumed after a specified time-out period. For other termtypes, the suspension is indefinite; the ENQ is repeated every few seconds until the ACK is received. Although the ADCC and ATP allow speeds greater than 4800 baud, some of HP's terminals cannot process the data at that speed. This protocol allows a user to run a slow terminal at high speed without losing data.

XON/XOFF (DC1/DC3) flow-control protocol is controlled by the device. When the device wants to suspend the output from the HP 3000, it sends out an XOFF. To resume output, the device sends an XON. Sometimes, the HP 3000 misses the XON or XOFF, causing either a device overflow or a hung port. Also, when pass-through parity is in effect, neither the ADCC nor the ATP strip off the parity bit. This means that either the XON or the XOFF will not be recognized if odd or even parity is used, because the controller checks all eight bits and has its parity bit set to zero.

The two methods of input flow-control are DC1 and DC1/DC2/DC1. The DC1 is a read trigger while in character mode. Only when a DC1 is sent to a device can a user input data. The DC1/DC2/DC1 method is better known as 'block mode'. The HP 3000 sends a DC1 notifying the terminal that input is allowed. A DC2 is sent to the HP 3000 alerting it that a block mode transfer is pending. The HP 3000 sends back another DC1 allowing the device to start the transfer. Block mode allows users to edit the screen locally, i.e., without interaction with the HP 3000.

Intermachine communication is done using synchronous devices. The Intelligent Network Processor (INP) is a device capable of two protocols: BInary SYNChronous (BISYNC) and Synchronous Data Link Control (SDLC). Using this communications device, two HP 3000s can communicate at speeds up to 56000 baud. An HP 3000 can also communicate with mainframe computers such as IBM, Honeywell, and others using HP software products such as RJE, MRJE, or NRJE, IMF, MTS.

With two INPs connected by cable, a synchronous modem, an X.25 network, or even satellites, a user can create a session on a remote machine. Then, the user can copy files from one machine to the other or even run a program on one machine using data files on either or both machines. If a user passes through more than one machine, the data files on any of the machines on which she or he has created a session can be used.

The problem with this is obvious. If the user's local machine is A, and A is connected to B, which is connected to C, which is connected to D, and the user needs to be on system D, the response time will be the cumulative total of the response times on A, B, C, and D. Two ways to avoid this are to connect each machine to every other using INPs (an expensive and limited option, since a finite number of expansion slots exist in each system) or to devise a method to connect each machine to every other with a single piece of hardware per machine.

In the mid-1970s, XEROX developed Ethernet. Often referred to as IEEE 802.3, it's more accurately called IEEE 802.2. Ethernet uses coaxial cables for connection of systems in a single building with a transmission rate of 10 megabits per second. It uses a Carrier-Sense, Multiple-Access/Collision-Detect (CSMA/CD) link protocol, which evolved into the IEEE 802.3 standard.

The HP 9000 uses this standard on its network. By the time HP started developing a Local Area Network (LAN) for the HP 3000, the medium-access control, or physical layer, of the 802.3 standard had been modified. This modification added new fields to the LAN 'packet', or unit of transmission. Although IEEE 802.2 and 802.3 can coexist on the same physical cable, a system using IEEE 802.2 cannot read a packet in IEEE 802.3 format, and vice versa.

The addition of the LAN to the HP 3000 repertoire of communication methods was indeed a welcome one. Sites with a large number of HP 3000s can now connect them directly rather than in a long chain (also called a 'ring topology'). Datafiles or programs on remote machines are now adjacent, which decreases response time and increases productivity and performance.

The MPE XL Approach

On the new HP 3000 900 Series computers, the LAN has been taken one step further. No longer are asynchronous terminals connected directly to the systems cabinet or an I/O bay. Now workstations are connected to a new Distributed Terminal Controller (DTC). The DTC is connected to the HP 3000 via the IEEE 802.3 LAN. This allows users the flexibility of placing the DTC anywhere in the building, subject to the LAN's cable limitations. The DTC will eventually allow any workstation to access any HP 3000 system on the LAN -- but not in first release of the product, when each terminal must be 'nailed' to a specific system. Write-only peripherals, such as printers and plotters, are required to be nailed to a single system as well.

HP offers two types of LAN cables: thick and thin. ThickLAN is based on the Ethernet (10BASE5) standard. It allows up to 500 meters of cable per segment and 100 nodes per segment. It uses .4-inch diameter, 50 ohm, double-shielded cable. Transceiver cables are required and can be up to 50 meters long. The typical connector for Ethernet is either a clamp-on tap or a type N connector.

ThinLAN is based on the 'Cheapernet' (10BASE2) standard. It allows up to 185 meters of cable per segment and 30 nodes per segment. It uses .2-inch diameter, 50 ohm, single- or double-shielded cable. Transceiver cables are not required. The typical connector for 'Cheapernet' is a BNC female connector.

So that DTCs can be placed even further from the system, HP has two repeater kits that increase the length of cable allowed on a single network. In addition, directly connected workstations using RS-232 can be placed up to 15 meters from the DTC. Those using RS-442 can be placed up to 1200 meters from the DTC.

DTC represents a marked departure for HP in its data communication strategy; in fact, the DTC is a cross-over device firmly planted in both the past and the future.

The DTC is similar to the ATP. There are three-pin, RS-232-C or five-pin, RS-422 local connections and 25-pin, RS-232-C modem connections. In general, HP is supporting only its newer terminals and printers. Thus, the 2392 and the Series 700 terminals are supported, but the 264x family is not. Some of the 262x family are supported only if certain ROMs are present. As far as printers are concerned, HP is in the process of validating the slower-line printers for use on the 900 Series. Currently, the 2934 and 2686 are supported. Non-HP devices are not supported.

In order to ensure compatibility with the ATP, HP developed the Asynchronous Serial Communications (ASC) software package for DTC control. There *are* differences, however: The ENQ/ACK handshake has been replaced by an enhanced XON/XOFF protocol; speed- and parity-sensing are the same as on the ATP, but not in the first release; baud rates of 110, 150, and 600 are no longer supported; turning the echo on and off is now done with the MPE XL command SET ECHO instead of 'ESC : ' and 'ESC ; '; and sessions are logged-off after a DTC power failure.

The DTC will support only two terminal types (10 and 18) and three printer types (18, 21, and 22).

Termtypes 10 and 18 on MPE XL use an enhanced XON/XOFF protocol instead of ENQ/ACK protocol. Printer types 18, 21, and 22 also use the enhanced XON/XOFF protocol. In addition, printer types 21 and 22 use the initialization string of MPE V's TTPCL22. Printer status checks are done less frequently on MPE XL; status requests are no longer done after each printed line.

HP is certainly not a pioneer in the concept of distributing terminals across a LAN. Digital Equipment Corporation's VAX computer line optionally employs a LAN-based terminal connection.

The DTC and DEC's terminal connections are significantly different. DEC offers three terminal servers: the DECserver 100, an inexpensive, eight-port unit designed for remote users; The DECserver 200, a high-cost-per-connection, 16-port unit designed for remote department use; and the DECserver 500, a 128-port unit that is cost-effective, space-conservative, and designed for centralized clusters of terminals. The terminal servers permit the user to select the system they wish to work on, thus eliminating the need for a dataswitch.

Unlike HP's, DEC's terminals support only character mode. The DECserver uses a different transmission approach than the HP DTC. The DECserver transmits all input received to all systems periodically. This means that each system must read the packet sent and weed out the data meant for its system. It then must also do another weeding out to buffer the data for the appropriate port. The HP DTC sends out one packet per port and only on completion of the read request or other interrupt (e.g., timeout, end-of-file, etc.). This lowers the overhead on the system, because the data in the packet received is only for a particular port on its system, and since the read request is complete, there is no need to buffer the data waiting for more. The data can then be delivered to the requesting program.

Comparing HP's DTCs to IBM's terminal connections is more difficult. IBM's high-end 4300 systems primarily use the 3270 Display Station, synchronous terminals that are highly integrated with the system itself. IBM is increasing its attention to the asynchronous market and has a controller that will connect up to 64 ASCII terminals to a 43xx system. However, the application support is limited.

The 900 Series of HP 3000 systems use the IEEE 802.3 LAN to communicate with other HP systems. This allows communications with any HP 3000 Series 37 through 70. In order to communicate with a Series III, 30, or 33, an intermediary must be used, as those systems don't support LAN.

The new MPE XL-based systems can use the communications capabilities of an MPE V-based system on the same LAN to access remote HP systems, X.25 networks, and IBM mainframes.

The 900 Series systems do not support DS/3000, DS/X.25, SNA NRJE/IMF, or BSC RJE/MRJE/IMF. Some of these products will be available in the future. Users on the HPPA systems must link to an MPE V-based system in order to use these facilities. Using DS/3000, DS/X.25, and BISYNC RJE/MRJE/IMF is rather direct. NS/3000 XL is used to link to the MPE V-based system, and then the appropriate subsystem, to complete the connection. HP has developed SNA Server Access/XL and SNA Server Access/V to use the SNA server on the MPE V-based system.

These SNA server access subsystems enable LAN users to transparently access the non-programmatic services of SNA IMF and SNA RJE on an HP 3000 node connected to an IBM host. The subsystem resides on each node that is not connected to the IBM host. It establishes the connection between the nodes and shares node address information. This allows the transparent transfer of data between the two nodes and allows the proper routing of data from the IBM to the appropriate node.

MPE V Versus MPE XL

The differences between MPE V and MPE XL in the area of data communication are numerous -- some are blatant, but most are subtle. These differences are important to anyone whose applications depend on any of the MPE V features.

On MPE V, the console can be moved to another logical device by the CONSOLE command. This allows another device to execute console commands, including CONTROL A commands. The console on the 900 Series is directly connected to the system cabinet on its own special card. The console can still be moved, but only from the hardwired console will the system be able to recognize the console-attention character (i.e., 'CONTROL A').

On MPE V, parity was sensed during logon. On MPE XL, it is not; the default is to use eight-bit characters with no parity.

On MPE V, when a user hits BREAK during a read, the system will remember what was typed in prior to the BREAK. On MPE XL, the input buffer is flushed upon the detection of a BREAK. For example, say the editor is running, and a user enters LIST at the / prompt, hits BREAK, and enters :RESUME at the : prompt. Upon returning to the editor and receiving the READ pending message, the user can hit the return key and the LIST will be executed. On MPE XL, the user will receive the READ pending message and a new read will be started; the LIST is lost.

On MPE V, the BREAK key is disabled while in the command interpreter during a read, except on a :REDO edit. On MPE XL, the BREAK key is not disabled.

On MPE V, a preemptive write will interrupt a read or another write. On MPE XL, a preemptive write interrupts only a read or a write that has not yet started. For example, on a read, when an operator sends a WARN message while a user is typing a command, MPE V loses the data entered before the WARN message, and the user has to retype the entire command. On MPE XL, the WARN message will be displayed while the command is being typed, but no data will be lost; the user just continues the command where it was interrupted. During writes on MPE V, a preemptive write will not interrupt a write that is already printing. On MPE XL, writes that have not yet started will be delayed until after the preemptive write. This is a minor difference.

MPE XL uses an enhanced XON/OFF protocol. In MPE V, an XON (DC1) or XOFF (DC3) are ignored in certain cases. In MPE XL, XON and XOFF are never ignored, except in binary transfer mode.

On MPE V, if a read is pending and a CONTROL S (XOFF) is pressed, the CONTROL S will be ignored, and any subsequent data will be transmitted immediately. On MPE XL, the CONTROL S is never ignored. If a CONTROL S is entered while a read is pending, any subsequent data will be queued until a CONTROL Q (XON) is pressed. At that time, the data will be echoed and transmitted.

XON and XOFF cannot be input while in an unedited terminal mode (FCONTROL 41). These characters are used strictly for flow control.

A side effect of having XON/XOFF always enabled also involves using CONTROL S at a terminal. When a user types CONTROL S to halt data flow to the terminal, the system waits for a CONTROL Q to resume output. This may cause a problem when the terminal is 'hung'. On MPE V systems, an :ABORTIO from the console will usually clear up the problem. On an MPE XL system, it is useless to use :ABORTIO on a terminal where a user has typed CONTROL S and not CONTROL Q since the XON/XOFF is handled by the DTC and not the system. In order to free the terminal, the user should first try to enter a CONTROL Q at the terminal. If this fails, an :ABORTIO must be entered from the terminal diagnostic program TermDSM, not from the console. If the :ABORTIO does not work, the terminal should be RESET from TermDSM.

On MPE XL, in a block mode transfer, the second DC1 is not sent to the terminal. Instead, the data is sent immediately following the DC2.

ENQ/ACK protocol is not supported by the ASC. At first release, speed-sensing is not supported. All devices must match the configuration file. Transmission speeds of 110, 150, and 600 baud are no longer supported due to rare use. The :EOF command is now obsolete. Printers that require carriage control delays are not supported by ASC on MPE XL. Backspace characters no longer are treated specially. On MPE V, some devices, usually hardcopy, do a backspace and a line-feed so characters will appear under the ones being typed over. On MPE XL, a backspace is echoed and the last character is deleted from the read data.

On MPE V, a line feed will cause a carriage return and line feed to be echoed to the terminal, and the line feed will be stripped from the input data. On MPE XL, the line feed is no longer stripped. This is different only during line block mode. On MPE V, some devices will have the form-feed character substituted as a line-feed character. The ASC software will not perform the substitution.

Using the ESCAPE key will no longer turn the echo facility on or off. The MPE XL :SET command will be used. The syntax is as follows:

```
:SET ECHO = { ON | OFF }
```

On MPE V, the character strings 'ESC : ' and 'ESC ; ', as well as the line-feed character (LF), are stripped from the input data. They are not stripped on MPE XL.

On MPE V, all writes to printers are critical writes. Control is not returned to the program until the file system reports that the write is completed. On MPE XL, the file systems report a successful write after the data is sent to the DTC. Since this happens before the data is actually printed, it does not guarantee that the write is successful.

On MPE V, printer status-checking is done after an FOPEN, FCLOSE, and every record print. Terminal types 19 and 20 also did status checks after receiving an XOFF. On MPE XL, status checks are done only after an FOPEN and FCLOSE. No status-checking is done on terminal type 18 on either MPE V or MPE XL, a condition that should lead to better performance.

On MPE V, it is necessary to enable the read timer with FCONTROL 20 before every read duration that needs to be measured. On MPE XL, the read timer is always enabled, so no programmatic enabling is necessary. FCONTROL 21 will not disable the timer.

On MPE V, there are 11 characters that may not be specified as the alternate end-of-record character. On MPE XL, that list is reduced to seven: NUL (null), BS (backspace), DC1 (XON), DC3 (XOFF), CAN (cancel), DEL (delete or rubout), and the current subsystem break, whose default is EM (end of medium, known better as CONTROL Y). The subsystem break can be redefined in transparent mode through FCONTROL 41.

Privileged Mode programs may issue QUIESCE I/O requests on MPE V. This is not supported by the ASC on MPE XL. It should be replaced by a read of zero bytes.

The Workstation Configurator is not supported with the ASC software. The JOB and (command) commands, sometimes used to log on terminals, are not supported. Also, the FCARD and PTAPE intrinsics are not supported on MPE XL.

IV

MPE XL
File System

10

$\mathbf{B}$its and Bytes

This chapter discusses the internals of the MPE XL file system as well as practical matters, such as how to open a file.

A disc file is a set of logically related records stored on disc. On MPE V, the basic unit of file storage is the sector, which consists of 256 bytes. On MPE XL, the basic unit of file storage is the page, which consists of 4096 bytes. Because MPE XL is an evolution of MPE V, the storage requirements of files are sometimes expressed in sectors; these can easily be converted to pages by multiplying them by 16. Files under MPE XL consist of a directory entry (holding a file title and other information); a binary tree (or "B-Tree") that keeps track of the data pages allocated to the file; and pages of actual data.

$\mathbf{D}$irectory Structure

The MPE XL directory is a large file consisting of a basic tree structures containing accounting information (users, groups, accounts) and file location information. The MPE V directory structure is quite similar. Directory entries in both operating systems point to file labels, the primary difference being their location. On MPE V, the file label is part of the first extent of the file; whereas on MPE XL, old file labels are stored in a label table.

Files have names, called 'filenames'. Under MPE, filenames have three mandatory parts (the file, the group, and the account) and two optional parts (the lock and the node). Using the normal Hewlett-Packard style of representing syntax, a filename is:

```
file [ / lock ]  [ . group  [ . account ] ] [ : node ]
```

Each part consists of one to eight letters or digits, except for the node part which can consist of up to 16 characters, The first character in each part must be a letter. Thus, the following is a legal filename:

```
catsup/bottle.kitchen.sink:hotel
```

The UNIX user can mentally map an MPE filename of FOO.PUB.SYS into a UNIX filename of /USR/SYS/PUB/FOO. (Because UNIX filenames accommodate more than a single level, they're much more expressive than MPE filenames.) In UNIX, for example, users can have /USR/SYS/PUB/FOO/A/B as well as USR/SYS/FOO/A/OLD-B. This is called a hierarchical filename.

MPE can be thought of as having only a three-level hierarchy: account name, group name, and filename.

In MPE V, files are opened with the FOPEN intrinsic. When FOPEN was written and documented, an unfortunate choice was made: A filename could be terminated by any special character. This allowed programmers to arbitrarily decide how to terminate their filenames. Most chose a blank ( ); some chose semicolons (;); some chose nulls (ASCII 0); some chose colons (:); and some chose other characters.

The result was predictable. As the file system was extended, characters that were valid as terminators under one release of MPE were suddenly part of the filename under the next release. The classic example of this is the colon (:), which now indicates the start of a node portion of a filename.

There are difficulties with FOPEN in MPE V beyond having a rather vague terminating character. For example, much code that calls FOPEN first parses user input to determine if a filename is valid, making future extensions to filenames difficult. To support UNIX-style filenames, a program would have to allow *any* character other than a space to be part of a filename. In that case, what could be used as a terminating character? Even a space can be part of a UNIX filename, if enclosed by quote marks.

With MPE XL, an alternative file-opening intrinsic, HPFOPEN, was introduced to address this problem powerfully, albeit in a way which requires extensive changes to the code. Instead of requiring a single terminator character (such as a blank or a null) for all file titles, HPFOPEN requires that the filename is started *and* terminated by a character chosen by a programmer. Thus, '/FOO/' and ' FOO ' and 'GFOOG' are equivalent legal methods of telling HPFOPEN to open the file 'FOO'.

This is the second most powerful choice possible, because it means that a filename can consist of almost any characters -- up to 255 of the possible 256 ASCII characters. The most powerful choice would have been a length count followed by any of the 256 possible characters.

With early versions of MPE, a program could determine the validity of a filename only by either trying to open it and waiting for an error or by parsing the name and manually checking the syntax valid at the time the program was written. Neither approach was good.

In MPE XL, and later versions of MPE V, HP solved this problem by providing the intrinsic FPARSE. FPARSE examines a string of text and reports whether or not it is a valid filename, and optionally picks apart the various fields of the filename for the programmer. Use of this procedure for filename parsing is highly recommended, as it can avoid problems if file parts become longer (up to 16 characters) and hierarchical files are available.

The B-Tree

Once MPE has located the directory entry for a file, it has access to the address of the associated binary tree (B-Tree) structure that records what pages are allocated for the file and where they are on disc.

From the internal viewpoint of the MPE XL file system, all files are mapped files (mapped files are discussed in detail in Chapter 11). This means that the file system sees a file of 1,000 records of 80 bytes each as a virtual space of 80,000 bytes. In MPE V, if a program created such a file, then wrote only to its first and last records, all 80,000 bytes would be allocated on disc. Although this works, it represents a waste of space.

The implementors of the file system leveraged off the MPE XL memory manager code, using B-Trees to keep track of which pages of a file have been allocated and where they are on disc. By doing this, they made it possible to allocate only those pages that have been used instead of allocating the entire file.

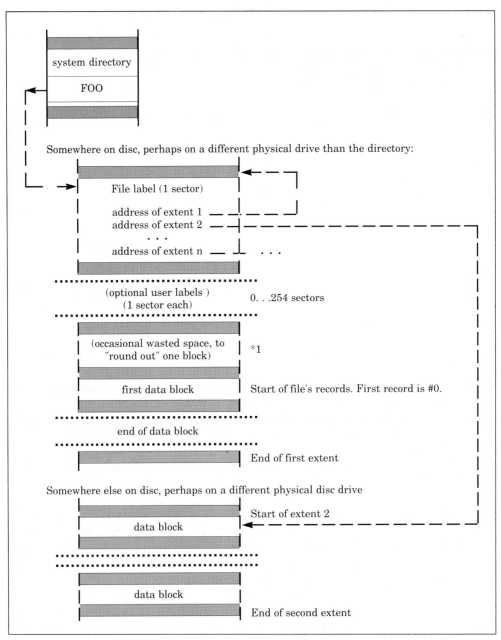

Figure 10.1 MPE V File Layout

The B-Tree and Empty Files

The :LISTF command will report the total number of sectors currently occupied by a file's data. The bytes of disc space occupied by the non-data pages are not reflected when MPE XL reports the file size. Thus, if a file is created normally but has never been written to, the :LISTF command would report it as occupying 0 sectors.

Here's an example of an empty file and use of the :LISTF command to display information about it:

```
:build foo;rec=-80,16,f,ascii;disc=1024
:listf foo,2
  ACCOUNT= SPLASH     GROUP= STAN


  FILENAME  CODE  ------------LOGICAL RECORD----------- ----SPACE-----
                  SIZE  TYP      EOF       LIMIT R/B SECTORS #X MX
MPE V:


  FOO             80B   FA       0         1024  16     45  1  8


MPE XL:


  FOO             80B   FA       0         1024  16      0  0  *
```

Notice the difference in the three columns marked 'SECTOR', '#X', and 'MX', under the '----SPACE----' heading. The MPE XL file allocation scheme differs from MPE V. Under MPE V, a file is made up of equal areas of disc called 'extents'. Each extent is an area of contiguous disc space a multiple of 256 bytes long. Every file occupies at least one extent and can have up to 32 extents. For backwards compatibility, MPE XL still allows files to be created by specifying the desired number of extents. Figure 10.1 shows a typical MPE V file on disc.

In MPE XL, logically consecutive pages do not need to be contiguous on disc or even located on the same disc drive. This freedom brings relief from two annoying limitations of MPE V: 1) that a file's maximum size has to be specified at file creation time and cannot be expanded later, and 2) that the storage for a file has to be partitioned into, at most, 32 areas of contiguous disc storage.

Like any new feature, it also has some bad points: A file that is created small, then expanded little by little over time, will end up with its pages scattered all over disc(s). Such fragmentation means that many, many disc I/Os might have to be done to read the entire file, with each I/O accompanied by a disc-head seek. Figure 11.1 (in the next chapter) shows a typical MPE XL file on disc.

Having pages of a file scattered across one or more discs implies difficulty in finding a file if the directory is scrambled. In MPE V, a file is fragmented into as many as 32 pieces, each of which is a contiguous area on disc. A program could attempt to locate 'lost' files by scanning sectors of disc for recognizable data. This task would be nearly impossible in MPE XL.

Data Records

When a file is created, the operating system remembers various attributes about the file, including record format (fixed, variable, undefined), record size (recsize), and block size (blocksize). These attributes stay with a file throughout its lifetime.

A record is the smallest amount of data directly addressable in a file. A file can be built with records as small as one byte or as large as 32,767 bytes (32,766 in MPE V).

MPE provides three lengths of record formats: fixed, variable, and undefined. Fixed-length records are the most commonly used and usually the most efficient for access, although not for disc storage. Variable-length records allow records of varying sizes to be efficiently stored on disc, but at the cost of additional file system overhead. In files with variable-length records, the record size specified at file creation is the maximum length of any record, and MPE allocates an extra two bytes per record to hold the actual size of each record. Undefined-length records are somewhat of an oddity; for magnetic tape files, they are necessary, but for disc files they are treated essentially the same as fixed-length records.

Although files are usually viewed as collections of records and accessed one record at a time, the file system typically manipulates them one 'block' at a time. A block is a grouping of one or more records and is the minimum unit of data moved to or from a file. The size of a file's blocks is controlled at file creation time by specifying the number of records per block (the 'block factor'). A block cannot exceed 65,280 bytes in MPE V or 65,535 bytes in MPE XL.

Within a block, records are placed end to end. If a record is an odd number of bytes long, a single, filler byte follows it. Variable-record format files have two extra bytes after the last record of each block. Undefined-record format files have a block factor of one. In MPE V, every block in a file starts at a sector boundary. Since a sector is 256 bytes, this means that blocks that are not multiples of 256 waste space. In MPE XL, records are laid end-to-end, with no wasted space at the end of a block.

So far, we have been talking about record size as if it was always specified in bytes, but it's not that easy. MPE has always had a schizophrenic view of the world -- sometimes eight-bit byte-oriented, sometimes 16-bit word-oriented. Although the internals of MPE XL are heading towards a consistent byte-orientation, the HPPA architecture has introduced a third personality: 32-bit word orientation.

The MPE file system calls 16-bit items 'words', because that's what they were called in MPE V. They now should be called 'half-words'. This problem of MPE's is shown in the way that a file's record size is specified. A positive value means the units are 16-bit words, and a negative value means the units are eight-bit bytes. MPE XL points the way to the eventual byte-oriented world: The new HPFOPEN intrinsic accepts record size only as a positive number of bytes.

Practical Matters: Opening Files

Files must be opened before they can be accessed. MPE XL provides two basic intrinsics for opening files: FOPEN and HPFOPEN. Both of these intrinsics are available to Native Mode programs, but only FOPEN is currently available to Compatibility Mode programs.

Parameter	Example
fid : = f open (file name,	'FOO'
foptions,	octal ('1004')
aoptions,	octal ('0')
recsize,	-80
device,	'DISC'
forms,	'PAYROLL-CHECKS'
user labels,	23
block factor,	16
buffers,	2
file limit,	1024
initial extents,	1
maximum extents,	32
filecode);	0

Figure 10.2 FOPEN Parameters

The FOPEN intrinsic is completely compatible with the MPE V FOPEN intrinsic. FOPEN provides no new functionality under MPE XL, hence all files created with FOPEN have the same size restrictions as files created under MPE V.

FOPEN's calling sequence, along with example values for the parameters, is illustrated in Figure 10.2. Parameters may be omitted, in which case documented defaults are used.

FOPEN is a very old intrinsic, written ignoring the possibility that new functionality might want to be added at a later date. Because MPE V programmers cannot simply add more optional parameters at the end, dangerous parameter overloading has occurred in the last few years. Some parameters, such as forms, are meaningless for disc and other types of files, so it's possible to redefine the forms parameter when the file opened is a disc file. This type of overloading makes some calls to FOPEN fairly difficult to code. Clearly, a better solution was needed.

MPE XL provides a new intrinsic, HPFOPEN, which can be used to create files that bypass the MPE V limits. With HPFOPEN, the following can be specified:

☐ Everything that FOPEN could specify.

☐ 'Fill' character, used to fill in every page allocated in the file from the end of the record the program writes to the end of the page. Under MPE V, this character was always either a blank for ASCII files or a null for binary files.

☐ New files are optionally created and placed into the directory at HPFOPEN time. Under MPE V, new files were not placed into the directory until they were closed.

☐ A short pointer to the file can be returned. (See Chapter 11 for a discussion of mapped files.)

☐ A long pointer to the file can be returned.

☐ Record sizes may be slightly more than the MPE V maximum of 32,766 bytes, since MPE XL allows 32,767 bytes.

☐ Tape density can be cleanly specified as an integer value (e.g., 1600, 6250).

- The amount of space initially allocated to the file is specified in units of records, instead of MPE V's extents.

- Access hints, to help improve disc access. Random or sequential are the two choices.

- Type of name syntax used. At first release, this is always MPE XL name syntax. The existence of this option leaves room for different name syntaxes in the future.

- File privilege level, saved with the file. This prevents all future opens of the file by users running at a less privileged level. This is similar to MPE V's privileged filecodes but is a cleaner concept.

- UFID (Unique File IDentifier). Normally, a file open causes the directory to be searched for the specified file. Every file on disc has a UFID, and once a file is opened, this UFID can be retrieved with the FFILEINFO intrinsic. Subsequent HPFOPENs of the same file are much quicker if the previously saved UFID is passed.

- HPFOPEN may be called on behalf of another process, by telling HPFOPEN the pin of the recipient process.

- A normal file-equate string may be supplied. This eases the programmer's task of calling HPFOPEN by allowing an ASCII string of desired file attributes (e.g., NEW;MSG;REC-80) to be passed to HPFOPEN.

- A file may be opened 'raw' by passing HPFOPEN a copy of an existing file's file label. The new file identical to the existing file will be built.

FOPEN and HPFOPEN both return 16-bit integers known as 'file numbers' ('file handles' in UNIX terminology) as the result of opening a file. A file number is a process-local index into a special table maintained by the file system for each process. Since file numbers are indices into a table, they tend to be small integers. Additionally, since it would be silly to let the size of this table grow without bounds when a process loops opening and closing files, an FOPEN/HPFOPEN will return with the lowest available file number. Don't count on this, but bear it in mind.

UNIX predefines files 0, 1, and 2 as stdin, stdout, and stderr. MPE avoids the mistake of using 0 as a file number, and predefines files 1 and 2 as $STDIN and

$STDLIST, respectively (currently, there is no $STDERR in MPE). Unlike in UNIX, a user in MPE cannot refer to files 1 and 2 directly unless running in Privileged Mode.

One interesting anomaly of file number allocation is that when a KSAM file is opened, three file numbers are allocated: one for the data file, one for the key file, and one for a temporary file used by the file system. This silent work allows KSAM files to be read in primary key order via the FREAD intrinsic without programs having special case code to handle KSAM input files.

Shortcuts for Opening Files

When opening a file, the operating system normally searches the directory for the specified filename -- an operation that could require a number of disc reads. Since many disc files never move once they are created, MPE XL provides a high-level, security-conscious way to open a file very quickly. The HPFOPEN intrinsic can be passed a Unique File Identifier (UFID) instead of a filename. This 20-byte record tells MPE XL the exact disc address of the file *and* provides information that allows it to determine if the disc address in question is a valid file label.

A timestamp within the UFID guarantees that when a user with an old copy of a UFID tries to open a file, even a new file with the same name and disc address as the old, MPE XL will be able to detect the UFID mismatch. This implies that purging a file causes MPE XL to erase the disc sector containing the disc copy of the UFID.

Where do programs get UFIDs for later use? After a file is opened (with either FOPEN or HPFOPEN), the FFILEINFO intrinsic is capable of fetching the UFID as follows:

```
ffileinfo (fid, 63, ufid);
```

The following pseudo-code fragment shows an example of obtaining and, later, using UFIDs. (It is taken from a hypothetical implementation of a database management system.)

```
procedure open_database (root_file_name);
    var root_fid, error : integer;
    var copy_of_ufid : packed array [1..20] of char;

    hpfopen (root_fid, error, 2, root_file_name, ...);
    if error <> 0 then
```

```
        return;
    ...
        (* loop, opening all of the associated datasets...*)
    for dataset_num := 1 to number_of_datasets do
      begin
      read (root_fid, copy_of_ufid, dataset_name);
      hpfopen (dataset_fids [dataset_num], error,
              44, copy_of_ufid);
      if error <> 0 then
        hpfopen (dataset_fids [dataset_num], error,
                2, dataset_name);

      end;
    end;
```

In the above example, each dataset is opened by giving HPFOPEN its UFID. Then, if that open fails, the open is tried again, but with the filename instead.

The :LISTF Command

The :LISTF command in MPE XL has been enhanced to reflect the changes in the implementation of the file system. In MPE V, :LISTF had 4 modes (-1, 0, 1, and 2). The MPE XL :LISTF command has 7 modes (-3, -1, 0, 1, 2, 3, and 4).

Modes 0 and 1 produce identical output in MPE V and MPE XL. Mode 2 is almost the same, as previously illustrated in this Chapter. MPE XL has replaced the utility program :LISTDIR5 with a new mode for the :LISTF command, mode 3. Note the presence of additional information (e.g., creation and access times):

```
FILE: XYZ.SAMPLE.BOOK

FILE CODE : 0              FOPTIONS: BINARY,FIXED,NOCCTL,STD
BLK FACTOR: 64            CREATOR : **
REC SIZE: 1022(BYTES)     LOCKWORD: **
BLK SIZE: 65408(BYTES)    SECURITY--READ    : ANY
EXT SIZE: 0(SECT)                   WRITE   : ANY
NUM REC: 0                          APPEND  : ANY
NUM SEC: 0                          LOCK    : ANY
NUM EXT: 0                          EXECUTE : ANY
MAX REC: 1023                    **SECURITY IS ON
                          FLAGS   : n/a
NUM LABELS: 0             CREATED : FRI, JUN 5, 1987 2:39PM
```

```
MAX LABELS: 0                MODIFIED: FRI, JUN  5, 1987  2:39PM
DISC DEV #: 2                ACCESSED: FRI, JUN  5, 1987  2:39PM
CLASS    : DISC              LABEL ADDR: **
SEC OFFSET: 0
```

The :LISTSEC command of :LISTDIR5 in MPE V has been replaced by :LISTF mode 4:

```
FILE: XYZ.SAMPLE.BOOK

ACCOUNT ------  READ : AC
               WRITE : AC
              APPEND : AC
                LOCK : AC
             EXECUTE : AC

GROUP --------  READ : GU
               WRITE : GU
              APPEND : GU
                LOCK : GU
             EXECUTE : GU
                SAVE : GU

FILE ---------  READ : GU          FCODE: 0
               WRITE : AC          CREATOR: SRN
              APPEND : AC          LOCKWORD:
                LOCK : AC          **SECURITY IS ON
             EXECUTE : AC

FOR SRN.BOOK: READ, WRITE, LOCK, APPEND, EXECUTE
```

The :LISTF, -1 output has changed in two major ways: It is in hexadecimal instead of octal, and the information reported is completely different in layout from MPE V.

```
F = A
00000000 4D504558 ...   5F564F4C 554D455F ....MPEXL_SYSTEM_VOLUME_
53455420 20202020 ...   41202020 20202020 SET        2..XYZ
20202020 20202020 ...   20202020 20202020          SAMPLE
00000000 5349454C ...   20202020 00000000 ....BOOK        ....
20202020 20202020 ...   5354414E 20202020          SRN.....
20202020 20202020 ...   03570000 2552B8A2          ....|....W..%R8"
```

```
00010401 00000000 ...    1F73113A 0001F422 ..............t".s.:..t"
1F73113A 0001F422 ...    1F73113A 00000000 .s.:..t".s+...t".s.:....
00000000 000003FF ...    00000000 00000000 ........................
000FF402 00000000 ...    000003FE 0000FF80 ..t...............~....
00400000 00000000 00000000 00000000        ..............
```

The output is 10 rows of six 32-bit words, followed by one row of four 32-bit words. The output shown above is compressed to fit on the page. Thus, 64 words of 32 bits each (256 bytes) are printed in hexadecimal.

The last new mode for :LISTF is mode -3. This mode is identical to mode 3, but it shows the usually suppressed security information (e.g., creator, lockword, label address). Thus, it serves as the replacement for the PASS and MAP options of :LISTDIR5's :LISTF command.

```
FILE: XYZ.SAMPLE.BOOK

FILE CODE : 0            FOPTIONS: BINARY,FIXED,NOCCTL,STD
BLK FACTOR: 64           CREATOR : SRN
REC SIZE: 1022(BYTES)    LOCKWORD:
BLK SIZE: 65408(BYTES)   SECURITY--READ    : ANY
EXT SIZE: 0(SECT)                 WRITE   : ANY
NUM REC: 0                        APPEND  : ANY
NUM SEC: 0                        LOCK    : ANY
NUM EXT: 0                        EXECUTE : ANY
MAX REC: 1023                   **SECURITY IS ON
                         FLAGS   : n/a
NUM LABELS: 0            CREATED : FRI, JUN  5, 1987  2:39PM
MAX LABELS: 0            MODIFIED: FRI, JUN  5, 1987  2:39PM
DISC DEV #: 2            ACCESSED: FRI, JUN  5, 1987  2:39PM
CLASS     : DISC         LABEL ADDR: $00000075 $00223220
SEC OFFSET: 0
```

With the information in the LABEL ADDR field, a privileged user can enter the debugging facility and display (or modify) part of a file label with the DV command. For example, to display the file label for XYZ from the debugging facility, the following command would work:

```
DV 75.223220,100,XYZ
```

More information about the debugging facility can be found in Appendix B.

11

$\mathbf{M}$apped Files

MPE XL has an exciting, powerful method of accessing data on disk: mapped files.

Prior to mapped files, if programmers wanted to access a large amount of disk-based data, they often had to write routines to convert from the file system's view of the data (typically fixed-size records) to the program's view of the data. This was not always easy, nor efficient. Programmers had to be continually conscious of the file system being between the disk and the program, and they often had to design the structure of the program's data to match restrictions in the file system.

Thus, with the advent of the tremendous addressability of the HPPA, coupled with a file system with newly designed internals, it became clear that a disk file could be treated as an object.

The intrinsic HPFOPEN, callable only from programs running in Native Mode, can be used to open a file in mapped mode. In this mode, the intrinsic returns a 32- or 64-bit pointer to the calling program. This pointer points to the first byte of the file. The program is then free to use this pointer to access any of the data in the file, in any manner desired.

The concept of mapped files did not originate with MPE XL. Earlier incarnations can be traced back to the file system provided by many implementations of the APL language, as well as to disk header arrays in ALGOL running under MCP on Burroughs equipment.

Although most HP 3000 users are probably unaware of it, MPE XL's mapped files are almost identical to the late, lamented 'virtual memory' feature of the HP 3000 Series III. When APL/3000 was written, some form of addressing that went beyond the 64Kb barrier was required -- and was provided by the APL expansion firmware for the Series III. This firmware added two new opcodes to the HP 3000 instruction set: virtual load and virtual store. SPL/V (aka SPL/3000) had a new declaration, 'virtual array', added and gave the programmer the ability to address a single disk file with a 32-bit index. In MPE XL terms, an SPL program could talk to a single, mapped file, and the mapped file was limited to the maximum size of an MPE V disk file.

Nonetheless, the mapped file facility of MPE XL represents a major improvement in the ease of handling of large amounts of data on disk. Many applications that would have been tedious to write have become simple programming exercises.

How Mapped Files Work

In MPE V, files could be opened only by calling FOPEN (or one of its variant entry points). This method of opening a file returned a 16-bit file number. The number was then used in subsequent file- system intrinsic calls (e.g., FWRITE, FREAD, FCLOSE) to specify the file to be used. The file number is meaningful only to the process that called FOPEN because the file number is used as an index into a process-local table of files. Hence, if three processes wanted to open the same file, each would call FOPEN and each would get a file number to use. Only by coincidence would any of the numbers be the same.

In MPE XL, FOPEN may be used to open files by both Compatibility Mode and Native Mode programs. Additionally, Native Mode programs can use an alternative intrinsic to open files: HPFOPEN.

Mapped files are opened by calling HPFOPEN and requesting that a pointer to the file be returned in addition to the file number. Normally, the memory manager creates an initially empty binary tree (B-Tree) for every data object (virtual array). In the case of a mapped file, the file system hands the memory manager a pointer to the base of the B-Tree that the file system uses to keep track of the file's pages. Thus, to the memory manager, a mapped file looks like any other data object. See Figure 11.1 for the physical and logical views of an MPE XL disc file.

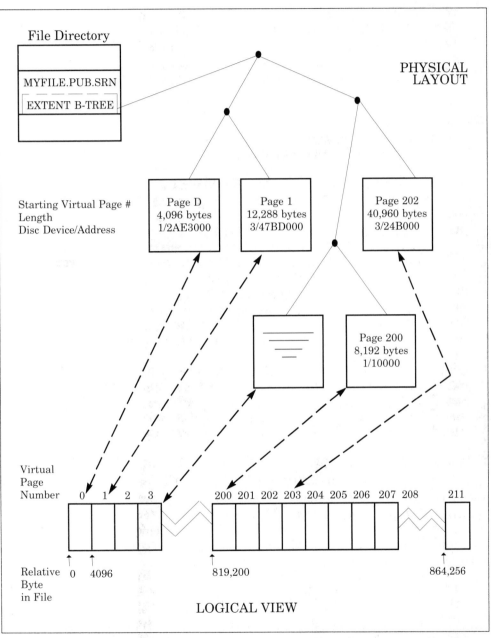

Figure 11.1 Physical and Logical Views of an MPE XL Disc File

Ordinary methods of accessing a file must go through the overhead of the file system intrinsics (FREAD, FWRITE, etc). Accessing a mapped file has no overhead at all, however. When a file is opened as a mapped file, a file number is returned as well as a pointer. This file number allows the normal file system intrinsics to be used to access the file. Intrinsic access may be mixed with mapped access.

An advantage of mapped files is that only the pages that have ever been accessed are actually allocated on disk. What this means is that a file whose limit is 2^{32} - 1 bytes (4,294,967,295) could occupy as few as zero pages of disk. If, for instance, a program puts data into the last byte of the file without touching any of the other pages, then only one page is allocated on disk. Essentially, the technique of using a binary tree (B-Tree) to keep track of the file's pages allows the equivalent of a 'sparse matrix' storage technique.

Pointers - the Long and Short of It

HPPA allows two basic types of pointers: short pointers (32 bits) and long pointers (64 bits). When a mapped file is opened with the long-pointer option, it is assigned an object number. Thus, one possible limitation on the number of long-mapped files open at a time is the number of possible objects (2^{32}-1). This limit will never be hit, as other resources will be exhausted first.

If a mapped file is opened with the short pointer option, it isn't given an object of its own. Instead, it is almost always allocated a range of pages within the third quadrant of object $B ($B is a hexadecimal constant equivalent to a decimal 11). Since MPE XL dedicates Space Register 6 to always point to object $B, a process can access pages in a short-mapped file by using a 32-bit short pointer. At times, MPE XL maps short-pointer files into the fourth quadrant of space $A, which is always pointed to by Space Register 7, but this seems to happen quite infrequently.

How short pointers work is not generally a concern to the programmer; however, some of the implications of short pointers *are* noteworthy. Since only 2^{30} bytes within object $B (and $A) are accessible via short pointers, short-pointer space is a valuable resource. Thus, MPE XL limits the size of any one short-mapped file to four megabytes, and the total size of all currently open, short-mapped files to six megabytes.

If two processes want to share data via a mapped file, they must both open the file in the long-pointer mode. Any interlock mechanism they want to use must be invented by the programmer, as none is provided by default.

Beyond RISC!

Normal file-system security is used to control access to a mapped file. This includes the 'EXClusive/SHaRe' (EXC/SRH) options, as well as the file access rights-mask.

When the pointer returned by the HPFOPEN is used to access data, a page fault will probably occur because the page containing the byte of data pointed to by the mapped file pointer is probably not in memory initially. When this happens, the operating system intervenes to handle the fault and has the memory manager look up the page the program is trying to access. The memory manager quickly realizes that the page in question is a member of the B-Tree for the mapped file, and it searches the B-Tree for the page. When it is found, a free page is found in physical memory and assigned to the virtual page, and a disk read is initiated. When the disk read is completed, the process will resume where it left off.

Accessing Files in Mapped Mode

Almost any existing disk file can be opened and accessed as a mapped file with HPFOPEN. The restricted files are databases (IMAGE, HPIMAGE, etc.), and files with sensitive internal structures (e.g., message files, RIO files, variable record size files). The major difference between opening an existing file and opening a new file is that the domain option must be 1, 2, or 3 (OLD, OLDTEMP, OLD/OLDTEMP) instead of NEW, and none of the creation-oriented parameters should be specified (record size, file size, etc.) When a mapped file is opened, a pointer is returned. Whether it is a short or a long pointer, it always points at the first byte of the first record of the file.

Looking at the offset portion of a long pointer to a mapped file provides some interesting insights. If the file has no user labels, then the offset portion is 0, indicating that nothing comes before the first record in the file. If a file *has* user labels, these are allocated on disk immediately before the first byte of the first record. Thus, if a file with two user labels is opened as a long-mapped file, the offset portion of the pointer will be 512 (2 x 256 bytes). This means that the user labels of files are accessible by adding negative offsets to the original mapped file pointer.

An alternative to HPFOPEN is available for accessing files in a mapped mode. A file can be opened by FOPEN (or HPFOPEN in a non-mapped mode) and a long pointer to the file can be obtained by calling the FFILEINFO intrinsic and requesting that item number 64 be returned. This is the same pointer that would have been returned if HPFOPEN was called with the long-pointer option. (The virtual address of the file label is returned by FFILEINFO item number 74.) FILEINFO returns an error if a program tries to get a long pointer to KSAM, message, circular, or RIO files.

Limitations of Mapped Files

When using mapped files, programmers must be aware of a number of restrictions. Whether a new or old file is being opened as a mapped file, only three languages give direct access to it: SPLash!, HP Pascal/XL, and HP C/XL. HPFOPEN is callable from other Native Mode languages (e.g.: HP FORTRAN 77/XL, COBOL II/XL), but no other languages have pointer data types.

When a new mapped file is created, it isn't sufficient to simply store all of the desired data into the file and FCLOSE it. If this were to be done, the data would seem to disappear, because the file system does not update the file pointer past the current End Of File (EOF) marker for a file. A ':LISTF,2' of the file would show the EOF unchanged even though the data is on disc. The correct procedure is to use the FPOINT intrinsic to set the current record pointer to the desired EOF, then call the FCONTROL intrinsic to post the EOF to disk. As an example, if a new mapped file is created with 100 records, the code necessary to correctly post the EOF and save the file would be:

```
fpoint (filenumber, 100);
if ccode <> cce then
    handle the error!
 fcontrol (filenumber, 6, dummy);
if ccode <> cce then
    handle the error!

fclose (filenumber, 0, 0);
if ccode <> cce then
    handle the error!
```

In the above example, the 100 means that records 0 through 99 are valid.

KSAM files and files with variable record sizes can be opened as mapped files for read access only. These types of files cannot be written upon, because a user might corrupt the internal data structures of the files. RIO, remote disk, message, circular, or device (such as printers or a tape drives) files cannot be opened as mapped files at all.

Only disk files may be opened as mapped files. While this makes sense, presumably the restriction will be lifted at some point to allow for user-written device drivers.

Simultaneous long-pointer and short-pointer access to the same mapped file is difficult. If a file is first opened by calling FOPEN or by calling HPFOPEN with long-pointer access, subsequent attempts to open it with short-pointer access will fail. This is because the first open allocated a 64-bit pointer with a new object number for the file. Since only four of the possible 2^{32} objects are easily accessible with short pointers, HPFOPEN rejects attempts to open a file in short-mapped mode. It is impossible to build a short pointer that would reference the same virtual address as the long pointer already allocated.

Conversely, if a program wanted to open a file as short-mapped but use a long pointer to it, there would be no problem. The long pointer can be built by converting the short pointer to the equivalent long pointer. If a file is already open without mapping, it cannot be opened for short-mapped access. Figure 11.2 shows the allowed interaction between FOPEN, short-mapped HPFOPEN, and long-mapped HPFOPEN.

First Open	Subsequent Opens		
	FOPEN	*Short HPFOPEN*	*Long HPFOPEN*
FOPEN	OK	NO	OK
Short HPFOPEN	OK	OK	OK
Long HPFOPEN	OK	NO	OK

Figure 11.2 Interaction of File Open Intrinsics

Because there is a limited amount of short-pointer space available, a maximum of six megabytes of mapped files can be opened with short-pointer access at any one time. Also, the largest file that can be opened as a short-pointer mapped file is four megabytes.

A possible performance problem could arise with the shared use of mapped files.

Unless a mapped file is opened with the 'unprotected' option, the file system will use Protection IDs (PIDs) to protect the pages of the file. When any page of a mapped file is brought into memory for the first time, it is tagged with the user's PID (the same PID used to protect the user's stack). If a second process tries to access a byte on a page of the file, HPPA hardware checks to see if the PID for the page matches any of the PIDs in the protection registers for the process. It won't find a match, because *no* user process is ever allowed access to the stack of another user process !

Since the PID of the page is not found in the protection registers, a fault occurs and the operating system intervenes. Every process has a list of PIDs associated with it. MPE XL searches this list for a PID that matches the one that caused the trap. It won't be found, so MPE XL then asks the file system, "Is this page one of yours?" The answer is yes, and the file system then changes the PID for the page to match the PID of the second user's stack, and the process resumes.

Why might this lead to a performance problem? Consider what happens if two processes (A and B) want to synchronize their actions via a mapped file. Here is process A:

```
var P_FOO : ^integer;
...
open shared short-mapped file, FOO, saving the pointer in
P_FOO.

while true do
   begin
   while odd(P_FOO^) do
      pause (one_second);
   P_FOO^ := P_FOO^ + 1;
   ... do some work ...
   end;
```

Process B is identical, except it replaces odd(P_FOO^) with not odd(P_FOO^). The effect of these two processes is that they treat the first four bytes of the file as a four-byte integer and take turns incrementing it. Thus, if FOO contains a transaction number, process A will work on even-numbered transactions, and process B will work on odd-numbered transactions.

Also, consider the performance implications. A accesses the file, and a protection trap occurs, so the file system changes the PID of the file to match A's PID. Then B accesses the file, and a protection trap occurs, so the file system changes the PID of the file to match B's PID. Then A accesses the file, and the process is repeated. Clearly, this is a worst-case scenario but one that must be kept in mind by programmers thinking of using mapped files.

One way to avoid this problem while using mapped files is to open the file with the unprotected option. This is done by calling HPFOPEN and passing in item 58 (HOP_OPTION_UNPROTECTED) with a value of 1. The result is a mapped file potentially accessible by anyone on the computer, without the overhead of 'protection'.

Mapped File Example

An explanation of mapped files is best given with an example. Consider how a text-editing program might make use of mapped files. Pascal is the programming language for this example (note that it is only a partial program, with some sections simply described in English rather than fully coded).

The example will edit only files with fixed-length records of 80 bytes, like numbered SPL, Pascal, and FORTRAN source files, so the following types will be declared:

```
type
    text_line            = packed array [1..80] of char;
    text_line_ptr_type   = ^text_line;

var
    cur_line_ptr    :  text_line_ptr_type;
    temp_line       :  text_line;
    text_base_ptr   :  text_line_ptr_type;
```

Notice there is no buffer declared as a 'current line' buffer, just a pointer cur_line_ptr. When a file to be edited is opened as a mapped file, the variable text_base_ptr will always point to the first byte of the file.

Here is how an existing file to be edited would be opened, then listed to a terminal:

```
...
prompt ('Enter name of file to be edited: ');
readln (user_input);
user_input := strltrim (strrtrim (user_input));
filename := '/' + user_input + '/';
```

```
        domain_old := 3;

        hpfopen (filenum, status,
                2, filename,            3, domain_old,
                18, text_base_ptr);                {short pointer}

    if status < 0 then
        begin
        writeln ('Unable to open the file: ', user_input);
        quit (1);
        end;
    ...
    ...
    procedure list_file;

        begin
        cur_line_ptr := text_base_ptr;
        done := false;
        while not done do
            begin
                {get a copy of the current line...}
            temp_line := cur_line_ptr;
                {display it to the user...}
            writeln (temp_line);
            cur_line_ptr := addtopointer (cur_line_ptr,
                                        sizeof(cur_line_ptr));
            ...
            end;
        end {list_file proc};
```

To someone not familiar with mapped files, the above code must surely look like nonsense. Where does the data come from?

The magic is in the `addtopointer` statement. The first time through the loop, `cur_line_ptr` is pointing to the first byte of the file. Assuming a 'list file' operation is the first command done after opening the mapped file, the act of de-referencing the pointer causes a page fault when we do a `temp_line := cur_line_ptr` because the pointer points to a page that is not in memory. When the page is eventually brought into memory, our process will resume where it left off at the start of the `temp_line :=` `cur_line_ptr` statement.

148   *Beyond RISC!*

At the end of the loop, the `cur_line_ptr` is bumped by 80 bytes, so it now points at the first byte of the next line of the file. Since files start on page boundaries (2048 bytes), and slightly more than 25 80-byte records fit within 2048 bytes, the following can be predicted:

☐ Lines 2 through 25 will be accessed with no page faults because their data is on the first page, along with line 1.

☐ Line 26 will cause a page fault because it is split across a page boundary. Technically, when the 26th `temp_line := cur_line` is being done, 48 bytes will be transferred from `cur_line` to `temp_line` and there will be a page fault on fetching the 49th byte.

Though many other examples could be developed, this brief discussion should demonstrate the power that mapped files offer.

The Pascal Packing Algorithm

When coding a mapped file application in Pascal, be careful that the Pascal packing algorithm doesn't give you a nasty surprise.

Consider a mapped file containing teller transaction records with three fields:

```
1) a 64-bit integer;   (a timestamp of some kind)
2) a 32-bit integer;   (a cash amount, in pennies)
3) a 16-bit integer;   (teller transaction number)
```

The record size of the file is 14 bytes, and there is a maximum of 20,000 records in it at any one time.

In HP Pascal/XL, it is easy to define a record that maps nicely onto this file structure:

```
type
   trans_type = record
                  tt_timestamp   : longint;  {64 bits, 8 bytes}
                  tt_cash        : integer;  {32 bits, 4 bytes}
                  tt_transaction : shortint; {16 bits, 2 bytes}
                  end;       {14 bytes total}
```

So far, a pretty straightforward translation of the external data structures into

Pascal. Now, consider the mapped file. If it is thought of as a giant array of records of type `trans_type`, it is tempting to declare:

```
type
    trans_type_array  = array [0..20000] of trans_type;

var
    trans_array       = ^ $extnaddr$ trans_type_array;

    ...
hpfopen (....
            21, trans_array_ptr,   {long mapped pointer}
            ...);
```

Note that "$extnaddr$" is a directive telling HP Pascal/XL that the pointer is a long pointer (64 bits).

Then, the program would try to access record N of the file by doing:

```
trans_array_ptr^ [n] := ...;
```

And -- it will *fail* because the array was not declared as a packed or crunched array. And, because the `sizeof(trans_type)` was not a multiple of 32 bits, HP Pascal/XL rounded up the size it thought each element of the array should have (to the next 32-bit boundary). The result was that the code emitted to calculate the address of `trans_array_ptr^ [n]` **was:**

```
trans_array_ptr + (n x 16).
```

However, the true data for record *n* starts at byte:

```
trans_array_ptr + (n x 14).
```

How can this problem be resolved? Either by being very careful to declare the array as a packed array or as a crunched array, or by using pointer arithmetic to access the array, as shown below:

```
var
    trans_ptr    : ^ $extnaddr$ trans_type;

    ...
```

```
           trans_ptr := addtopointer (trans_array_ptr,
                                    n x sizeof(trans_type) );
           trans_ptr^ := ...;
```

Another observation: HP Pascal/XL and HPPA like to work on 32-bit boundaries, but this is hidden from Compatibility Mode (CM) programs by the file system. Although the code shown just above does build a pointer pointing to the very first byte of record *n*, the code emitted by HP Pascal/XL to de-reference the pointer and access the fields of the record will be incorrect, because it assumes that the record starts at a 32-bit boundary, which it doesn't. It starts at a 14-byte boundary.

One workaround, useful for accessing files designed for CM programs, is to do the pointer arithmetic shown above, then move the bytes via the pointer into a variable that *is* 32-bit aligned, as shown in the following example:

```
           var
              tt     : trans_type;

           ...

           move_bytes (localanyptr (addr(tt)),
                        trans_ptr, sizeof(trans_type));
```

12

General File Access Methods

MPE XL provides several types of files: standard (or flat) files, indexed sequential files (KSAM), Relative I/O (RIO) files, circular files, message files, mapped files, and databases. This chapter explores the first five file types. Mapped files are a variant of standard files and were discussed in Chapter 11. Databases are covered in the three chapters comprising Section V.

If the reader is familiar with MPE V features, he or she may want to skip this chapter since MPE V and MPE XL differ very little in the implementation of these file types.

Flat Files

A flat file consists of a series of records of fixed or varying length, a concept discussed in Chapter 10.

The type of access allowed to a file is specified at file open time, but some types can be mixed at run time. Files of fixed-length records can be accessed in any of the following manners: sequential read; append (sequential write, starting at the end of the file); sequential write (starting at the beginning of the file, losing the old data); random read; random write; or random I/O.

Sequential I/O is done with the FREAD and FWRITE intrinsics. Each call reads or writes the current record, then advances the record pointer by one. The initial value of the record pointer is either 0 or 1 plus the record number of the last record of the file, depending on how the file was opened.

Random read/write is done either with the FREADDIR/FWRITEDIR intrinsics or by positioning the record pointer and using FREAD/FWRITE. FREADDIR and FWRITEDIR have a parameter that specifies the record number to read/write. Using either of these intrinsics accesses the desired record and advances the record pointer to the next record. Alternatively, the record pointer can be set to any specified record with the FPOINT intrinsic; moved forward/backward by a specified number of records with the FSPACE intrinsic; or set to 0 (rewound) with the FCONTROL intrinsic.

An FREAD or FWRITE following an FPOINT/FSPACE/FCONTROL effectively simulates an FREADDIR or FWRITEDIR.

MPE provides six modes for opening a file. These modes are selected either with an ACCESS= phrase in a file equation or by four bits in the 'aoptions' parameter to FOPEN. Figure 12.1 shows the ACCESS= keywords and the aoptions bits required to open a file in all of the available modes. It also shows the effects of the various modes on where the record pointer is set, and whether or not all data is thrown away.

Note that Execute Read is available only to privileged MPE XL programs. All other modes are available to all MPE V/E and MPE XL programs, except that Execute is available only in Privileged Mode for both. Read mode allows the file to be read but not written to.

Write mode allows the file to be written to but not read. Any records already in the file are thrown away when the file is opened. The old data is irretrievably lost when the file is opened.

Write (Save) mode allows the file to be written to, but it does not throw away the old data in the file. However, since the record pointer starts at 0, the programmer must take care to write only to records that are to be replaced. FPOINT, FSPACE, and FWRITEDIR allow a program to selectively write over specified records.

Append mode positions the record pointer at the EOF of the file and allows new records to be added. The old data in the file is not lost. Nothing may be read from the file, either before or after the old EOF.

Mode	ACCESS =	aoptions	record pointer	EOF after open
Read	IN	0	0	unchanged
Write	OUT	1	0	0
Write (Save)	OUTKEEP	2	0	unchanged
Append	APPEND	3	EOF	unchanged
Input/Output	IO	4	0	unchanged
Update	UPDATE	5	0	unchanged
Execute	N/A	6	0	unchanged
Execute Read	N/A	7	0	unchanged

Figure 12.1 File Access Modes and Options

Input/Output mode allows unrestricted access to the data in the file. This is similar to combining IN and OUTKEEP modes. The old data in the file is not lost. All of the file system intrinsics are allowed except FUPDATE.

Update mode allows unrestricted access to the data in the file. It is identical to Input/Output mode, except that the FUPDATE intrinsic is allowed. FUPDATE is used to rewrite the record most recently accessed.

Execute mode is used by the MPE V loader when a file is being loaded for execution. Execute Read mode is a new mode in MPE XL used by the Native Mode loader.

KSAM Files

KSAM stands for Keyed Sequential Access Method, a method of organizing records of a file according to the value of one or more key fields in each record. When a KSAM file is created, the user (or program) tells the file system important information about the file: how many keys it has; which is the primary or most important key; whether or not any key can have more than one record with the same value (duplicate keys); the name of the data file; the name of the key file; the expected number of primary keys; and the usual MPE file information (record size, fixed/variable, binary/ASCII, etc.).

A KSAM file actually consists of two MPE files: a data file and a key file. The data file contains only the data provided by the user in a normal FWRITE call. The key file is maintained for the user by the MPE file system and contains a copy of the keys from every record along with the information necessary to form a binary tree of all the records in the data file. When a program FOPENs a KSAM file, the corresponding key file is automatically opened by the file system for the program.

KSAM allows the following types of access: random write (records are written without regard to key order); sequential write (records must be written in key order); append (sequential write, starting at the end of the file); sequential read ordered by a selected key; sequential read in chronological order (the order in which the records were added to the file); random read by key value or by a chronological record number; random read with a generic key or approximate matches; and update access (a record is read, then updated, perhaps with key fields changed).

KSAM offers two powerful methods of locating records not available to flat files or IMAGE databases: generic keys and approximate matches. A generic key allows a program to specify the first few bytes of a key value instead of the entire key value. KSAM will then search for the first record whose key starts with the same bytes.

As an example of this, consider a file with a key called LICENSE-PLATE, which is a seven character ASCII field allowing digits, letters, and blanks -- a typical automobile license plate for many locations in the United States. If a request comes in to locate a license plate starting with the letters 'ORG', a generic lookup would retrieve "ORG123," "ORGANIZ," and "ORGELLA."

An approximate match allows a program to request all records that satisfy a particular relationship to a key value. The relationships supported are 'greater than', 'greater than or equal to', and 'equal to'.

At the option of the creator of the file, keys are allowed to have duplicate values (i.e., two or more records with the same value in the key field). At creation time, each key is specified as either unique or duplicate. Duplicate keys, while often necessary, should be used sparingly, as they can greatly increase the cost of adding new records.

A record with a duplicate key is, by default, always positioned so that it comes after all other records with the same key value. This, however, is also controllable at file creation time. The option RDUPLICATE may be specified for a duplicate key. RDUPLICATE allows duplicate keys but adds them in a random manner -- without preserving the chronology as the DUPLICATE option does. The advantage of RDUPLICATE is that it makes adding records much faster.

KSAM allows up to 16 keys. The key values may overlap but no two keys may start at the same byte. This limitation sounds silly at first but is necessary because KSAM does not assign either names or numbers to keys. A program tells KSAM which key it wants to use by specifying the byte it starts at within a record. If KSAM allowed two keys to start at the same byte, it would have no way of distinguishing between the two of them. (Once a KSAM file is created, no commercial tools are available to restructure it. This contrasts with IMAGE databases, which have a host of tools for restructuring.)

KSAM files are particularly vulnerable to corruption caused by system crashes. Indeed, the KSAM Reference Manual states, "If the system fails when a KSAM file is open for any type of access except read-only, the file cannot be reopened until it has been recovered." Recovery is done by running a utility program, KSAMUTIL, and using the KEYINFO command. Unfortunately, KEYINFO is not able to recover serious problems, such as key values that are missing or out of sequence, and potentially requires that the file be reloaded.

Relative I/O Files

Relative I/O (RIO) is an interesting method of file access provided by MPE primarily for the use of COBOL programs. RIO keeps a deletion flag for every record, and allows records to be logically (but not physically) deleted from a file by using the FDELETE intrinsic. When an RIO file is read sequentially with the FREAD intrinsic, the file system simply skips over the records that have been flagged as deleted. These so-called 'deleted' records may be read by explicitly asking for them with the FREADDIR intrinsic. Records may be deleted with FDELETE -- even if the file is open for read access.

RIO files were designed to be used by COBOL, and although they work transparently with programs that read input files one record at a time with FREAD, many programs will not be able to correctly handle them if they were not designed with RIO in mind. For example, the MPE V version of EDIT/V (aka EDITOR/3000) uses FREADDIR to retrieve a workfile, so all records from an RIO file are read in -- even the deleted records! Unfortunately, no utilities exist to efficiently compact RIO files by removing deleted records or to sweep through RIO files and reactivate deleted records.

Circular Files

Circular files are similar to normal files, but with one interesting difference: They never fill up. If a program writes 1,000 records to a circular file whose limit is 20 records, then when the program closes the circular file, the LAST 20 records it wrote are the only ones in the file.

Consider an analogy of a cassette recorder with an auto-reverse feature. These cassette recorders automatically switch to recording on the flip side of a cassette when they hit the end of one side. Thus, with a C-60 cassette (30 minutes per side), two hours of the HP Management Round Table at a conference could be recorded, but only the last 60 minutes would be captured on the tape.

The MPE file system keeps an internal pointer to the oldest record in the file, using this record as the logical record 0 when someone tries to read from the file.

One nice feature of circular files is in addition to serial reading, random read access is supported. The FREADDIR intrinsic can be used to access arbitrary records, just as in normal files.

The cassette recorder analogy also illustrates a few limitations of circular files. Just as a cassette being recorded upon cannot be listened to by someone else at the same time, a circular file that is in use for WRITE access cannot be opened for READ access. (It can, however, be opened by multiple readers when no one has it open for WRITE access.)

On the cassette recorder, there is a glitch when the tape reverses. In a circular file, glitches can also occur whenever a new block is touched. For example, consider a circular file created as:

```
:BUILD C; CIR; REC=-80, 4, F, ASCII; DISC = 12, 1, 1
```

The first four records are placed in the first block of the file (because the block factor is 4). The next four records are in the second block, and the last four records are in the third block. When the next record is written, the file system wraps around to the first block, so the thirteenth record will overwrite the first record. This would be fine -- indeed it is what one would expect -- but the flaw is that the file system discards the rest of the records in a reused block. Thus, if a program wrote thirteen records to the circular file shown above (records 1-13), then closed the file, it would have only nine records (5, 6, 7, 8, 9, 10, 11, 12, 13) and the records with 2, 3, and 4 would be lost.

The only way around this problem is to always create circular files with a block factor of 1, but the price that is paid for not losing data is decreased performance.

Message Files

Message files are a means of allowing two processes to link and share information. Unlike the UNIX 'pipe' facility, message files exist as named files on disc. This powerful concept allows them to exist independently of processes that access them. It also provides a rendezvous method for separate processes to access the same message file. Thus, it's easy to have an interactive process (e.g., an order entry program) talk to a batch process (e.g., an inventory program) via a message file. Each process simply does an FOPEN of the message file.

A message file is a cross between a normal file (which can be accessed randomly) and a First-In/First-Out (FIFO) queue. Message files were added to MPE at the same time as circular files and share some common implementation code. Internally, a message file is simply a circular file that does something special when the file is empty and when the file is full. Message files allow multiple readers and multiple writers simultaneously. Like a UNIX pipe, the flow of data in a message file is one-way. If two processes want to communicate both ways, a single message file is not enough -- each process must open two (one for reading messages from the other process, and one for writing messages to the other process).

Like circular files, MPE maintains an internal pointer to the first logical record of a message file. As soon as that record is read, it is discarded, and MPE advances the record pointer. If no records are available for reading, a process attempting to read a record from a message file will be suspended (blocked) until a message is available.

Historically on MPE V, message files were very susceptible to corruption caused by system failures. The System Status Bulletin had many bug reports describing this class of problem. The Transaction Management facilities of MPE XL should improve this aspect of message files.

V

Data Base Management Systems

13

The HPPA
Approach to DBMS

This chapter explores the database management systems for Hewlett-Packard's newest generation of computers. It begins by taking a general look at what a database system is and does, and then examines HP's database history, for that history provides insights into the directions HP is taking with its new database management systems.

Since their appearance on the computing scene, database management systems have had a profound impact. Database management systems have changed the way system designers design and the way programmers program. They have simplified these tasks as surely as the introduction of operating systems and third- and fourth-generation languages have simplified them. In order to *truly* appreciate this fact, you must have designed or programmed a complicated system without one.

A database management system can be defined as a series of programs or procedures which logically relates a group of disc files, collectively known as the database, and allows access to the information these files contain. With a database management system, the system designer still has to figure out how the system being designed can be modeled into a set of files, and must still specify the information to be stored in each file. Depending upon what type of database management system is being used, the designer may also have to decide how system data is most likely to be used in order to specify fast-access paths into and between the files. For the most part, however, how the model is physically implemented (disc files, data structures, pointers, etc.) is no longer the system designer's concern, because that is carried out and controlled by the database management system.

Data security and integrity are important issues and database management systems have made major contributions in this regard. Most database management systems have implemented fairly sophisticated security mechanisms to control access to data. In general, the system designer defines various levels of access to data and then assigns individuals and/or groups an access level. Again, physical implementation is no longer a concern because once the security matrix is defined, the database management system enforces it. It should be noted, however, that while a security matrix controls programmatic access to a database, it *does not* protect the database from operating system-level commands such as those which allow disc files to be deleted, renamed, copied, or stored to tape. The database management system must make specific provisions for security at this level. Many allow no access to database files through the operating system, but instead provide a special utility to perform typical operating system functions such as copying the database to tape. The utility program typically requires use of a password and/or operation by the database creator. Database management systems often include a mechanism for keeping an audit file of all accesses to the database. Audit files provide an extra level of security because they permit monitoring of what is being read from and written to the database.

Redundant data storage is usually equivalent to inconsistent, erroneous data. Database management systems help to improve data integrity because they make it easier for data which is common to many files and applications to be stored in one place and shared. In general, they also perform some data type and validity checking. Additionally, database management systems often provide a mechanism for maintaining both the logical and structural consistency of the database in the event of a system failure.

In short, database management systems save time in the system-design phase because the building blocks of system design are already in place. Similarly, database management systems save time in the program-development phase because the building blocks of program development are already in place. The routines to add, retrieve, update, and delete data already exist, so the programmer can concentrate on writing the routines to accomplish higher-level programming tasks. And finally, the many database management systems that implement their own security-checking, auditing, and recovery mechanisms save time because the programmer does not have to code these features into the system design.

Database management systems also facilitate program maintenance. Throughout the life of a system, as processing requirements evolve and the usefulness of data is evaluated, some data restructuring will undoubtedly be necessary. The logic of application programs which use conventional file management techniques is intricately interwoven with the file design, which makes it impossible to do data restructuring without necessitating major changes to program code. With database management systems, application programs are much more independent of the data files, so data restructuring can be accomplished with only minor modifications to programs.

Database management systems come in several varieties with names such as hierarchical, network, and relational. Each one has, of course, its advantages and disadvantages. Typically, there is an inverse relation between the time it takes to add a new record versus the time it takes to find the record subsequently. Where multiple database management systems are available to choose from, a careful analysis must be done to ensure that the system chosen has the right benefits with a cost that is acceptable.

Hewlett-Packard's DBMS

Until very recently, HP offered only one database management system. When it first appeared in 1974 on the HP 3000, it was called 'IMAGE'. Now, years later, it is still called 'IMAGE' by most traditionalists, even though HP has renamed the latest version 'TurboIMAGE'. It really is the same IMAGE in most respects, but new features allow it to deal with the needs of a computer family that has grown much larger than the original HP 3000 for which it was designed.

It is hard to quantify how important IMAGE has been to HP. Normally, the sales figures for a software product determine its relative importance. But that is not possible in this case, because in a somewhat unusual (and in retrospect, insightful) move, HP packaged the IMAGE database management system with the MPE operating system. Consequently, anyone who buys an HP 3000 gets IMAGE, too. How important is IMAGE in selling the HP 3000? A seemingly difficult question to answer, but some facts speak for themselves.

When Hewlett-Packard introduced the HP 3000, the company was well-respected in the scientific, industrial, and educational markets but relatively unknown in the business market. Yet, the HP 3000 soon became a significant competitor in business computing. It is safe to speculate that IMAGE had a lot to do with that. Why? Because database management systems, for all the reasons mentioned earlier, had become important in the commercial market, and IMAGE was making a name for itself as an extremely reliable, versatile, and effective database management system.

In 1987, thirteen years after its introduction, IMAGE/TurboIMAGE is still going strong. There are thousands of IMAGE-based applications and tools run every day. It is an understatement to say that IMAGE is an exceptional software product that has been important to HP. But it is *not* an exaggeration to say that IMAGE is one of the best database management systems in the computing industry -- and the most successful software product HP has ever developed.

The HPPA Generation

HP has now introduced its next generation of computers, based on the RISC-oriented Precision Architecture. The HP 3000 900 Series is an addition to the line of MPE-based business computers, while the HP 9000 800 Series is an addition to the line of HP-UX based scientific computers. When HP first announced its next generation database offerings, the marketing names of ALLBASE, HP IMAGE, and HP SQL were bandied about as Native Mode database solutions, with TurboIMAGE offered only in Compatiblity Mode on MPE XL as a temporary migration solution.

However, in late 1986, in recognition of an installed MPE customer base with millions of dollars invested in IMAGE-based software and a need for both database performance *and* compatiblity, HP decided to provide a Native Mode version of TurboIMAGE on the 900 Series systems. To its credit, HP has always emphasized upward compatiblity across its entire computer line. The Native Mode TurboIMAGE decision is ultimately a reaffirmation of this commitment.

Now, about the marketing names mentioned before. Each of them actually has a suffix that designates the operating system for the product. 'ALLBASE' is the general name that can be used to describe *the* database management system for HPPA computers. Under HP-UX, ALLBASE/UX consists of HP IMAGE/UX and HP SQL/UX. Under MPE XL, ALLBASE/XL consists of TurboIMAGE/XL and HP SQL/XL.

TurboIMAGE, as noted earlier, is a network database system available on MPE V and MPE XL. HP IMAGE/UX is similar in many respects to TurboIMAGE, but since it runs only on HP-UX, it will not be a focus of this discussion.

HP SQL is a Native Mode relational database management system that is modeled after IBM's relational system, SQL (structured query language). Relational databases are popular in the industry right now, largely because they provide simpler and more flexible access to data than network database systems traditionally do. As always, there are costs for increased simplicity and flexibility, and the application should be the determinant for whether or not a relational system is more appropriate than a network system.

This overview of the database options available with HPPA has addressed some of the more important issues and concerns. In the following chapters, TurboIMAGE and HP SQL are examined in depth, and the design of each database illustrated. Information is also included on how to access the databases, both programmatically and through the HP-provided query utilities. Also covered are the important issues of security, concurrent usage, locking, recovery from failure, and database performance. The intent is not to provide comprehensive 'how-to' information, but rather to provide a thorough understanding of how each database management system works. Information on migrating database applications from the current MPE V-based HP 3000 to the MPE XL-based HP 3000 is also included.

14

TurboIMAGE

This chapter provides a comprehensive look at TurboIMAGE, the database management system that is currently used on the HP 3000 family, including the 900 Series in Native Mode. It also includes a section on the steps involved in getting TurboIMAGE applications to work on the 900 Series.

TurboIMAGE is what is known as a 'network', or limited-hierarchical, database management system. In such a database system, information is stored on various levels. Information on a lower level is generally accessed by traversing a path from the highest level, or hierarchy, of the network to the desired lower level.

TurboIMAGE has two levels of hierarchy: the master level and the detail level. At the master level, files called 'master datasets' keep information about a uniquely identifiable entity. At the detail level, files called 'detail datasets' keep detail information on the entities in the top level. Detail datasets are also used to relate the entities in the master level to each other. (see Figure 14.1)

Some people tend to look at their data in terms of entities and relationships that exist between these entities. This view maps nicely into this type of database management system: the entities are placed into master datasets and are linked to their relationships represented by detail datasets.

All of the examples shown in this chapter use an abbreviated version of SRNDB, a database used in a Chemical Processing Quality Assurance (QA) Project. SRNDB is used to keep an inventory of QA-tests, record the results of automated QA tests, and keep track of problems discovered during these tests. The basic unit of QA-testing is the test. Related tests are grouped into cadres. Cadres are then grouped into stanzas. As shown in Figure 14.1, master datasets are used to store information about tests, cadres, and stanzas. Detail datasets are used to relate tests to cadres and to relate cadres to stanzas. (As we walk through this example database, follow along on Figure 14.1. As is common practice, the master datasets are shown as inverted triangles and the detail datasets as trapezoids.)

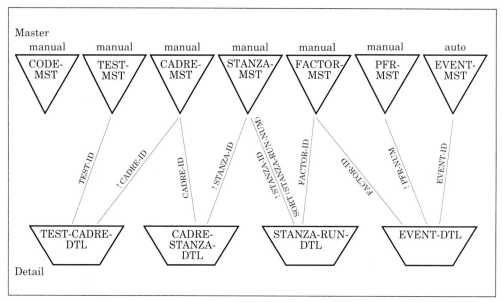

Figure 14.1 TurboIMAGE Database Diagram for SRNDB

In QA-testing, certain factors related to a QA-test must be tracked in order to be able to correlate the appearance of problems to the factors that might have caused them. As shown in Figure 14.1, all of the factors to be monitored are stored in the FACTOR-MST master dataset. When a stanza of tests is run, those factors of interest during the run are recorded and stored along with the information in the STANZA-RUN-DTL dataset. When a problem occurs during a stanza-run, the factors related to the appearance of the problem are recorded in the EVENT-DTL dataset.

Beyond RISC!

In addition to FACTOR-MST, Figure 14.1 shows two other master datasets which are linked to EVENT-DTL. In this quality control environment, detection of problems in the run of a stanza of tests is almost entirely automated, as is the logging of these problems to the database. When a problem is first detected, it is assigned both a problem identifier (which is stored in EVENT-MST) and a Production Follow-up Request (PFR) number (which is stored in PFR-EVENT-MST). The PFR number is initially the same as the problem identifier. The details of the problem occurrence are stored in the EVENT-DTL dataset.

Later analysis of problem reports usually shows that some of the newly recorded problems are actually duplicates of problems that have already been recorded. The PFR numbers for these duplicates are then changed in the EVENT-DTL dataset so that they match the PFR number for the first unique occurrence of the problem. The PFR numbers originally assigned to the problem are then deleted from the PFR-MST. You can then track information not just on problems, but on problems that are *truly* unique to that run, which is much more useful. The information in the EVENT-DTL dataset, then, is really the detail on each occurrence of some unique problem.

Note that it is not necessary for a master dataset to have detail datasets attached to it. CODE-MST is an example of a stand-alone master dataset. This dataset is used to look up the value of the SRNDB data items which are stored as codes. Stand-alone detail datasets may also exist. These are in effect just random access files with the full features of TurboIMAGE.

It is important to understand that a dataset is a file, whether it is of the master or detail variety, and that the file is made up of records of information. The record layout of each file is defined by specifying which items of information are to be stored in the dataset record. Once an item of information is defined to be part of a record, it is called a 'field'. (One item of information can be defined as a field in multiple dataset records.)

TurboIMAGE has various kinds of fields. The most common kind of field is just a piece of information stored in a record. Other fields, however, are more interesting. A 'key' field is found *only* in a master dataset. Each master dataset must have one -- but only one -- key field. This key field serves two purposes. Its first purpose is to provide fast, direct access to an entry in the master dataset. Its second purpose is related to the purpose of another kind of field called a 'search' field.

A search field is found *only* in a detail dataset. When a search field is defined, it establishes a relationship between a detail dataset and a specified master dataset.

This relationship is commonly referred to as a 'path'. Because of this path, the search field in the detail dataset can take on only values which correspond to values of the key field in the associated master dataset. A search field and its corresponding key field are usually the same data item, although it is required only that the search field be of the same type and length as its corresponding key field.

Once a path is established between a master and detail dataset, you can quickly access all the detail entries associated with a particular key/search field value. The master entry for the key value and any associated detail entries constitute what is known as a 'chain'.

Figure 14.1 shows the key field for each master dataset and the search fields for each detail dataset. Note that while each master dataset can have only one key field, detail datasets can have multiple search fields. In fact, a single detail dataset can be linked to as many as sixteen different master datasets.

In SRNDB, the EVENT-DTL dataset has three search fields: FACTOR-CODE, EVENT-ID, and PFR-NUM. This means that problem details can be retrieved via three paths. The first path leads to all the problem details associated with a particular factor code. The second path leads to all the problem details associated with a particular problem identifier. And the third path leads to all the problem details associated with a particular PFR number.

The last kind of field to be examined is the 'sort' field. Ordinarily, when a detail entry is added to a chain for some key/search field value, the entry is added to the end of the chain. However, if a sort field is associated with the search field, the entries in the chain are kept sorted by the value of the sort field. So when entries are added, their placement in the chain is dependent upon the value of the sort field.

For example, in Figure 14.1, the STANZA-RUN-DTL has two search fields. One of these search fields, STANZA-ID, has a sort field, STANZA-RUN-NUM, associated with it. This sort field is used as follows. Each unique run of a stanza of tests is assigned a unique run number. Because this run number, STANZA-RUN-NUM, is a sort field, the details on all the runs of a particular stanza are stored in the STANZA-RUN-DTL sorted by this run number.

When all the detail information is retrieved on a particular run of a stanza, it is retrieved in the same order in which it is stored, which is to say, in sorted order by run number. Note that in this case, because run numbers are sequentially assigned, run details for a particular stanza would actually be stored in sorted order even without a sort field. However, the sort field is necessary to ensure that TurboIMAGE keeps the information in sorted order throughout all of its operations.

Before completing this explanation of the basic mechanisms of TurboIMAGE, two final points need to be mentioned. First, master datasets actually come in two varieties: manual and automatic. The most commonly used variety is the manual master. A manual master record contains a key field plus some number of additional fields. The addition of a record to a manual master requires an explicit action. An automatic master record, on the other hand, can contain only one field, the key field. Records are not *explicitly* added to an automatic master; they are *automatically* added when a record is added to one of the detail sets which is linked to the automatic master. Similarly, records are *automatically* deleted from an automatic master when all the associated detail entries are deleted.

Second, the most frequently accessed path in each detail dataset should be defined as the 'primary path'. This is done by designating one search field in each detail dataset as the primary path search field. Whenever data is loaded into the database with the TurboIMAGE DBLOAD utility, detail dataset entries will be stored so that optimum retrieval times are achieved along the primary path.

TurboIMAGE Security

TurboIMAGE security gives you specific control over who is allowed to add, read, update, and delete items of information in the database. Up to sixty-three user classes can be defined. A user class is identified by an integer from one to sixty-three and is associated with a password consisting of eight or fewer characters. For each dataset in the database, you can specify which user classes will be allowed to read and/or write to the dataset. At the data item level, you can specify which user classes will be allowed to read and/or update the data item. This specification is referred to as a 'read-and-write class list'.

Every programmatic access to a TurboIMAGE database requires a password. If the supplied password is associated with one of the user classes defined in the database, the program has access to any data that is allowed to that user class. If no password is supplied, or the supplied password does not match any of the passwords defined in the database, the program has access only to that data which is allowed to the user class 'zero'. When logged onto the computer as the user who created the database, you need only supply a semicolon as the password in order to gain complete access to the database.

TurboIMAGE databases are protected at the operating system level by the fact that all database files are created as privileged files. Most MPE commands, such as purge, rename, and fcopy, will not work on privileged files. In order to perform these kinds of activities, you must use DBUTIL, an HP-provided utility program. Only the database creator or a user who knows the database's maintenance password can use this utility. However, the MPE commands to store a file to tape or to restore a file from tape *do* work on TurboIMAGE database files, so in a database environment, you must set up the tightest MPE security possible -- and be aware of who has access to the tape drive.

Defining and Creating a TurboIMAGE Database

In order to define a TurboIMAGE database, you must specify such things as the name of the database, which data items are to be stored in the database, which datasets are in the database, what the record layout is for each dataset, and which fields are key, search, and sort fields. You also need to specify the level of data access various user classes are allowed, the type of data to be stored in each data item, how much storage space is needed for each data item, and the capacity of each dataset.

Once all of these pieces of information have been specified, the database can be formally defined. This formal definition is known as a 'schema'. The schema used to create SRNDB, the sample database, is shown in Figure 14.2. The schema file is processed by a program called 'DBSCHEMA'. If no syntax errors exist in a schema, the DBSCHEMA program creates a special file, called the 'root' file. This file contains the definition of the database in a format that the database management system understands.

To create the actual database, the CREATE command in the DBUTIL program is used. This program creates the database files according to the definitions it finds in the root file. One MPE file is created for each dataset in the database.

Accessing a TurboIMAGE Database Programmatically

The procedures which access TurboIMAGE databases are callable from HP Business BASIC, COBOL II, FORTRAN, Pascal, RPG, and SPL under MPE V and MPE XL. Under MPE XL, all of these languages, except for SPL, RPG, and HP Business BASIC, are supported in both Compatibility Mode and Native Mode and can be used to access TurboIMAGE databases. HP's SPL only runs in Compatibility Mode, but can make TurboIMAGE calls. SPLash!, the Native Mode SPL compiler available from Software Research Northwest, also supports TurboIMAGE calls.

There are sixteen TurboIMAGE procedures. To understand what is involved in writing a program to access a TurboIMAGE database, you must examine how to use

```
$PAGE "Schema for SRNDB Database"                         NAME:    STANZA-MST, MANUAL (10/20);
                                                          ENTRY:   STANZA-ID (2),
BEGIN Data Base SRNDB;                                             STANZA-TIMESTAMP;
                                                          CAPACITY: 101;
PASSWORDS:                                                <<---------------------------------------------------->>
   10   DBREAD;              <<Data Base Reader>>         NAME:    FACTOR-MST, MANUAL (10/20);
   20   DBWRITE;             <<Data Base Modifier>>       ENTRY:   FACTOR-ID (2),
                                                                   FACTOR-DESCRIPT;
$PAGE "SRNDB Data Items (Alphabetical Order)"             CAPACITY: 53;
                                                          <<---------------------------------------------------->>
                                                          NAME:    EVENT-MST, AUTOMATIC (10/20);
ITEMS:                                                    ENTRY:   EVENT-ID (1);
   CADRE-CATEGORY,          X06(10/20);                   CAPACITY: 503;
   CADRE-DESCRIPT,          X72(10/20);                   <<---------------------------------------------------->>
   CADRE-ID,                X04(10/20);                   NAME:    PFR-MST, MANUAL (10/20);
   CADRE-TIMESTAMP,         X06(10/20);                   ENTRY:   PFR-NUM (1),
   CODE-ID,                 X06(10/20);                            PFR-TYPE,
   CODE-VALUE,              X50(10/20);                            PFR-CATEGORY,
   EVENT-ID,                X10(10/20);                            PFR-DESCRIPT-1,
   FACTOR-DESCRIPT,         X30(10/20);                            PFR-DESCRIPT-2,
   FACTOR-ID,               X04(10/20);                            PFR-STATUS;
   FACTOR-VALUE,            X10(10/20);                   CAPACITY: 307;
   PFR-CATEGORY,            X06(10/20);                   <<---------------------------------------------------->>
   PFR-DESCRIPT-1,          X72(10/20);                   NAME:    CODE-MST, MANUAL (10/20);
   PFR-DESCRIPT-2,          X72(10/20);                   ENTRY:   CODE-ID,
   PFR-NUM,                 X10(10/20);                            CODE-VALUE;
   PFR-STATUS,              X06(10/20);                   CAPACITY: 211;
   PFR-TYPE,                X06(10/20);                   <<---------------------------------------------------->>
   STANZA-ID,               X04(10/20);                   NAME:    TEST-CADRE-DTL, DETAIL (10/20);
   STANZA-RUN-NUM,          X04(10/20);                   ENTRY:   CADRE-ID (!CADRE-MST),
   STANZA-TIMESTAMP,        X06(10/20);                            TEST-ID (TEST-MST);
   TEST-CATEGORY,           X06(10/20);                   CAPACITY: 250;
   TEST-DESCRIPT,           X72(10/20);                   <<---------------------------------------------------->>
   TEST-ID,                 X08(10/20);                   NAME:    CADRE-STANZA-DTL, DETAIL (10/20);
   TEST-TIMESTAMP,          X06(10/20);                   ENTRY:   STANZA-ID (!STANZA-MST),
                                                                   CADRE-ID (CADRE-MST);
$PAGE "SRNDB Data Sets"                                   CAPACITY: 500;
                                                          <<---------------------------------------------------->>
SETS:                                                     NAME:    STANZA-RUN-DTL, DETAIL (10/20);
                                                          ENTRY:   STANZA-ID (!STANZA-MST(STANZA-RUN-NUM)),
   NAME:    TEST-MST, MANUAL (10/20);                              FACTOR-ID (FACTOR-MST),
   ENTRY:   TEST-ID (1),                                           FACTOR-VALUE,
            TEST-CATEGORY,                                         STANZA-RUN-NUM;
            TEST-DESCRIPT,                                CAPACITY: 1000;
            TEST-TIMESTAMP;                               <<---------------------------------------------------->>
   CAPACITY: 101;                                         NAME:    EVENT-DTL, DETAIL (10/20);
<<---------------------------------------------------->>  ENTRY:   PFR-NUM (!PFR-MST),
   NAME:    CADRE-MST, MANUAL (10/20);                             EVENT-ID (EVENT-MST),
   ENTRY:   CADRE-ID (2),                                          STANZA-ID,
            CADRE-CATEGORY,                                        STANZA-RUN-NUM,
            CADRE-DESCRIPT,                                        FACTOR-ID (FACTOR-MST),
            CADRE-TIMESTAMP;                                       FACTOR-VALUE;
   CAPACITY: 53;                                          CAPACITY: 1000;
<<---------------------------------------------------->>  END.
```

Figure 14.2 The TurboIMAGE Schema for SRNDB

some of these TurboIMAGE procedures to do the basic types of data entry and retrieval typically found in a database application.

For example, how is an entry added to a dataset in a TurboIMAGE database? The process is started by opening the database with DBOPEN.

The mode that is used to open the database must be one which allows modification of the database, and the password sent to DBOPEN must be associated with a user class that has write access to the dataset to be opened. DBOPEN returns a ten-word status array, as do all the TurboIMAGE procedures. The first word, called the 'condition' word, indicates whether or not the call has been successful. If the condition word is zero, the call has been successful. Any condition word other than zero indicates that an exception condition has been encountered.

Information about what caused the condition can be found by looking up the value of the condition word in the TurboIMAGE reference manual -- or by sending DBERROR the status array and letting it translate the condition word into an appropriate message. The condition word should *always* be checked after a call to *any* TurboIMAGE procedure, and if the call has been unsuccessful, the appropriate action should be taken.

Once the database has been successfully opened, DBPUT can be called to add an entry to the database. DBPUT requires an array which identifies what field values are being added. A special value for the array exists which indicates that all field values in the dataset are being specified.

When you add entries to a master dataset, the key field must be included in the array. When you add entries to a detail dataset, search and sort fields must be included in the array. DBPUT also requires a second array which contains the values of the data items referred to by the first array. Attempts to add an entry to a master dataset with a key field value that already exists in the dataset will not be successful, because keys in master datasets must be unique.

Once the database has been opened by a call to DBOPEN (which provides *at least* read access to the dataset), you can read entries in the database by calling the DBGET procedure. DBGET requires a mode parameter to indicate the type of read being done. It must also know which data items are to be read, and where to store the values of the data items being read. When DBGET performs a directed read, it must know the record address of the entry to be read. In a calculated read, it must know the value of the key field for the entry to be read.

For example, to read the entry in a master dataset associated with a particular value of the key field, you must call DBGET with a mode of 7 in order to indicate a calculated read and include the value of the key. To read all the entries in either a master or detail dataset that meet some criteria unrelated to the key or search field values (or to read all the entries in a dataset), you must call DBGET with either a mode of 2 or 3. This will enable you to read serially through the dataset either forward or backward, respectively. To read all the entries in a detail set that are associated with some value of the key field in a master dataset -- assuming that a path was established between the master and detail dataset when the database was created -- you must call DBGET in either a 5 or 6 mode to do a forward or backward read of the chain, respectively.

Before a chained read can take place, however, TurboIMAGE needs to find the beginning of the chain. To establish the beginning of the chain (or end of the chain, for backward chained reads), call DBFIND, which requires specification of a search field and a search field value in order to establish which chain is to be read.

TurboIMAGE internally keeps track of the address of the record it last retrieved. This address is known as the 'current address'. When DBGET mode 2 is called to do a serial read of a dataset, the entry retrieved is the first entry whose record address is greater than the current address. To serially read a dataset from beginning to end, first call DBCLOSE in mode 3. This mode of DBCLOSE does not really close anything, but it *does* reinitialize some dynamically changing variables for the dataset, including resetting the current address to the beginning of the dataset. You can then keep calling DBGET mode 2 to read each of the entries in the dataset until the desired entries are found, or until the end of the dataset is reached. (The way to tell that the end of a dataset has been reached is by checking the condition word value after each TurboIMAGE call.)

To update an entry in the database, first call DBGET to retrieve the entry. Then call DBUPDATE, which requires an array of data item names as well as an array of corresponding updated data item values. Note that the user class which opened the database must have write access to the fields being updated for the DBUPDATE call to succeed.

To delete an entry from the database, call DBGET to get the entry. Once the entry to be deleted has been retrieved, the deletion is accomplished with a call to DBDELETE. Note that in order for this call to succeed, the database must be opened in a mode which allows write access, and the user class must have write access to the dataset from which an entry is being deleted.

Concurrent Usage of a TurboIMAGE Database

The previous explanations about accessing a TurboIMAGE database assumed that only one program was accessing the database at a time. In reality, single user systems are the exception rather than the rule. Consequently, it is necessary to understand the implications of multiple users simultaneously accessing the same database, and to write programs that anticipate and deal with the various scenarios which might develop in a multi-user system.

One such scenario might have database users A and B reading the same record. User A updates the third field in the record. User B updates the same field. The new value that user B is writing into the field is calculated based on the original value of the field and does not take into account the change user A has just made to the field. So, because user B is not aware of the changes user A made to the record, user B is writing erroneous data in the record.

Another possible scenario has user A read a record. User B then deletes this record. Along comes user C who adds a record which resides at the same location as the record which was just deleted. User A then proceeds to update the last record read. The newly added record, of course, will consequently be updated with the values intended for the recently deleted record. And because these users are making changes to the database in blissful ignorance of what other users might have done or be doing, erroneous data is being written to the database.

TurboIMAGE offers a solution to this kind of chaos with a mechanism called 'locking'. Locking allows a program to gain exclusive control of part *or all* of a particular database. When and how locking is implemented is entirely up to the programmer, and there are many possible strategies that can be adopted.

TurboIMAGE locking is available on three levels: the database level, the dataset level, and the item level (also known as the predicate level). Locking comes in two varieties: conditional and unconditional. Conditional locking immediately returns control to the program if it is not possible to obtain the requested lock right away. Unconditional locking waits until the resource to be locked is available -- no matter how long it takes.

The problem with both of the multi-user database scenarios presented above is that user A is reading and then updating a record, and in between the occurrence of the read and the request for the update, other users have changed the record. Locking can solve this by giving user A exclusive control of that record by locking either the entire database, the dataset that contains the record, or just the record itself. It is important to recognize, however, that granting user A exclusive control to a resource causes other accessors of this resource to wait. To minimize this wait, it is desirable to lock *as little data as possible for as little time as possible*.

Obviously, global database locks should be avoided except for those processes that make database changes of a global nature and typically run in batch mode. Less clear-cut, however, is the choice between dataset-level locking and item-level locking. It may seem that item-level locking is the way to go, because only entries with a particular value for the lock item will be locked. However, item-level locking is more complex to program -- and to administer -- than the other types of locking.

For example, TurboIMAGE allows only one item in a dataset to be the lock item, and all programs must use this same lock item. If it happens that different programs select different lock items in the same dataset, TurboIMAGE will revert to set-level locking. So, if locks are held for short periods of time and there is not severe contention for the same dataset, dataset-level locking may be the most appropriate solution.

An important question to ask is: "What is happening between the time user A reads and updates a record?" If database user A is a *program* that reads a record, makes some calculations, and updates the record, dataset-level locking *is* a possible approach. If database user A is a *person* who is reading the record, thinking about it, keying in changes, and then updating the record, dataset-level locking is *not* the best approach. The terminal user's 'think time' (the time between the read and the update) could be a few seconds -- or a few hours.

To put some kind of limit on think time, a time-out mechanism should be programmed in. If an update does not occur within the specified time limit, the transaction is canceled and the lock is released. Unless contention for the dataset is very low, however, it is best to use item-level locking rather than dataset-level locking when locking around a terminal read.

A second approach to handling terminal reads is *not* to lock around them at all. This approach, which requires more programming effort, works in the following manner. When the user first reads the record, it is not locked. After the user thinks about it, keys in the updates or requests a deletion, and the terminal read completes, the record is locked. The program then reads the record again to ensure that it has not been deleted or changed. If it hasn't, the update or delete proceeds. If the record has been deleted or changed, the transaction is canceled, and the record is unlocked.

With TurboIMAGE, it is important to define a locking strategy and require all database programs to follow it. TurboIMAGE makes an attempt at enforcing this with DBOPEN mode 1. If all the database programs open the database in mode 1, then all are required to do at least an item-level lock in order to perform a DBPUT, DBDELETE, or DBUPDATE. Additionally, a DBPUT or DBDELETE to a master dataset requires *at least* a dataset-level lock.

Using HP's QUERY Program

QUERY is an HP-provided utility program that can be used to access and modify a TurboIMAGE database. QUERY is a powerful programmer's tool which, during program development, is useful for adding test data to the database and for checking the results of programs. It is also useful in the program-maintenance stages because it shows what is *really* in the databases, as opposed to what is *believed* to be in them. It also provides complete information about the structure of the database (datasets, key fields, search fields, paths, capacities, etc.) so it is not necessary to rely on out-of-date or non-existent schema listings.

At best, QUERY is an awkward tool for the general user population. At worst, it is a dangerous tool to allow them to use. It is command-driven, and for the most part, the commands are not intuitive. Users who truly have some understanding of the structure of their database may be able to extract the desired information. Typically, however, users wind up doing more serial reads than are truly necessary. This, of course, can quickly degrade system performance. It is also dangerous to allow users write access within QUERY because QUERY allows all kinds of modifications, as well as deletions of a global nature. In short, QUERY in the wrong hands can reduce a database to a worthless bit bucket.

TurboIMAGE Recovery Mechanisms

TurboIMAGE provides three mechanisms for recovering a database from a system interruption. The first of these mechanisms is called 'Intrinsic Level Recovery' (ILR). When ILR is enabled on a TurboIMAGE database, every call to DBPUT or DBDELETE causes a copy of the as-yet-unchanged data to be written to a file created by TurboIMAGE exclusively for this purpose. If a system failure occurs, the first DBOPEN to a database following the failure checks a special flag to see if a DBPUT or DBDELETE was in progress at the time of the failure. If the flag is set, TurboIMAGE uses the contents of the ILR file to restore the database to its state before the last DBPUT or DBDELETE call.

Essentially, ILR is protecting the database from structural inconsistency -- namely, broken chains. (As previously defined, a chain is a linking of all the detail entries in a detail dataset whose search field value equals the master entry's key field value.)

A chain's linkage is held together by pointers. Each entry in the chain has a pointer to the next and previous entry in the chain. A DBPUT or DBDELETE necessitates the reworking of some of these pointers. If a system failure occurs while pointers are being reset, the result is a broken chain, *unless* ILR is enabled so that the effects of the interrupted DBPUT or DBDELETE can be backed out. ILR is enabled through the DBUTIL utility program. Once enabled, ILR is automatic, and no other intervention is required.

ILR does not protect the database from disc media failures, nor does it protect the database from logical inconsistencies due to system failures. Logical inconsistencies occur when a logical transaction, such as the entry of the information on a purchase order, is interrupted while still in progress.

The remaining two TurboIMAGE recovery mechanisms, however, do provide a level of protection from these occurrences through 'transaction logging'. With transaction logging, every call to DBOPEN, DBUPDATE, DBPUT, DBDELETE, DBCLOSE, DBBEGIN, DBEND, and DBMEMO causes a record to be written to a logfile, on either disc or tape. This record contains information about who made the call, when the call was made, and what database, dataset, and data fields were involved. The logical consistency of a complex transaction can be maintained only if DBBEGIN and DBEND are used to bracket the calls that make up the transaction.

In order to use TurboIMAGE's second recovery mechanism, called 'Roll-Back Recovery', both transaction logging and ILR must be enabled. Additionally, the database must be enabled for Roll-Back Recovery through the DBUTIL utility program. In the event of a system interruption, ILR restores structural consistency. Then, a recovery program called 'DBRECOV' is run to begin Roll-Back Recovery, which restores logical consistency to the database by backing out incomplete logical transactions.

In order to use TurboIMAGE's third recovery mechanism, called 'Roll-Forward Recovery', transaction logging must be enabled and you must have a backup copy of the database. The database must also be enabled for Roll-Forward Recovery through the DBUTIL utility program. In the event of a system failure, the database must be purged from the system and the backup must be restored. DBRECOV is run to reapply all of the complete logical transactions that have been recorded in the logfile.

While the Roll-Back and Roll-Forward mechanisms each provide a greater degree of protection against system interruptions than ILR, they also require more human intervention to set up and maintain. Also, with ILR, the time for recovery after a system failure is negligible. While Roll-Back Recovery is a fairly short process, Roll-Forward Recovery is generally a lengthy process. Exactly how long it takes depends upon the size of the logfile that is being reapplied. The size of the logfile, in turn, depends upon how active the database is and how frequently it has been backed up to tape using DBSTORE.

There are gaps worth noting in TurboIMAGE's recovery mechanisms. One is that there is no reasonable means of protecting against logical inconsistencies due to program aborts. Although a program abort logs a special DBEND record to the logfile, you would need to shut down the database and do a Roll-Back Recovery using DBRECOV with the NOABORTS option to restore the database to its logically consistent state.

Also, if a logical transaction spans multiple databases, there is no way to enclose that transaction within a single DBBEGIN-DBEND construct. Therefore, the recovery of that system of databases to a logically consistent state after a system interruption cannot be assured.

TurboIMAGE Performance: How It Really Works

The purpose of the following discussion is to provide an understanding of how some of the primary features of TurboIMAGE really work -- and to identify some of the classic TurboIMAGE pitfalls to avoid.

At their best, TurboIMAGE master datasets allow you to locate a particular entry from among the thousands of others with just one disc access. This kind of retrieval is possible because of the way an entry is added to a master dataset. To add an entry to a master dataset, you must specifiy a value for the key field. TurboIMAGE does some manipulations on this key field value in order to yield a number between 1 and the capacity of the master dataset, inclusive. This technique is known as 'hashing'.

The manipulations performed on the key field value are dictated by the hashing algorithm. The number generated by hashing the key field value is the primary address of the master entry. This primary address is where TurboIMAGE attempts to store the master entry. It is possible, however, that this location is already occupied. If it is, this situation is known as a 'collision'. Collisions can occur in two ways. The primary address location may be occupied by a synonym, an entry whose key value hashed to the same primary address. If this is the case, TurboIMAGE will begin searching at the beginning of the primary address block and place the new entry in the first available location. The new entry is linked to the entry at the primary address by means of pointers, namely a doubly linked list. Each entry that hashes to a primary location, but is located elsewhere, is known as a 'secondary'.

The second way for a collision to occur is for an entry to hash to a location occupied by a secondary. If this occurs, the secondary must be relocated. This is known as the 'migrating secondaries phenomenon'.

What all this means is that when a master entry is added, the first thing that TurboIMAGE does is hash the key value. Then, because the key value must be unique in the master dataset, TurboIMAGE checks to see if a synonym already exists in the primary address. If so, TurboIMAGE checks the key value of this entry and every secondary that might be chained to it to verify that the key value is in fact unique.

If the key value *is* unique, what TurboIMAGE does next depends on what it finds in the primary address. If nothing is found, the entry to be added is simply stored at the primary address. If a synonym is found, TurboIMAGE goes searching for an alternate location. Once found, the entry to be added is stored there and the pointers in the synonym chain are updated to reflect the newest addition.

If a secondary is found in the primary address, an alternate location for this secondary is sought. Once that is found, the secondary will migrate to this new location, and the synonym chain of which it is a member will be updated to reflect its new location. The entry to be added can then locate in the primary address.

To retrieve an entry in a master dataset, TurboIMAGE hashes the key value to find the primary address. The entry at the primary address, and subsequently the entries, if any, in the synonym chain are searched until the correct entry is found.

To delete an entry in a master dataset, it must first be retrieved. What happens next depends on where the entry is located. If the entry was at its primary address and had no synonym chain, it is simply deleted. If the entry was a member of a synonym chain, the entry is deleted and the pointers of the chain are updated appropriately. If the entry was at a primary address with a synonym chain, the entry is deleted, the first entry in the synonym chain is relocated to the vacated primary address, and the synonym chain pointers are updated accordingly.

It should be obvious by this point that synonyms are to be minimized because they add steps to every type of access to a master dataset. There are two factors within the database administrator's control that directly affect collision rate.

One is the capacity of the master dataset. For non-numeric keys, it is generally desirable to have a master dataset capacity that is a prime number. A detailed examination of numeric keys, which are hashed differently than non-numeric keys, is beyond the scope of this discussion. Suffice it to say that numeric keys should only be used when absolutely necessary and with a complete understanding of the ramifications of the hashing algorithm, given the likely distribution of the numeric keys and the dataset capacity.

The second item directly related to collision rate is the degree of fullness of the master dataset. It has been found that a master dataset more than 80 percent full generally experiences a marked increase in collisions. Therefore, when a master dataset gets approximately 80 percent full, *its capacity should be increased*.

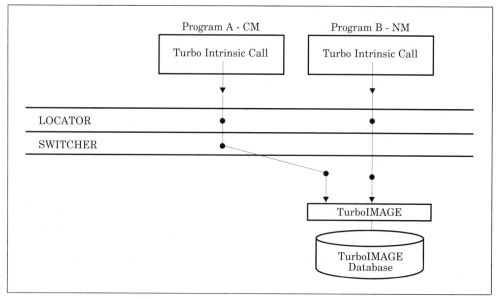

Figure 14.3 TurboIMAGE Migration Tools

When adding an entry to a detail dataset, the entry is stored in either the location occupied by the most recently deleted entry or in the first available never-been-occupied location. If the detail entry contains one or more search field values, the entry is added to the end of each chain of which it is a member. If there is a sort field associated with any of the chains, TurboIMAGE starts at the end and reads up the chain until it finds the correct location for the entry and updates the pointers in the chain accordingly. Obviously, the more paths defined for the detail dataset, the more chains that have to be maintained when an entry is added. The more sort fields defined, the longer it will take to add a detail entry to a chain if the detail entries are not entered in already-sorted order.

The benefit of maintaining all of these chains is the fast (non-serial read) access to detail entries. To retrieve one or more entries in a chain, you must first establish the beginning of the chain by locating the associated master entry using a call to DBFIND. Then, the pointers can be followed until the desired entries are found. A sort field on the chain will cause the entries to be retrieved in sorted order.

One of the factors to be aware of in a detail dataset is the free-entry chain. For each dataset, TurboIMAGE keeps a pointer to the highest record ever used and a pointer to the beginning of the free-entry chain (a chain of all the locations in the dataset that are free due to deletion). When a detail entry is added, the locations on the free-entry chain are used first.

Detail entries on the same chain are often input at the same time. If there are *no* entries on the free-entry chain, these entries will locate in contiguous locations, which usually means that they can then be retrieved with just one disc access. But, if there *are* entries on the free-entry chain, the entries to be added will be put in these locations, which are likely to be scattered all over. (So much for one disc access!) The only solution for this is to regularly repack the detail datasets by doing a DBUNLOAD-DBLOAD or by using one of several third-party database utilities.

Using TurboIMAGE on the HP 3000 900 Series

HP has recognized the concerns of current TurboIMAGE users in regards to moving their TurboIMAGE applications to the Series 900 systems and has strived to create a relatively painless path of migration from TurboIMAGE to TurboIMAGE/XL. HP's level of success in this regard is impressive, particularly since TurboIMAGE on the MPE V-based HP 3000 systems employs a fair amount of machine-specific code.

A typical migration scenario might read as follows: An HP 3000 user restores TurboIMAGE programs and database files from an MPE V-based HP 3000 to a 900 Series system. The user immediately begins running applications in Compatibility Mode, with TurboIMAGE calls operating in Native Mode. For optimum performance, the user eventually converts the application to Native Mode following the guidelines for the specific application language being used.

In order to allow database application programs running in either Compatibility Mode or Native Mode such transparent access to TurboIMAGE/XL databases, HP placed a layer of software between the database application programs and the database system. As shown in Figure 14.3, this layer of software is essentially a set of switch stubs and interface routines that determines the execution mode of the calling process and then interfaces to the appropriate TurboIMAGE/XL intrinsic.

There is one known incompatibility between TurboIMAGE and TurboIMAGE/XL. Both TurboIMAGE and TurboIMAGE/XL return a status array at the completion of every call. This array consists of ten 16-bit storage locations. Virtually all of the TurboIMAGE/XL calls return the same information to this status array as do the TurboIMAGE calls. However, in certain error conditions, the status array contains the PB-relative location of the erroneous call and the DB-relative address of certain data items. On MPE-V based HP 3000 computers, these are 16-bit addresses, and therefore fit quite nicely in the status array. On HPPA computers, however, these are 32-bit quantities. For these cases, the format of the status array has changed. Applications which rely on these 16-bit quantities for error condition checking will have to recode their applications to allow for the 32-bit quantities under HPPA.

15

Hp sql

HP SQL is the relational interface to HP's new ALLBASE database management system. It is available on both the MPE XL-based HP 3000 900 Series and the HP-UX-based HP 9000 800 Series. HP SQL is also a fairly recent addition to the software offered on the MPE V-based HP 3000. HP SQL is a relational database management system, as opposed to TurboIMAGE, which is a network system. It uses the industry standard relational language, SQL (Structured Query Language).

Relational databases have been around since the late 1970s, but it is only recently that 'relational' has become a buzzword. With the current trend of end users taking and/or being given increased responsibility for meeting their own computer-generated report requirements, relational databases have become quite popular. In short, relational databases tend to provide as much, if not more, functionality than their hierarchial counterparts -- in an easier-to-use package. However, in the minds of many system managers, relational databases also tend to be synonymous with poor system performance. But the truth is that there is nothing inherent in the formal definition of a relational database that requires it to be highly functional, easy to use, and slow. These characteristics are entirely dependent upon how the model is implemented.

HP's implementation, HP SQL, provides all the functionality that relational databases are known for. At the same time, HP has obviously put some thought into performance. For instance, programs containing embedded SQL commands are pre-processed at compilation time, and the SQL commands are translated into their executable form so that programs are not slowed down by SQL translation at run time. HP SQL also provides the database administrator with a wide array of statistics with which to monitor performance and with the necessary tools to tune this performance. So, TurboIMAGE users, read on and find out what it's all about.

Fundamentals of HP SQL

If you are a TurboIMAGE user, you are going to have to make a few adjustments. The jargon of relational databases is slightly different from that of network databases. The HP SQL dataset is called a 'table'. A data record in an HP SQL table is called a 'row'. A field in an HP SQL table is called a 'column'. So instead of thinking of datasets filled with records made up of fields, think of tables filled with rows made up of columns.

A 'table' is one of the basic structures of HP SQL and defines data that is physically stored in an HP SQL database. This is opposed to a 'view', another of the basic structures in HP SQL. A view is, as its name implies, a particular way of looking at the data that is physically stored in a database, a 'window' into a database that shows only those aspects of the database that are included in the view definition.

Views are a very powerful concept in HP SQL for two reasons: security and independence. Suppose you have a table which contains complete information on employees, including salaries. You can define a view of this data which excludes salaries. Those departments that should not be able to see salaries are given access only to this view of the data, rather than all the data in the table. This is comparable to TurboIMAGE's read and write class lists for items, but better, because new views can be created dynamically (while the database is up and running), and who has access to views can also be changed dynamically.

Views can also be used to increase independence of data and programs. If programs are using views to access data in a database, they know nothing about the true structure of the database. It is the view definition that specifies where to go to get the information. If the structure of the database changes, only the view -- not the program -- must be modified. Also, by specifying commonly accessed and complex data combinations in a view, the definition process only occurs once rather than every time the data needs to be accessed.

Another of the basic structures in HP SQL is an 'index'. An index is similar in functionality to the key or the search field in TurboIMAGE. As do TurboIMAGE's keys and search fields, HP SQL's indexes provide a way of finding data that meets certain criteria that is faster than doing a serial read. However, HP SQL's indexes are different from their TurboIMAGE counterparts in several ways.

First, there is no hashed indexing. All HP SQL indexes are implemented as modified B-trees. The pointers are stored separate from the data. You can define as many indexes for a table as you want. The index item can be made up of a single column or as many as 15. The index can be defined as 'unique', which means duplicate values in the index column(s) are not allowed (in the same manner as TurboIMAGE requires unique key field values). One index per table can be defined as a 'clustering' index, where HP SQL will attempt to physically store rows with similar values in the clustering index near one another in a manner similar to TurboIMAGE's primary path. An index may also be defined as both unique and clustering -- or neither.

Here's how the HP SQL indexes compare with the keys, search, and sort fields used in TurboIMAGE. In general, a key field is defined as a unique index in HP SQL. A search field with an associated sort item is defined as a unique, clustering index made up of the columns that correspond to the search and sort fields. A search field without an associated sort item would be defined as a clustering index. HP SQL's implementation of indexes is remarkably different from TurboIMAGE's in two primary respects. In HP SQL, just as in TurboIMAGE, you define indexes for commonly accessed data paths in order to avoid serial reads and improve performance. But in HP SQL, if your initial suppositions about the commonly accessed paths prove incorrect, you can easily drop the useless index and add a new one. Indexes in HP SQL can change dynamically, just as your data access needs can change dynamically.

For instance, when you do end-of-year processing and access data in an unusual manner, you can temporarily define indexes to optimize this processing. In HP SQL, you specify only what data you want, not how to get it. Based on what data you have asked for, what indexes are defined, and the performance of these indexes, HP SQL figures out how to best retrieve the data. This is one of the reasons relational databases are generally easier to use than their network counterparts. The database accessor needs only to be familiar with the data stored in the database, not the index structures.

Figure 15.1 shows the series of SQL commands which define the initial structure of the HP SQL implementation of SRNDB. You may recall from previous chapters that SRNDB is a modified version of a database used in a Chemical Processing Quality Assurance (QA) Project. The database is used to keep an inventory of automated QA

```
CREATE PUBLIC TABLE     SRNDB.TESTS              PFR_NUM              VARCHAR(10),
  (TEST_ID              VARCHAR(08)    NOT NULL,  EVENT_FACT1          VARCHAR(10),
   TEST_CATEGORY        VARCHAR(06)    NOT NULL,  EVENT_FACT2          VARCHAR(10),
   TEST_DESCRIPT        VARCHAR(72),              EVENT_FACT3          VARCHAR(10))
   TEST_TIMESTAMP       VARCHAR(06))            IN PFR_INFO;
 IN TEST_INVENTORY;
                                              CREATE VIEW          SRNDB.PFR_EVENTS
CREATE PUBLIC TABLE     SRNDB.CADRES             (PFR_NUM,
  (CADRE_ID             VARCHAR(04)    NOT NULL,   EVENT_ID) AS
   CADRE_CATEGORY       VARCHAR(06)    NOT NULL,  SELECT SRNDB.PFRS.PFR_NUM,
   CADRE_DESCRIPT       VARCHAR(72),                     SRNDB.STANZA_EVENTS.EVENT_ID
   CADRE_TIMESTAMP      VARCHAR(06))             FROM  SRNDB.PFRS,
 IN TEST_INVENTORY;                                    SRNDB.STANZA_EVENTS
                                              WHERE SRNDB.PFRS.PFR_NUM = SRNDB.STANZA_EVENTS.PFR_NUM
CREATE PUBLIC TABLE     SRNDB.STANZAS                AND SRNDB.PFRS.PFR_STATUS = '04OPEN'
  (STANZA_ID            VARCHAR(04)    NOT NULL,  ORDER BY PFR_NUM;
   STANZA_TIMESTAMP     VARCHAR(06))
 IN TEST_INVENTORY;                           CREATE UNIQUE INDEX     TEST_NDX
                                                ON  SRNDB.TESTS (TEST_ID);

CREATE PUBLIC TABLE     SRNDB.TEST_CADRE
  (CADRE_ID             VARCHAR(04)    NOT NULL,  CREATE UNIQUE INDEX     CADRE_NDX
   TEST_ID              VARCHAR(04)    NOT NULL)  ON SRNDB.CADRES (CADRE_ID);
 IN TEST_INVENTORY;
                                              CREATE UNIQUE INDEX     STANZA_NDX
CREATE PUBLIC TABLE     SRNDB.CADRE_STANZA         ON SRNDB.STANZAS (STANZA_ID);
  (STANZA_ID            VARCHAR(04)    NOT NULL,
   CADRE_ID             VARCHAR(04)    NOT NULL)  CREATE CLUSTERING INDEX  CAD_IN_STAN_NDX
 IN TEST_INVENTORY;                                ON SRNDB.CADRE_STANZA (STANZA_ID);

CREATE PUBLIC TABLE     SRNDB.CODES            CREATE INDEX            STAN_IN_CAD_NDX
  (CODE_ID              VARCHAR(06)    NOT NULL,  ON SRNDB.CADRE_STANZA (CADRE_ID);
   CODE_VALUE           VARCHAR(50))
 IN CODES_LOOKUP;                             CREATE CLUSTERING INDEX  TEST_IN_CAD_NDX
                                                ON SRNDB.TEST_CADRE (CADRE_ID);
CREATE PUBLIC TABLE     SRNDB.STANZA_RUNS
  (STANZA_ID            VARCHAR(04)    NOT NULL,  CREATE INDEX            CAD_IN_TEST_NDX
   STANZA_RUN_NUM       VARCHAR(04)    NOT NULL,  ON SRNDB.TEST_CADRE (TEST_ID);
   STANZA_RUN_FACT1     VARCHAR(10),
   STANZA_RUN_FACT2     VARCHAR(10),             CREATE UNIQUE INDEX     CODE_NDX
   STANZA_RUN_FACT3     VARCHAR(10),               ON SRNDB.CODES (CODE_10);
   STANZA_RUN_FACT4     VARCHAR(10))
 IN STANZA_RUN_INFO;                          CREATE UNIQUE CLUSTERING INDEX    STANZA_RUN_NDX
                                                ON SRNDB.STANZA_RUNS (STANZA_ID, STANZA_RUN_NUM);
CREATE PUBLIC TABLE     SRNDB.PFRS
  (PFR_NUM              VARCHAR(10)    NOT NULL,  CREATE INDEX            STAN_RUN_EVENT_NDX
   PFR_TYPE             VARCHAR(06)    NOT NULL,  ON SRNDB.STANZA_EVENTS (STANZA_ID, STANZA_RUN_NUM);
   PFR_CATEGORY         VARCHAR(06)    NOT NULL,
   PFR_DESCRIPT1        VARCHAR(72),             CREATE UNIQUE INDEX     PFR_NDX
   PFR_DESCRIPT2        VARCHAR(72),               ON SRNDB.PFRS (PFR_NUM);
   PFR_STATUS           VARCHAR(06)    NOT NULL)
 IN PFR_INFO;                                 CREATE UNIQUE INDEX     EVENT_NDX
                                                ON SRNDB.STANZA_EVENTS (EVENT_ID);
CREATE PUBLIC TABLE     SRNDB.STANZA_EVENTS
  (STANZA_ID            VARCHAR(04)    NOT NULL,  CREATE CLUSTERING INDEX  PFR_EVENT_NDX
   STANZA_RUN_NUM       VARCHAR(04)    NOT NULL,  ON SRNDB.STANZA_EVENTS (PFR_NUM);
   EVENT_ID             VARCHAR(10)    NOT NULL,
```

Figure 15.1 HP SQL Definition of SRNDB

tests, record the results of QA runs, and keep track of problems that are discovered during these runs. Problems are assigned event identifiers. Unique occurrences of a problem are assigned a Production Follow-up Request (PFR) number and tracked through SRNDB. The basic unit of QA testing is the test. Related tests are grouped into 'cadres'. Cadres are then grouped into 'stanzas'.

Note that the tables defined for the HP SQL database are very similar to the datasets defined for the TurboIMAGE versions of this database. The most notable difference is that all of the factors recorded about a particular stanza run or a problem occurrence are stored in one table row as opposed to recording multiple rows, storing one factor per row in the manner of a detail dataset. The primary reason these factors were stored in detail form in the TurboIMAGE implementations was that it was not clear at design time how many factors would need to be tracked as the system progressed. With TurboIMAGE, it would be a fairly difficult procedure to add fields to a record later in the system's life in order to store additional factor information, so this information was put in a detail. In HP SQL, columns *can* be dynamically added to a table if it becomes necessary later in the system's life to store additional factor information.

Figure 15.1 also includes a view definition. It is common to report all of the problem occurrences that are asociated with outstanding (PFR_STATUS = 04OPEN) PFR's. View PFR_EVENTS combines the information in the Table PFRS and STANZA_EVENTS to create such a view of the data.

Defining and Creating an HP SQL Database

One of the steps in defining and creating an HP SQL database is to specify the tables, indexes, and views in that database through a series of SQL commands, as was done in Figure 15.1. There are several points that have not yet been noted about defining a table. A table is defined to be accessed in either PUBLIC, PUBLICREAD, or PRIVATE mode. A PUBLIC table can be read and updated by concurrent transactions. A PUBLICREAD table can be read concurrently but can be updated by only one transaction at a time. A PRIVATE table can be read *and* updated by only one transaction at a time. The data stored in a column can be one of six types recognized in HP SQL. Additionally, if it is mandatory that a value be specified for a particular column, the column can be specified as NOT NULL.

You will note that there is an IN clause associated with the CREATE TABLE command. This command is specifying the DBEFileset in which the table is to be stored. Unlike TurboIMAGE, where the process of creating physical storage on the disc was an automatic part of creating the database, in HP SQL creating the database and creating physical storage for the database are related -- but very distinct -- steps. You need to define the structure of the HP SQL database before you can figure out how much physical storage space the database requires. But you need to create the physical storage before you can actually create the structure you have defined.

Every HP SQL database resides in a 'database environment' (DBE). A DBE consists of databases that are logically related to one another and are likely to be accessed simultaneously. Databases in different DBE's cannot be interactively accessed at the same time. The DBE is the basic unit of logging and recovery in HP SQL and is created by using the START DBE MULTI NEW command. The MULTI keyword signifies that the database can be accessed by multiple users simultaneously. When the DBE is created, several files are *automatically* created: the DBECon file, the DBE logfile(s), and DBEFile0 in a DBEFileset belonging to a special HP SQL user called 'SYSTEM'.

The DBECon file contains start-up parameters for the DBE. The DBE logfile is created to store database transactions for recovery purposes. The DBEFile0 contains the DBE's system catalog, which includes complete DBE structural information as well as information on DBE users and DBE performance.

DBEFiles correspond to actual MPE V, MPE XL or HP-UX disc files. DBEFilesets are logical groupings of one or more DBEFiles. All DBEFiles for a given table's data and indexes are stored in one DBEFileset. Figure 15.2 is a diagram showing a DBE viewed as a set of databases containing tables and indexes. Figure 15.3 is a diagram of the same DBE, but highlights the relationships between DBEFilesets, DBEFiles, tables, and indexes.

After creating the DBE, the next step is to create DBEFilesets for the tables in the database. Tables that are closely interrelated are generally grouped into one DBEFileset. For instance, in SRNDB all of the tables involved in keeping an inventory of tests, cadres, and stanzas are grouped in the DBEFileset TEST_INVENTORY. Once the logical DBEFilesets are created, physical DBEFiles are allocated to the DBEFilesets. DBEFiles can be used to store table data pages, table index pages, or a combination of both. In general, it is better to create separate DBEFiles for data and indexes in order to ensure, for performance reasons, that data and indexes are on separate discs.

The exception to this occurs when there is just one index to a table. If you create a DBEFile large enough to hold both data and index for this table, HP SQL will attempt to place rows and keys on contiguous pages.

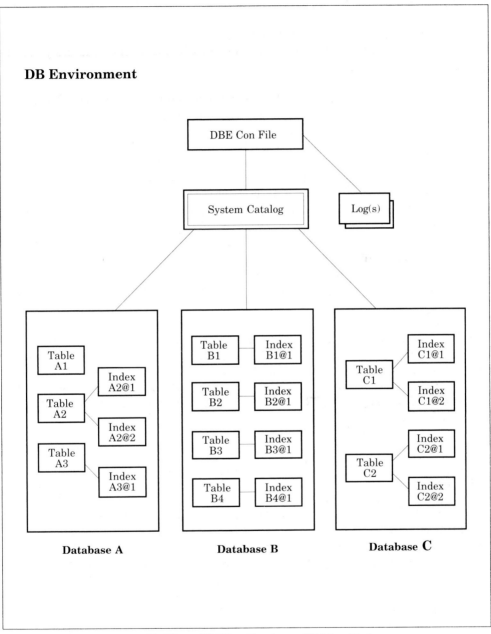

Figure 15.2 View of DBE as Databases / Tables / Indexes

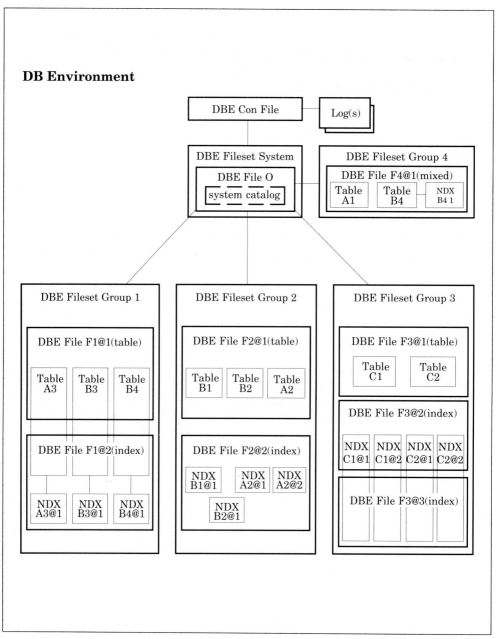

Figure 15.3 View of DBE as DBEFilesets / DBEFiles

Beyond RISC!

HP SQL Security

An important part of creating and maintaining a database is securing it. HP SQL provides several very useful security features. One of these, using views to restrict data access, has already been mentioned. The other security features reference the two types of entities that are assigned capabilities in HP SQL.

One is a user, represented in HP SQL security by his or her logon identifier. The second is a group, such as PERSONNEL, to which users can be assigned. HP SQL groups simplify granting authorities: Multiple users can be granted authority with just one command; new users can be added to existing groups that are already defined with the appropriate capabilities.

HP SQL ensures that control over the type of data access allowed has been completely separated from *who* has that type of data access. For instance, the owner of a table can grant various accesses to the table to different groups. Who is in those groups, however, is controlled by the database administrator or the owner of the group.

HP SQL has four basic groupings of authority: the special authorities (DBA, RESOURCE, and CONNECT); the OWNER authority; the table and view authorities (ALTER, DELETE, INDEX, INSERT, SELECT, and UPDATE); and the RUN authority. DBA authority is the authority to issue all commands. The DBE creator is assigned this authority automatically and can assign it to others. The RESOURCE authority is necessary to create or become the OWNER of an HP SQL entity. The CONNECT authority is necessary to connect to a DBE. You must be able to connect to a DBE to execute any of the SQL commands interactively.

What you can do with the OWNER authority depends upon what you own. If you own a table or view, you have all the table and view authorities. If you own a module, which is a preprocessed program containing SQL commands, you can RUN the program. If you own an authorization group, you can add to or delete from the list of users in that group. The various table and view authorities grant permission to use the SQL command named by the authority on the table or the view the authority is granted for. The RUN authority allows you to run a preprocessed program containing SQL commands.

Accessing an HP SQL Database

Whether you are accessing an HP SQL database from a program or using HP's interactive utility, ISQL, the basic commands are the same. The first step in accessing an HP SQL database is to establish an SQL session/process in the DBE using the CONNECT command. The next step is to define the beginning of your SQL transaction using the BEGIN WORK command. SQL is a transaction-oriented language and requires that every SQL command be enclosed inside a transaction delimited by a BEGIN WORK/COMMIT WORK construct. Locks are held around transactions. In a system failure, complete transactions are recovered. Incomplete transactions are rolled back.

The next step is to define the data access you wish to accomplish in terms of one or more SQL commands. Almost all of the data manipulations necessary in HP SQL can be done using either the SQL SELECT, INSERT, UPDATE, or DELETE commands. The SELECT command is used to retrieve data and is composed of the following components, all of which are optional except for the select list and the FROM clause: the select list, an INTO clause, a FROM clause, a WHERE clause, a GROUP BY clause, a HAVING clause, an ORDER BY clause.

The select list identifies what columns you wish to report. The select list can contain mathematical expressions involving the addition, subtraction, multiplication, and division of columns, as well as columns that are being operated on by one of HP SQL's aggregate functions, such as AVG, which computes the arithmetic mean. The INTO clause is used only in application programs to identify host variables for storing the query results. The FROM clause identifies tables and views from which data will be retrieved.

The WHERE clause specifies a search condition for screening rows. The comparisons that can be done in the search condition include the standard comparisons, such as greater than, less than, and equal to; a BETWEEN comparison to check if a value is between the value of two expressions; a LIKE comparison to do pattern-matching; and a check for NULL and non-NULL values. Very complex compound search conditions can be created using the logical AND, OR, and NOT operators.

The GROUP BY clause tells HP SQL how to group rows before performing an aggregate function in the select list. The rows that satisfy the WHERE clause are grouped. The HAVING clause further screens rows once they are grouped. The ORDER BY clause sorts the rows resulting from the query in order by the specified column(s).

The SELECT command can be used to retrieve data from single tables or from multiple tables. The following sample SELECT statement reports on all the PFRs in

SRNDB which have occurred more than once. It reports the PFR number, the number of times the PFR occurred, and the average time to failure for the PFR (EVENT_FACT2).

```
SELECT PFR.NUM, COUNT(Y.PFR.NUM), AVG(EVENT_FACT2)
  FROM SRNDB.PFRS X, SRNDB.STANZA_EVENTS Y
 WHERE X.PFR_NUM = Y.PFR_NUM AND PFR_STATUS = '04OPEN'
 GROUP BY PFR_NUM
HAVING COUNT(Y.PFR_NUM) > 1
 ORDER BY PFR_NUM
```

The INSERT command is used to add rows to a table and is made up of the following components: table or view name, column names, and column values. You can only insert data into a single table or view at a time. An example of a simple INSERT command follows.

```
INSERT INTO SRNDB.PFRS
          (PFR_NUM, PFR_TYPE, PFR_STATUS)
      VALUES ('1650026641', '02QASF', '04OPEN')
```

The UPDATE command is used to change the data values in one or more columns and has the following components: a table or view name, a SET clause to specify the change(s) to be made, and a WHERE clause to specify which rows are to be updated. An example of an UPDATE command follows.

```
UPDATE SRNDB.PFRS
   SET PFRS_STATUS = '04OPEN'
 WHERE PFR_NUM = '1650026641'
```

The DELETE command, which is used to delete rows, has two components: the table or view name and a WHERE clause to indicate the rows to be deleted.

```
DELETE FROM SRNDB.PFRS
      WHERE PFR_NUM = '1650026641'
```

Because HP SQL does not have any predefined paths between tables as TurboIMAGE has between datasets, some automatic data integrity checking is lost. For example, you can enter a PFR number in the STANZA_EVENTS table that is not defined in the PFRS table. You can also delete a PFR number from the PFRS table that is still being referenced by an entry in the STANZA_EVENTS table.

The final step in completing an SQL transaction is to commit the transaction using the COMMIT WORK command. All locks on behalf of the transaction are released at this point. HP SQL also provides the capability to roll back an uncommitted transaction if an abnormal or abort condition is detected. It enhances this feature, however, with 'savepoints'. A savepoint is a point in a logical transaction that has been marked by a call to the SAVEPOINT command. If later in the transaction, you need roll back, you have the option of either rolling back to the beginning or rolling back to one of the previously defined savepoints.

Some Notes on Programmatic Access to HP SQL

As has been previously mentioned, the commands to access an HP SQL database from a program are basically the same as the commands to access an HP SQL database interactively. But instead of typing the commands in at a terminal, the commands are embedded in a program. However, there are certain versions of and additions to the SQL commands that are used only programmatically. Also, some considerations apply in a programmatic environment which do not apply in the interactive environment.

Data is passed back and forth between HP SQL and a program by host data variables. Host variables are defined in the program between the SQL command BEGIN DECLARE SECTION and the SQL command END DECLARE SECTION.

When you embed SQL commands in an application program, you must accompany each SQL command with several language-dependent keywords. For example, in Pascal, embedded SQL commands are preceded by 'EXEC SQL'. In COBOL, embedded SQL commands are preceded by 'EXEC SQL' and succeeded by 'END-EXEC'. Programs that contain embedded SQL commands are preprocessed using the preprocessor provided for that language. On the MPE V-based HP 3000 and the MPE XL-based HP 3000 900 Series, there is a preprocessor for COBOL II and Pascal. On the HP-UX-based HP 9000 800 Series, there is a preprocessor for C and Pascal, and there will be a pre-processor for COBOL II when that compiler is available.

When an application program is preprocessed, a 'module' is stored in the system DBEFileset for the DBE. This module is composed of a 'section' for each SQL command embedded in the application program. A section contains an uncompiled version of the command and a compiled, executable form of the command. At run time, HP SQL checks a section to see if it has been flagged as invalid. A section is marked as invalid whenever any of the database structures it references are modified. If the section is still valid, it is immediately executed. If HP SQL finds that the section has been flagged as invalid, it then determines if the referenced structures still exist and authorization criteria are still satisfied. If so, the section is marked as valid and HP SQL dynamically recompiles and executes the section. If not, the command is not executed, and an error condition is returned to the program.

Some Notes on Interactive Access to HP SQL

The SQL commands are executed interactively by running the ISQL interactive utility program. The program operates in several ways that are worth noting. The end of an SQL command is signaled by a ';' *and* a carriage return, not just a carriage return by itself. This means that multi-lined commands can be easily input.

If you do not specify all of the parameters to an SQL command, ISQL will prompt for them. Most SQL commands entered through ISQL will automatically generate a BEGIN WORK command if no transaction is active. However, the COMMIT WORK command must be explicitly entered to end a transaction.

By responding to the 'scroll display' prompt that follows every query result, you can browse through its results. There is a command history buffer which contains a history of the commands executed in the current ISQL session. This history buffer can be used to edit and redo the commands contained within it. SQL commands can also be stored in a file referred to as a command file. The commands in this file are executed using the ISQL START command.

Several special purpose commands are available in ISQL. The UNLOAD command unloads the data from a table into a file. If the INTERNAL option of the UNLOAD command is used, HP SQL structural information is stored with the file. The file can be used only to load the data back into HP SQL in the exact format it was unloaded. If the EXTERNAL option of the UNLOAD command is used, the file is stored as a flat ASCII file. The LOAD command is used to read data from a file back into an HP SQL table and also has an INTERNAL/EXTERNAL option similar to the UNLOAD. More information is presented later on the reasons for using these commands.

Because program development usually entails quite a bit of programming and debugging, preprocessing programs which are in the development stages in a production DBE is generally not recommended. Preprocessing a program reduces concurrency in a multi-user DBE because the system catalog is locked until preprocessing finishes. A preprocessing session is treated as a single transaction and tends to quickly fill buffers and log files. Also, a module that is not fully debugged may cause problems for other DBE users. The solution, then, is to develop and preprocess the program in a development version of the DBE. The module is stored in the development DBE as a file, which can be installed into the production DBE by using the INSTALL command in ISQL.

Concurrent Usage of an HP SQL Database

As mentioned earlier, HP SQL automatically locks around transactions. HP SQL does either page-level or table-level locks. If a table is defined as PUBLIC or PUBLICREAD, HP SQL holds shared-read locks at the page level and exclusive-write locks at the table level. If the table is defined as PRIVATE, HP SQL holds exclusive-read locks at the table level and exclusive-write locks at the table level. The LOCK TABLE command can be used to override certain aspects of the default locking scheme. A page-level lock can be increased to a table-level lock. The mode of a table-level lock can be changed from shared to exclusive -- or from exclusive to shared.

All locks, whether automatic or explicitly created by LOCK TABLE, are held until the end of a transaction. For this reason, it is important that transactions be as short as possible. However, even when transactions are carefully defined, deadlock situations can occur. A deadlock occurs when two processes suspend, each waiting for a resource that is held by the other suspended process.

HP SQL handles deadlocks in the following manner. Before suspending a process that requires an unobtainable lock, HP SQL checks to see if the suspension would cause a deadlock situation to develop. If so, HP SQL aborts the transaction with the larger priority number. Priorities can be assigned to transactions via an option of the BEGIN WORK command. If two transactions have the same priority, HP SQL aborts the more recently started transaction. Any partial effects of the aborted transaction are rolled back.

HP SQL Recovery Mechanisms

HP SQL's logging and recovery mechanisms require every HP SQL transaction to be logged to a file. The default logfile is a no-archive-mode logfile. Basically, it stores transactions only until they are committed. Then logfile space is reclaimed. With this type of logging, you can recover the DBE to a logically consistent state after a soft system failure. The first START DBE or CONNECT command issued to a DBE initiates a Roll-Back Recovery of the DBE. All logical transactions that were incomplete at the time of the failure are rolled out of the database. Because there are relatively few transactions in a no-archive-mode logfile, the recovery time is short.

Archive-mode logging is provided for those who require a higher level of recovery assurance. In archive-mode logging, every transaction made against the DBE since the last time it was stored on a backup medium is kept in the archive-mode logfile. In the event of a soft system failure, the standard Roll-Back Recovery is run. However, in the event of a disc media failure, where the DBEFiles are damaged, a Roll-Forward Recovery is necessary.

In Roll-Forward Recovery, the corrupted DBE is purged, a backup copy of the DBE is restored from the backup medium, and assuming that the archive-mode logfile was not also corrupted by the media failure, all the transactions that were complete at the time the failure occurred are reapplied to the database. How long this recovery takes depends upon the complexity and number of transactions in the archive-mode logfile. If it should happen that both the DBE files *and* the logfiles are damaged by the media failure, the only recovery alternative is to restore the latest version of the DBE from the backup medium -- that is, unless you were using dual logging. Dual logging is provided for those who require maximum assurance that recovery will be possible if there is a serious media failure. The cost of this kind of assurance is increased overhead. Dual logging causes every logfile record to be written to two logfiles, which are on separate storage media.

Some Performance Notes

At the start of the chapter it was mentioned that relational databases are often noted for poor performance. HP SQL has some design features that are obviously geared towards improving performance.

For instance, all programs are preprocessed into executable code at compilation time to cut down on run-time overhead. HP SQL also stores extensive information on DBE activity in the system catalog, which can be viewed by the database administrator as a guidepost to tuning the DBE. For a database to perform well, its indexes must be effectively reducing the amount of disc I/O necessary to retrieve information. Stored in the system view is information on the cluster count of an index. This count indicates how many times HP SQL has to access a different data page in order to retrieve the next row during an index scan. The greater the cluster count, the more potential I/O when a query that uses that index is processed.

A good guideline to follow is that if the cluster count is greater than half the value of the number of pages in the table (another piece of information in the system view), the clustering index is no longer performing well. Over the course of time, it is expected that the performance of indexes will deteriorate. As rows are inserted into a table, the indexes expand in number of pages and levels. As rows are deleted, the number of index pages may decrease, but the number of levels remains at an unnecessarily high level.

When the system view shows that the performance of a clustering index has deteriorated, the table should be unloaded using the UNLOAD INTERNAL command with an ORDER BY clause to ensure maximum clustering. All rows and indexes on the table should be deleted. Then the clustering index should be recreated and the table reloaded using the LOAD INTERNAL command. All remaining indexes should then be recreated. Periodic use of this procedure ensures good clustering on the clustering index.

Care needs to be taken about configuring too much space for table pages. Not only does it waste disc space, it also degrades the performance of serial scans because they have to read lots of empty space in order to find the entries. It is particularly pointless to over-configure storage space for an HP SQL database, because additional storage can be easily and dynamically added.

VI

Languages

16

An Overview of Compiler Features

The intention of this chapter is to introduce the new compiler features of MPE XL. We begin with a review of the MPE V Segmenter process, and continue with discussions of the new MPE XL Linkedit process, the Optimizer, and the Object Code Translator. The chapter contains specific information regarding new features of interest to programmers creating software explicitly designed for MPE XL.

The Segmenter Process

Compatibility Mode (CM) compilers produce User Subprogram Libraries (USL), that must be prepared into program files before they can be run. This preparation is done with the :PREP command, which runs a program called the 'Segmenter'. The Segmenter on MPE XL is the same segmenter as on MPE V. It accepts only CM code (RL, SL, USL) and produces CM program files (file code = 1029 = PROG).

The Segmenter is an old product, dating from the first days of the HP 3000. It provides a bare bones mechanism for users to maintain libraries of compiled code. One serious limitation of the Segmenter is its handling of Relocatable Libraries (RL). An RL contains one or more compiled procedures, and is built by copying them from USL files over a period of time. At :PREP time, the Segmenter allows the specification of a single RL file which will be searched for otherwise missing procedures. All external procedures that are found in the RL are bundled into a single segment, which is added to the program file being built by the Segmenter. The limitation here is that the RL may contain only a single segment, and all procedures imported from an RL must reside in a single segment of the resulting program file. This limitation severely restricts the usability of RL files for many applications.

The last important file maintained by the Segmenter is the Segmented Library file (SL), which contains procedures in segmented form, i.e. they exist as executable code segments. SL files are intended for procedures that are used by many programs. For example, system intrinsics such as FOPEN are in an SL. While RL files contain code that is bound to each program, code in an SL is shared by many programs. SL files are used for final resolution of external references at run-time.

MPE allows only three possible choices for using SL files with the :RUN command:

□ look only in SL.PUB.SYS for external procedures. This is the default option.

□ look first in SL.PUB.*programaccount* for external procedures, then in SL.PUB.SYS. This is requested by specifying ';LIB=P' as an option on the :RUN command.

□ look first in SL.*programgroup.programaccount* for external procedures, then in SL.PUB.*programaccount*, then in SL.PUB.SYS. This is requested by specifying ';LIB=G' as an option on the :RUN command.

MPE will look for SL files in the account and group of the program being run, not that of the user running the program. Also, the only file name examined by the loader is 'SL' -- no other names are allowed.

One of the few recent enhancements to the Segmenter was the ability to request that information concerning the names of procedures in the USL and RL be carried over to program and SL files. This is requested with the FPMAP option of the :PREP and :ADDSL commands.

In different terminology, the USL file and RL file interaction is an example of link time binding, and the PROG file and SL file interaction is an example of load time binding.

Both MPE V and MPE XL provide run time binding. This type of binding is where a program calls an intrinsic to request that a particular procedure be 'loaded' and made available to be called. On MPE XL, run time binding is available for both Compatibility Mode and Native Mode programs. Note that run time binding in MPE V and CM is resolved from different SL files than load-time binding.

The Linkedit Process

Native Mode (NM) compilers produce Spectrum Object Modules (SOM files) that must be linked into program files before they can be run. This linking is done with a Native Mode program called 'Linkedit'. Linkedit, often referred to as the linker, accepts only NM code and produces NM program files (file code = 1030 = NMPRG).

Linkedit provides many advances over the capabilities of Segmenter. One of the most important is the ability to specify a list of libraries at link time, and a list of libraries to be used at load time.

Linkedit is invoked either by the :LINK command or by running LINKEDIT.PUB.SYS. The syntax for the :LINK command is:

```
:LINK FROM=file [,file]... [;TO=destfile]
      [;RL=rlfile [,rlfile]...]
      [;XL=xlfile [,xlfile]...]
      [;PRIVLEV=privlev]
      [;XLEAST=privlev]
      [;CAP=caplist]
      [;ENTRY=entryname]
      [;STACK=maxstackpages]
      [;HEAP=maxheappages]
      [;UNSAT=unsatname]
      [;NODEBUG]
      [;PARMCHECK=checklevel]
      [;MAP]
      [;SHOW]
```

When Linkedit resolves references to external procedures, functions, or global variables, it checks to see if the types in actuality match those that were declared by the caller. The ';PARMCHECK' option specifies what should happen if type mismatches are detected.

A valuable feature of Linkedit is the ability to specify a procedure to be linked to satisfy any unresolved external procedure or function name. On MPE V, if a program cannot be run because of the error 'UNRESOLVED EXTERNALS', the user is stuck; nothing short of providing the missing routines will allow the program to be run. On MPE XL, if a Native Mode program is missing one (or more) routines, the :LINK (or :RUN) command's ';UNSAT' option allows the user to specify:

```
:LINK ...;UNSAT=QUIT

or

:RUN  ...;UNSAT=QUIT
```

Then, when the program is run, it will load with no problems. If one of the missing routines is called, QUIT is called instead.

Linkedit is obviously part of a new generation of tools. The user interface is dramatically better than that of Segmenter, which makes firm distinctions between SL, USL, RL, and program files, and has a separate set of commands to manipulate each type of file. Linkedit links all types of files (NMPRG, XL, and RL) with one command (:LINK), and a uniform user interface.

The Optimizer

The purpose of an optimizing compiler is to create more efficient procedures. However, optimization can be a two-edged sword. While it often can clean up poor coding practices, it can also generate code that is totally cryptic.

Long code paths are a characteristic of RISC-based software. Anything that can reduce the length of a path will invariably speed up execution of a procedure. High level optimization can significantly reduce the length of code paths, but there is a cost: the resulting code is meaningless when compared to the original source. Humans simply do not write software in this fashion.

Most of the NM languages (COBOL II/XL, HP Pascal/XL, HP FORTRAN 77/XL) share a common code emission mechanism, called 'Universal Code' (UCODE), which can be viewed as a machine code for a hypothetical 32-bit machine. UCODE is translated into Spectrum machine code in a special format known as 'SLLIC' (Spectrum Low Level Interface Code, pronounced 'slick') by the UCODE routines. A set of routines known as the SLLIC package reads the SLLIC format and generates a SOM file after doing optional optimization. The optimization is possible only because the compilers that generate UCODE pass optimization information to the UCODE routines which in turn passes the information to the SLLIC package. Thus, all of the compilers emitting UCODE share the same optimizer. The HP C/XL compiler, perhaps reflecting its origins on another machine, bypasses UCODE and directly emits SLLIC without optimization information. Because of this, SLLIC is unable to further optimize the code emitted by the HP C/XL compiler. However, the C compiler can do its own optimization before emitting SLLIC code, if requested.

SPLash!, for reasons discussed later in this chapter, tends to produce better unoptimized code than the UCODE compilers. As a result, its need for an optimizer is less, and at first release has a fairly simple one. SPLash! does not emit either UCODE or SLLIC, but builds SOMs directly.

COBOL II/XL, HP Pascal/XL and HP FORTRAN 77/XL provide for three levels of code optimization. By default, no optimization is performed, allowing the symbolic debugger to be used to debug the program. Level 1 optimizing makes the most common type of improvements to reduce code space and shorten execution time. This type of optimization is done over smaller portions of source code. Level 2 utilizes all of the optimizing algorithms to reduce space and shorten execution times by optimizing over an entire procedure.

Code optimization is only done at the request of the programmer. In HP Pascal/XL, COBOL II/XL, and HP FORTRAN 77/XL, a new compiler directive must be used to specify the level of optimization: '$optimize'. The effects of the various types of optimization are covered in chapter 6.

In the default case, none of the languages emit optimized code, but they do emit debugging and tracing information that is absolutely invaluable during the debugging and development phase of a writing a program. Turning on optimization loses *all* of this extra information.

Unoptimized code from the UCODE based compilers inefficient. This may sound like a nasty comment, but the reasons behind it are simple and predictable. The compilers emit very unoptimium UCODE *by design*, since the theory was that *all* optimization should be done by the optimizer. According to this theory, compilers would often optimize incorrectly if they were allowed to do it themselves. Additionally, every compiler would have to have tailored optimizing code written for it. In fact, the design of UCODE specifically forbids certain types of compiler optimization from being done while generating UCODE. The result is pretty obvious -- if you don't turn on the optimizer (at least at level 1), you get poor code.

As mentioned earlier, neither HP C/XL nor SPLash! use the UCODE mechanism, so they tend to produce more optimum code from the start.

The Object Code Translator

When MPE XL 'executes' CM code, it is really emulating it with an assembly language program executing in Native Mode. The process of emulating the stack-based HP 3000 code works very well. It is interesting to note that the emulator is, in effect, a microcoded implementation of a CISC instruction set, just like the implementation of all prior HP 3000s (II, III, 4x, 3x, and 6x families). However, no matter how well written an emulator is, it always has certain inefficiencies that could be removed if a program written in the emulated instruction set were to be translated into the native mode instruction set. HP realized this even on the older HP 3000s -- the HP 3000 Series 70 gained some of its extra speed by translating part of MPE to microcode.

On MPE XL, there are two ways of speeding up CM code: using a Native Mode compiler to compile a program; and using the Object Code Translator (OCT). Using a Native Mode compiler is covered in Chapter 18, and is really a 'sideways' solution to the speedup problem -- it simply avoids CM code entirely. What if your program cannot be recompiled with an NM compiler? This could be the case if it was written in COBOL/3000, FORTRAN 66, BASIC/3000, if the source code was lost, or if some aspects of the program prohibit easy recompilation (e.g.: dependence on 16-bit addresses). For these problems, HP has provided a solution called the 'Object Code Translator' (OCT).

The OCT takes a CM program file (or a CM SL) as input and translates the CM code into NM code. The resulting output file still looks like a CM program (the filecode is PROG), albeit that the file is from eight to seventeen times larger than the original input file.

OCT analyzes the CM code sequences and attempts to produce an efficient NM instruction sequence to accomplish the same goals. Consider the CM code emitted by the SPL fragment:

```
BEGIN
    DOUBLE X;              ! 32-bit integer
    DOUBLE A, B, C;       ! 32-bit integers
                          ! A is at DB+2, B at DB+4, C at DB+6
    A := B + C;
```

The code sequence produced by SPL/3000 and the translation of it produced by OCT are:

```
SPL/3000    OCT                 Comments


LDD DB+4    LDH  8(1,10),12     ; R12 := DB+4 (B's upper 16 bits)
LDD DB+6    LDH  10(1,10),13    ; R13 := DB+5 (B's lower 16 bits)
            LDH  12(1,10),14    ; R14 := DB+6 (C's upper 16 bits)
            LDH  14(1,10),15    ; R15 := DB+7 (C's lower 16 bits)
            DEP  14,15,16,15    ; R15 := C (combined R14 & R15)
            DEP  12,15,16,13    ; R13 := B (combined R12 & R13)
DADD        DEPI 0,20,1,5       ; R5.(20:1) := 0  reset overflow flag
                                ; R5 is emulated CM STATUS Register
            ADD,NSV 15,13,13    ; R13 := R13 + R15
            BLE  720(7,20)      ; call millicode for overflow check
                                ; note: branch is skipped if the
                                ;       add did not overflow
            OR   13,0,6         ; R6 := R13
            ADDC 0,0,8          ; R8 := carry flag
            EXTRS 13,15,16,12   ; R12 := upper 16 bits of R13
STD DB+2    STH  12,4(1,10)     ; upper 16 bits A := R12
            STH  13,6(1,10)     ; lower 16 bits A := R13
```

Note that the NM code took 14 instructions to implement the 3 instructions of CM code, not even counting the amount of code used by the millicode routine.

A program can be translated with the command:

```
:OCTCOMP OLDPROG, NEWPROG
```

If it looks like a duck, and it walks like a duck, and it quacks like a duck -- is it a duck? Just what is a program produced by the OCT? Is it a 'CM program' or an 'NM program'? The answer is: neither, either, or both -- it depends on your viewpoint.

The 'NM program' argument is based on the fact that a translated program will *usually* be executing Native Mode code and thus should be called an NM program.

The 'CM program' argument is based on two interesting facts: first, the NM code is still bound by the 16-bit limitations of the CM code. In fact, the data being manipulated is still within the CM stack of the program, not the NM stack. This argument recognizes that the NM instructions being executed are conceptually nothing more than the same NM instructions that the emulator would have executed to emulate the original code, but without the overhead instructions. The second interesting fact is that the NM code can, and often does, drop back into emulation mode from time to time. For example, if the CM code contained an instruction like 'XEQ 0' (execute the CM instruction found on the top of the stack), the translated code calls the emulator to execute the instruction. Furthermore, when the translated code calls an intrinsic, it is the CM version of the intrinsic that is executed.

The OCT can translate segmented libraries (SL) as well as program files. On MPE XL, the system segmented library (SL.PUB.SYS) is already translated.

If a file produced by OCT were transported to an MPE V-based HP 3000, it could still be executed with the :RUN command. The NM loader looks at previously unused information located in record 0 of the :PROG file that OCT changes to be a pointer to the start of the NM code. Since the older HP 3000s ignore this field, they will continue to access only the CM code. (These words are at octal %25, %26, %130, and %165.) This capability appears to be a "feature"; that is, it certainly works this way *now*, but there is no guarantee it will work this way in the future. Certainly, Hewlett-Packard does not officially support this feature.

Programs produced by the OCT are almost always faster than emulated programs, but are not as fast as recompiling in a Native Mode language.

17

HPPA Languages

The good news about languages that work under MPE XL is that just about everything that works on MPE V will continue to work, in one fashion or another. In Chapter 16 we discussed the fundamental changes in the methods used to create executable program code -- the changes were significant and revolutionary. In this chapter, you will see that remarkably little has changed in the languages themselves.

Some compilers, transported from MPE V, produce Compatibility Mode code, which executes slowly under MPE XL. These are known as 'CM compilers'. These compilers do have the advantage though, that programs will compile and run without modification on both MPE V and MPE XL. Newer compilers produce Native Mode code, allowing access to the speed and huge addressing space of the HPPA computers, but requiring varying degrees of migration if the same program needs to run under MPE V. These are known as 'NM compilers'.

The focus of the chapter will be HP Pascal/XL, the Native Mode compiler of choice for the HP 3000 900 Series. It is one of the few languages that is significantly different from the corresponding MPE V implementation. A summary of other languages will also be presented, outlining the fundamentals of each and the treatment under MPE XL. The chapter will conclude with a discussion of interlanguage calls.

Pascal

Pascal was designed by Niklaus Wirth in Switzerland in 1968. It was intended as a language to be used to teach the fundamentals of structured programming. A block-structured language in the tradition of PL\I or ALGOL 60, the language is quite intolerant of 'sloppy' coding techniques, flagging as syntax errors such things as type mixing within a statement. Pascal began to get a foothold in university computer science courses in the mid 1970's when Dr. Ken Bowles of the University of California at San Diego implemented Pascal on inexpensive microcomputers. When students trained in Pascal graduated, Pascal found its way into the world of commercial data processing.

A sure sign of Pascal's 'arrival' occurred when the American National Standards Institute (ANSI) developed a standard definition for it. Soon after, a superset of the ANSI standard was defined by the International Standards Organization (ISO). Hewlett-Packard then developed a superset of both the ANSI and the ISO standards to be used for all Pascal compilers to be developed at HP. This is referred to as HP Standard Pascal. It should come as no surprise that HP Pascal/XL was developed as yet another superset -- this time of HP Standard Pascal.

Some of the extensions in HP Pascal/XL allow the programmer to 'turn off' much of the rigorous error checking inherent in the original Pascal language. Together with other system programming extentions, this has allowed HP to do almost all of its system programming for the HP 3000 900 Series in HP Pascal/XL. The MPE XL operating system is written primarily in HP Pascal/XL, and the HP Pascal/XL compiler is itself written completely in HP Pascal/XL.

If there are any 'nits to be picked' regarding the extensions that HP has implemented, it has to do with the *semantics* that have been chosen to describe them. They are constantly referred to as *system programming* extensions, when in fact the extensions are essential to and vitally necessary for *application programming*. While this wordplay may seem trivial, you must recall that HP has frequently taken action to prevent user program access to features that are deemed to be of a 'systems' nature. If these extensions are really classified as not being of interest to applications programming, it is doubtful that corresponding improvements can be expected in Pascal/V.

Due to HP's obvious commitment to Pascal and due to Pascal's growing acceptance in the data processing world, HP Pascal/XL is destined to be a major language of choice for many application systems for the HP 3000 900 Series. It offers the advantages that come with a block-structured language, along with features such as record structures that are often required for commercial applications. For financial applications however, one drawback exists: there is no direct support for packed decimal data types. One is forced to store dollar amounts as pennies or tenths of pennies in an integer variable, or be prepared for ten dimes to equal $0.9999999999 if real variables are used, or write the financial portions of the application in COBOL.

As noted earlier, Pascal/V is an extended version of ANSI standard Pascal. It emits code for MPE V-based HP 3000s, but both the compiler and programs compiled by it will run on MPE XL. Note, however, that Pascal/V is not officially supported on MPE XL. Pascal/V extensions include: strings, structured constants and constant expressions, longreal data type, separate compilation, I/O extensions (direct file access), and interface to MPE intrinsics.

HP Pascal/XL is also an extended version of ANSI Standard Pascal, and it emits Native Mode code. There are extensions that facilitate using it for real world programming applications. Among the features available in HP Pascal/XL are: Pascal/V extensions, modules, exception handling, type coercion, procedure/function variables, crunched data structures, pointer arithmetic, extensible procedures, 32-bit and 64-bit pointers, and predefined 'shortint' type.

Programs written in Pascal/V can be migrated, with some effort, to HP Pascal/XL. Migration issues are documented in Section VII and include:

☐ address manipulation differences

☐ 'shortint' (predefined in HP Pascal/XL, manually defined in Pascal/V -- the manual definition does *not* result in an identical type to the predefined type)

☐ data alignment differences

The ability of Pascal to call routines written in other languages has not improved at all with MPE XL. As will be discussed later in this chapter, interlanguage calls with Pascal demand greater care than with any other language.

Other Languages

There are, of course, other languages available under MPE XL. The majority run in Compatibility Mode, and those that are Native Mode are little changed from their MPE V counterpart. The most obvious difference between CM and NM versions is the speed of execution of the resulting object code.

There are several versions of **BASIC** available, but only as CM programs. BASIC stands for Beginners All-purpose Symbolic Instruction Code, and while very impressive extensions of the language are available in the Personal Computer marketplace, the HP 3000 implementations have been somewhat, well -- basic.

BASIC/V and HP Business BASIC/V are available in both compiled and interpreter versions on MPE V. HP will only support HP Business BASIC/V on MPE XL, and only in CM at first release. The other versions actually work, however.

Two implementations of the **C** programming language are available. The C which has been running on HP 3000's prior to the 900 Series is a third-party product tailored to MPE V and earlier systems. It is supported by its maker on MPE XL as a CM program emitting Compatibility Mode code. HP's implementation of C is called HP C/XL, a Native Mode program emitting NM code only. HP C/XL follows Harbison & Steele, which confers a good deal of ANSI compatibility.

C on MPE V and MPE XL is of interest primarily to those programmers enamored of its notational idiosyncrasies and those who want to transport significant programs written in C from another computer family to the HP 3000. Both interests are somewhat thwarted, however, by implementation compromises necessitated by differences between UNIX and MPE and the architectures of C's traditional host computers versus the stack-based HP 3000. Conversely, these same compromises ease the task of an HP 3000 programmer learning C, and facilitate the translation to C of applications written in other HP 3000 languages. MPE intrinsics, and thus the subsystems they support, are callable directly.

Though well over twenty years old, **COBOL** (COmmon Business Oriented Language) continues to be a major language in industry and government data processing applications. Hewlett-Packard offers two versions of the language, each virtually identical to the other. The COBOL II/V and COBOL II/XL compilers are based on the 1985 ANSI standard, known as 'COBOL X3.23-1985'. They both have entry points to compile programs written to the 1974 standard, COBOL X3.23-1974. Neither is a full high level implementation.

COBOL II/V emits Compatibility Mode code, and COBOL II/XL emits Native Mode code. Both compilers have HP extensions to the language, including a pre-processor that provides macro ($DEFINE) and file inclusion ($INCLUDE) functions. Also, numerous debugging aids allow the programmer to debug programs in an efficient manner. Both provide symbol and verb cross references and high level access to MPE intrinsics.

By using ANSI Standard COBOL Input and Output operations, both MPE files (for sequential and random access) and KSAM files (for indexed sequential access) can be accessed. Other HP subsystems, such as VPLUS/V for terminal handling, or TurboIMAGE/XL for data management can be accessed through the use of procedure libraries and intrinsics.

COBOL II is the second COBOL compiler from HP. The first, originally called 'COBOL/3000', is COBOL I. COBOL/3000 is an implementation of the 1968 ANSI COBOL standard. It has been obsoleted by HP and removed from their price list. Nevertheless, programs compiled with COBOL/3000 will run in Compatibility Mode on MPE XL.

The most recent ANSI standard for **FORTRAN** (FORmula TRANslator) is FORTRAN 77 X3.9-1978. HP FORTRAN 77/V and HP FORTRAN 77/XL are CM and NM implementations of this standard. Both compilers provide: FORTRAN 66/V compatibility support; HP extensions; MPE access; and MIL-STD-1753 language extensions.

Although the NM and CM versions of the FORTRAN 77 compiler appear to be completely compatible, migration problems can arise if the '$HP 3000_16$' option is not used in HP FORTRAN 77/XL.

Prior to FORTRAN 77, the standard was FORTRAN 66 (ANSI standard X3.9-1966). HP FORTRAN 66/V has a number of HP extensions, which aid in the development and debugging of programs. Although this language is not officially supported on MPE XL, both the compiler and programs produced by it will run. The two FORTRAN 77 compilers come with a conversion utility to aid migrating FORTRAN 66 code to FORTRAN 77 code.

Introduced by IBM in 1964, **RPG** (Report Program Generator) has evolved through RPGII and RPGIII to its current status as one of the most widely used languages for minicomputer business systems. RPG/V closely follows the standard set by RPGII on the IBM System/36. It is available in Compatibility Mode under MPE XL at first release, and will execute in Native Mode as RPG/XL at second release.

RPG differs from other standard languages in that it uses a non-procedural source code language made up of 'specifications' which define the job to be accomplished. The compiler processes the specifications according to the RPG Cycle, a predefined logic framework that reads records, calculates and outputs records. The programmer defines the file and processing environment through a set of specifications.

RPG/V provides a complete applications development environment on the HP 3000. MPE, KSAM and TurboIMAGE file interfaces are fully implemented and the programmer has a choice of two HP supported screen interfaces for interactive programming: VPLUS and RSI (RPG Screen Interface). In fact, RPG is the *only* language with two supported screen interfaces.

HP provides an easy migration path for RPG programs from IBM System/3X (/3, /32, /34 and /36) computers with the TRANSFORM software and services. The IBM programs and procedures are converted and recompiled to run identically under MPE V and MPE XL.

SPL is the Systems Program Language for MPE V, and it is based on ALGOL 60. While it lacks several of the features of ALGOL 60, it provides impressive extensions including: macros, INCLUDE files, MOVE/SCAN statements/expressions, ASSEMBLE, direct usage of hardware stack, bit manipulation, and access to stack-based HP 3000 registers.

SPL/V emits Compatibility Mode code and is supported by HP on MPE XL. Some of MPE XL is written in SPL.

When speed-critical applications are being written for MPE V, SPL is the language of choice. SPL's leanness means that the compiler emits very clean code for all of the high level constructs. SPL allows the programmer to have total control over data layout, stack manipulation and (via the ASSEMBLE statement) over the emitted code. Like C, SPL allows the programmer to write unreadable programs. Also like C, SPL's macro facilities allow high-level 'extensions' of the language -- a feature sorely lacking in Pascal.

SPLash! is an implementation of SPL that is very compatible with SPL/V. SPLash! emits Native Mode code and has extensions to SPL that include:

- 32-and 64-bit pointers

- procedure and function variables

- very large arrays

- it calls -- and is callable by -- other NM languages.

In the early days of HPPA, HP decided against developing a Native Mode compiler for SPL. One reason given was that SPL was tied too closely to the stack architecture of the MPE V-based HP 3000s. Fortunately, some SPL afficionados realized what HP had not: the basic premise of a RISC machine is that all compilers emit microcode. Furthermore, this microcode is emitted with a software-imposed model of a machine in mind. With this insight, they realized that the NM compilers were emitting microcode that modelled a 32-bit stack machine which happened to have a lot of general purpose registers. They then realized that they could write a compiler for SPL that would emit microcode modelling the stack-based HP 3000.

SPLash! maintains a 16-bit wide stack in the middle of the ordinary 32-bit wide Native Mode stack. With this stack, nearly every stack-based HP 3000 machine instruction and SPL construct can be translated to NM code. SPLash!, however, does not slavishly use the stack. For some expressions, for example:

```
A(I := I + 2) := A(K) * J;
```

the stack is never used. Instead SPLash! makes use of the many general purpose registers of HPPA. As a result, some NM code sequences to implement SPL constructs take as few HPPA instructions as they did stack-based HP 3000 instructions.

SPLash! is available from Software Research Northwest, Inc.

Interlanguage Calls

On MPE V, calling routines written in one language from a program written in another varies from mildly difficult to nearly impossible. On MPE XL, things haven't gotten any better. In fact, they are worse, but for an understandable reason: there are more languages, and two execution modes (NM and CM). For information on calling routines in different execution modes, see Chapter 18.

Most languages have constructs to allow the programmer to call an 'external' routine, where an external routine can be defined as one whose body is not declared within the same compilation unit. The following example shows how some of the languages would call an external routine, FOO, with two parameters. Parameter 1 is a 16-bit integer by value, parameter 2 is an 80-byte character array by reference:

```
BASIC                call foo (i, a$)

HP Business BASIC/V  call foo (i, a$)
```

```
C/XL                    extern void foo();
                        int i;
                        char a[80];
                        foo (i,a);


COBOL II/XL             call "FOO" using \i\, @a.


HP FORTRAN 77/XL        call foo (\i\, a)


HP Pascal/XL            procedure foo (i : shortint; var a : pac 80);
                                external;
                        foo (i, a);


SPL                     procedure foo (i, a);
                                value   i;
                                integer i;
                                byte array a;
                             option external, check 3;
                        foo (i, a);


RPG/XL          C                       MOVEL'FOO      PNAME
                C                       EXIT RUNPGM
                C                       PARM           PNAME
                C                       PARM           STATUS
```

When calling an external routine, the ideal is to have the computer, and not the programmer or user, automatically verify the answers to the following four questions. Does the external routine exist? Is the caller calling it with the correct number of parameters? Are all of the parameters of the correct type? Does the caller of the routine know what type of result, if any, the routine returns? Some languages provide constructs to request this, some do not.

In SPL, for example, the programmer may specify a 'check level' from 0 to 3 (0 is the default). Each level causes MPE to check more stringently:

```
Level                   Checking
-----           ------------------------------------


0               Routine exists?


1               Routine exists?
```

```
                          Type of routine matches what program expects?


              2           Routine exists?
                          Type of routine matches what program expects?
                          Proper number of parameters?


              3           Routine exists?
                          Type of routine matches what program expects?
                          Proper number of parameters?
                          Parameter types match?
```

The 'check level' applied to a link-time or load-time reference to an external routine
is the lesser of the check level the actual routine was compiled with, and the check
level the calling program specified for the external reference.

Prior to Pascal/V, all compilers on the HP 3000 adhered to this convention. These
compilers built USL files which contained compiled code and, for every actual
routine or reference to an external routine, the checking information. This
information simply consisted of a single 16-bit word for every routine and one word
for every parameter of every routine. It was the responsibility of the SEGMENTER
(see Chapter 16) to check call compatibility at link-time and the LOADER to check at
load-time.

The implementors of Pascal/V muddied the issue of interlanguage calls, and those
responsible for HP Pascal/XL did nothing to clarify it. Faced with Pascal's ability to
define new types via the RECORD statement, they chose to emit a much more
sophisticated data structure to properly describe the parameters of a routine and its
functional result (if any). Unfortunately, they failed to extend the SEGMENTER
(and later, the LINKER). Instead they chose to re-use checking levels 1, 2, and 3.

As a result, programs written in Pascal can correctly call external routines written in
languages other than Pascal *only* if the external declaration declares these routines
to be in a language other than Pascal. Similarly, programs written in languages other
than Pascal must turn off checking (i.e.: use level 0) when declaring calls to routines
written in Pascal. If Pascal is involved in any way, the inability to easily change the
specification of the external routine's language compounds the difficulty.

VII

Migration
Issues

18

From MPE V to MPE XL

In any discussion of HP Precision architecture, migration of applications is a major concern. This chapter explains some of the difficulties that can be encountered in migrating applications from an MPE V-based HP 3000 to an MPE XL-based system.

The word 'migration' refers to the process by which a large group of items moves from one location to another. A central concept of migration is that this movement does not occur all at once, but is gradual over a period of time. The migration path defined by HP has many possible stops along the way and many options: Compatibility Mode, translated mode, and Native Mode.

What is Migration?

The image presented by HP during the initial product announcement -- and in subsequent public events -- gives the impression that conversion to Native Mode is just a matter of 'a simple recompile'. This is an oversimplification of the problem and can mislead a potential customer. More accurately, migration from MPE V to MPE XL, *while simple when compared to the classic mainframe computer migration scenario*, can involve varying degrees of code and database changes.

Word Lengths: 16-bit Versus 32-bit

The major difference between MPE V-based HP 3000s and HPPA-based machines is the difference in word length: 16 bits for the MPE V-based HP 3000s and 32 bits for the HP Precision Architecture machines. The MPE V-based HP 3000s *can* manipulate 32-bit integers, but not in Native Mode. (They use a microcode loop, which takes longer.) HPPA systems can perform 32-bit integer arithmetic in a single clock cycle.

The primary benefit of the 32-bit word length on HPPA systems is the increased address space, which makes migrating from the MPE V-based HP 3000 to an MPE XL-based HP 3000 quite worthwhile. The old stack limitation of 64K bytes is a thing of the past, because you can have very large arrays of data within the stack. Even larger arrays are possible using mapped files (see Chapter 11).

One migration difficulty arises because of MPE XL's 32-bit words and their address alignment in memory, which is dictated by the design of the hardware which accesses memory. In order to retrieve the proper number of bytes from memory, the hardware must use the correct addressing scheme.

In a CISC (Complex Instruction Set Computing) machine, microcode easily accesses and fetches until the total number of bytes requested by the operation is fetched. Then the whole package is presented to the requesting software. The MPE V-based HP 3000s perform this function in a similar fashion, but rather than accessing memory a byte at a time, the hardware fetches 16-bit words. If a byte-aligned operation is requested, such as an MVB (Move Bytes) instruction, the 16-bit words are masked by the microcode to deliver the proper number of bytes.

A prime goal of HPPA is to keep the hardware as simple as possible while still incorporating the needed functionality. This is done by defining separate machine instructions for every type of memory access length. For example, STW (STore Word) stores a full 32 bits to memory; STH (STore Half-word) stores 16 bits; and STB (STore Byte) stores only 8 bits. There is a corresponding set of load instructions. In this way, the hardware is made simpler by pre-defining the word size to be accessed, rather than interpreting the proper size at run time. As with other facets of RISC, this places a greater burden on the software.

HPPA instructions demand that the data be aligned on specific boundaries within memory. For example, data accessed by a 32-bit operation (STW or LDW) must be aligned on a byte address divisible by 4. Half-word operations demand 16-bit (divisible by 2) alignment, and byte operations require the data be on a byte boundary. For example, if a 32-bit integer was stored at the memory location $40000088, the data in a register could be stored to this address, since it is divisible by 4. A store would not be possible at address $4000008a, since it is not evenly divisible by four. Although the requirements seem somewhat arbitrary, they simplify the hardware design and achieve fast machine-execution time.

Whether an address can be divisible by two or four can be determined by looking at the low-order two bits of the address. If the last bit is 0, then the address is divisible by two and is 16-bit aligned. If both bits are 0, then the address is divisible by four and is 32-bit aligned.

Some problems, however, can occur because of this feature. Specifically, data imbedded in a record structure can be aligned on different boundaries. Data that is correctly aligned on an MPE V-based HP 3000 could cause problems on an MPE XL-based machine. For example, take the following COBOL data definition:

```
01  DATA-RECORD.
    03  FIRST-ITEM        PIC S9(04) COMP.
    03  SECOND-ITEM       PIC S9(08) COMP.
    03  THIRD-ITEM        PIC S9(08) COMP.
```

Since all COBOL '01 level' structures are 32-bit aligned, the first item is a 16-bit data item and will be properly aligned in all cases. The second and third items, however, are 32 bits each, and are not 32-bit aligned. If 'FIRST-ITEM' resides at some base address X, then 'SECOND-ITEM' is at X+2, and 'THIRD-ITEM' is at X+6. Thus, the statement:

```
ADD SECOND-ITEM TO THIRD-ITEM.
```

could cause a problem, because the two arguments are not on 32-bit boundaries. It is up to the compiler to resolve these differences. In this case, the COBOL compiler would have to generate two half-word loads for each item, perform a 32-bit add, then do two half-word stores of the result.

But a far worse problem can be created. The previous example assumed the storage allocation scheme was the same as that which exists on the MPE V-based HP 3000s. Data items of the type PIC S9(04) COMP are always assigned 16 bits, and anything larger is assigned 32 bits, until the limit for 32-bit storage has been reached. If the MPE XL COBOL compiler chooses to align data by default, the problem with performing calculations with non-aligned data disappears. But if this data record represents the COBOL working storage for an application disc data structure, this data alignment (packing) scheme poses grave problems for application migration, since the data already on the disc will not be the same as that represented within the migrated COBOL application.

A great number of these problems are extremely language-dependent. Many options exist in the languages to modify the defaults -- not only for data packing but for other options as well. (The specifics for each language will be discussed in Chapter 19.)

Compatibility Mode Versus Native Mode

To make migration from the MPE V-based HP 3000 easy, Hewlett-Packard added Compatibility Mode to MPE XL. (Compatibility Mode is an environment which allows programs compiled on MPE V-based HP 3000s to run on MPE XL with no recompilation.) The environment has two major components:

☐ A software emulator which reads each machine instruction from the MPE V program file and executes an equivalent set of HPPA instructions.

☐ Interfaces to all intrinsics (file system, TurboIMAGE, VPLUS, etc.) necessary for running user applications.

In effect, Compatibility Mode is a large program which treats an MPE V-based program file like a data file. Each word (machine instruction) of the program file is treated as a word of data, and a different routine is executed for each type of machine instruction encountered. When an external procedure is called, the emulator establishes the linkages to that routine and continues running, retrieving 16-bit machine instructions from the new procedure, and emulating them as well. Some of the Compatibility Mode procedures (such as the file system) also exist as Native Mode routines in MPE XL. For them, a small procedure is provided which receives the parameters provided by the Compatibility Mode program and remaps them to the addressing format of the Native Mode procedure. This small intermediate procedure, called a 'switch stub', is discussed later in the chapter.

In addition to executing the proper code sequences, the emulator must maintain a data structure that imitates the MPE V-based HP 3000 stack format. The different registers (Q, DL, DB, etc.) are emulated in software to allow code that relies on this format to run properly. Again, this adds overhead to Compatibility Mode emulation.

Along with the emulation of the MPE V-based HP 3000 instruction set goes the emulation of the limitations of the MPE V-based computers. Stack limits are still

64K, segment sizes are the same, and there is no access to any new features of MPE XL, such as mapped files. The program files used in Compatibility Mode have the same format and file designation (PROG) as those under MPE V.

Native Mode is the ideal execution mode under MPE XL. In this mode, the HPPA instruction set is used and the full benefits of the optimizer are realized. The machine instructions are executed directly in the hardware, just as the MPE V-based HP 3000 executes the 16-bit instruction in firmware. Program externals provided are also written in a Native Mode language, usually HP Pascal/XL or C/XL.

The Object Code Translator

Another type of Compatibility Mode exists which philosophically lies somewhere between the Compatibility Mode and Native Mode described above. As discussed in Chapter 16, this special brand of Compatibility Mode, called 'translated code', is created through a special program called the Object Code Translator (OCT). Translated object code is created by executing a command called 'OCTCOMP' which specifies a Compatibility Mode program file as input. OCT then translates each MPE V-based machine instruction into a sequence of Native Mode machine instructions, which is placed in the output file. This file can then be run like any other program.

The benefit of this type of scheme is that the translation is done once (at translate time) and not every time the machine instruction is fetched from the program file. The Native Mode machine instructions contained in the translated program file can be directly fetched by the hardware like a normal Native Mode program.

Theoretically the OCT could produce a program file with the filecode of NMPRG. Because there is a consistent one-to-many correspondence between Compatibility Mode and Native Mode instructions, you should be able to produce such a program file by this translation process. In reality, however, several factors prevent this from occurring.

The Compatibility Mode code in the source file runs under the assumption that the user stack exists and has a certain format. The procedures called by this Compatibility Mode program also assume this, and often the procedures execute operations totally dependent upon the stack being in a certain configuration. For example, virtually all intrinsics pass a condition code back to the caller by setting two bits in the Status Register of the stack marker laid down by the calling procedure. The Status Register is accessed by creating a dummy variable and assigning it the address of Q-1, which is the location of the Status Register placed by the PCAL instruction. When the EXIT instruction executes, the value at Q-1 is used to set the Hardware Status Register. Since the two bits containing the condition code were set by the called procedure, the hardware condition code is set to that value after the EXIT instruction is finished.

Because so much Compatibility Mode code runs under these assumptions, the OCT must create this environment at run time, just as the emulator does. Since the Native Mode instructions and stack format are different, you cannot have a truly Native Mode program which runs under the assumption that a Compatibility Mode stack exists. Because of this hybrid characteristic of translated programs, the code produced by OCT is itself a hybrid. Part of the translated program file is true Native Mode code, but the entire Compatibility Mode program file is retained. When the program is run, the emulator jumps back and forth between true Native Mode and Compatibility Mode. Compatibility Mode is entered whenever necessary, such as when an intrinsic is called. The Native Mode code maintains the complete CM stack structure.

The choice of which mode to use when migrating an application involves trade-offs in two areas: performance and ease of migration. Straight Compatibility Mode offers the easiest migration path. Essentially, the data files and program files are stored from the MPE V-based HP 3000, then restored onto the MPE XL-based system. Assuming all external factors are correct, such as the I/O configuration and accounting structure, the application will probably run as it did on the MPE V-based system. After the application is up and running, the programs can be migrated to Native Mode by compiling them with the appropriate MPE XL compiler. This seemingly trivial task is complicated by the way the compilers treat data areas and some required control statements.

If all of the source code for an application is available, migration to Native Mode is mostly a matter of recompilation, with a few minor changes. If some routines do not exist in a language available on MPE XL, or if the amount of code does not justify the purchase price of the Native Mode compiler, then a hybrid Native Mode-Compatibility Mode environment is called for.

The Switch

In order for Native Mode and Compatibility Mode code to co-exist in the same application, a method for alternating between the two modes is provided by what is generically known as the 'switch facility'.

A set of intrinsics is provided which allows user code to switch between Native Mode and Compatibility Mode, or vice-versa. There are basically two intrinsics which allow the alteration of execution mode:

- □ HPSWTONMNAME - This intrinsic is provided to switch from Compatibility Mode to Native Mode and is used if an application must remain in Compatibility Mode and must call a facility that is provided only in Native Mode. An example of this might be an application in SPL that calls the HPCICOMMAND intrinsic.

- □ HPSWITCHTOCM - This intrinsic is provided to switch from Native Mode to Compatibility Mode and is used to call code which must remain in Compatibility Mode from a migrated application. Compatibility Mode code might be appropriate for SL routines for which no source exists or when there is a small amount of code and purchasing the compiler is not cost effective.

Each process on the system is assigned both Native Mode and Compatibility Mode environments at run time, and the SWITCH facility transfers from one to the other. It builds the appropriate stack markers and transfers control to the MPE V-based emulator when desired, as in the case of HPSWITCHTOCM, or to the native hardware instruction set, as in the case of HPSWTONMNAME.

The main program mode is determined by the file code (NMPRG or PROG), and it is the responsibility of the system loader to determine the proper execution type at runtime. The switch facility comes into play when subroutines and procedures running in one mode must be called by a main program (or another procedure) running in the other. Thus, switching is done at the procedure level. A facility also must be provided to handle the high-level mapping of the procedure parameters. This facility is not automatically provided by the operating system, as might be expected, but must be explicitly provided by the programmer. This parameter conversion is done by writing a switch stub.

Switch stubs are simply small procedures which accept parameters in the format dictated by the caller. They use this information to format the parameters to HPSWTONMNAME or HPSWITCHTOCM and to call the proper switch intrinsic.

This sounds easy, but it can be somewhat tedious. The SWITCH intrinsics are part of MPE XL, and are written in HP Pascal/XL. The possible combinations of parameter types (simple or array; value or reference; input, output or both) and data types (integer, byte, etc.) make for a difficult translation job. All of this information about each parameter must be passed to the SWITCH intrinsic, which uses it to copy the parameters from the calling environment to the new environment. The SWITCH intrinsics then use this data to determine how the data is aligned and whether or not the data must be passed back to the caller, as is the case for output or I/O parameters.

Because of the many possible combinations of parameter attributes and the desire to pass this information to the SWITCH intrinsics in the most compact form, the SWITCH intrinsics were written using a Pascal feature called 'variant records'. A variant record allows a redefinition of the memory space associated with a record type, similar to the COBOL REDEFINES verb. These types of records allow the type of data passed to the SWITCH intrinsic to vary with the data itself.

For example, if one of the parameters of the called intrinsic is an integer, then the data type, location in memory, and whether the parameter is input, output, or both, are all that is necessary to pass on to the SWITCH intrinsic. If, however, the parameter is an integer array, it is necessary to also give the parameter length to SWITCH. Using a variant record, you could make the record format vary with whether or not the parameter type was simple or an array.

The Switch Assist Tool

The Pascal variant record and syntax are somewhat complicated for the uninitiated, and this complexity adds to the difficulty of writing a switch stub. If a user doing the migration has never used Pascal before, being forced to use this approach could pose a problem.

HP has anticipated this problem and has created a migration tool to aid in the creation of switch stubs. The tool, called 'SWAT' (for SWitch Assist Tool), leads the user through a set of VPLUS screens. The user fills in the screens with the name of the called routine and the names of the parameters and their attributes. When done, SWAT generates a Pascal source program, which can be compiled and either installed in the proper executable library (XL) or linked directly into the program.

SWAT is capable of generating *only* Native Mode HP Pascal/XL switch procedures. This has several implications. First, if you want a CM program to call a 'new' Native Mode intrinsic (e.g., HPCICOMMAND), you must write the switch stub yourself -- manually. Second, if you are migrating both a CM program and a CM library in stages, you should migrate the program first and use SWAT to generate stubs to call the CM library routines until the library is migrated. If the library is migrated first, SWAT will be of no assistance.

The CM program being migrated will then be able to call the switch stub routines, which will appear to be the originally called subprograms. When the switch stub is entered, it formats the parameters for the proper destination procedure, then calls it.

This method of calling procedures can add a substantial amount of overhead to the execution of a program. If a large amount of code is left in Compatibility Mode and called from a Native Mode program, or if frequent switches must be done, the overhead incurred by the switch mechanism could negate the performance gains of migrating to Native Mode in the first place. The performance penalty of leaving code in Compatibility Mode must be weighed against the potential gain of compiling the code into Native Mode or rewriting it in another language.

The motivation behind the switch facility was twofold. First, HP did not develop an SPL compiler for Native Mode. Since much of the code called from applications were utility procedures written in SPL, which could not be compiled to NM code, the switch facility seemed absolutely necessary. Since the advent of SPLash! (from Software Research Northwest), the necessity of switch stubs for SPL code has been removed.

HP also realized that people would have code they wanted to migrate for which the source was lost or otherwise not available. For this, the switch facility can be invaluable.

Floating Point

Another issue in migration is the floating point formats used by the MPE V-based and MPE XL-based machines. HP decided early in the Spectrum project to standardize the format used to store and process floating point numbers, and the IEEE standard for floating point was adopted.

Most floating point formats have many things in common. First and foremost is that the number is stored in two parts, called the 'mantissa' and the 'exponent'. This can best be seen by using the scientific notation convention to express real numbers. For example, the number 4324.00 is expressed as 4.324×10^3. Scientific notation always expresses the number as a mantissa between 1 and 9 with some number of decimal places multiplied by an exponent, which is 10 raised to some power. In the example, 4.324 is the mantissa and 3 is the exponent. Numbers less than 1 are expressed with negative exponents, indicating that the decimal place is shifted to the left instead of the right. In this case, the number .02334 would be expressed as 2.334×10^{-2}. Second, an entire number can be negative, so a sign is associated with the mantissa. For any real (floating point) number format to be useful, the mantissa, exponent, and their associated signs must be stored.

Some adjustments are made in the number format to make the storage and manipulation easier in the computer. Typically, the 1st bit (from left to right) is the mantissa's sign bit. Unlike integer numbers, real numbers are not stored in two's complement format. The sign bit is a simple binary 1 or 0 indicating the number is negative or not. Next usually comes the exponent. Instead of storing this number in the usual two's complement, the number is biased to a certain base value. Biasing involves adding some constant (always the absolute value of the largest negative exponent) to the real number. For example, if the exponent is biased by 127 and the exponent value is 0, the number stored as the exponent is 127. If the exponent is -45, the number 82 is stored, and an exponent of 54 will cause the number 181 to be stored.

What this accomplishes is to simplify comparison of real numbers. With the exponent stored as the leading bits in the storage area and properly biased, a simple byte comparison can determine the inequality of two numbers.

The mantissa is stored as an absolute value, since its sign is the leading digit of the real number. The other main difference in real number formats is the total number of bits used for storage and the number of bits assigned to the mantissa and the exponent.

The HP 3000 stores real numbers in single precision (32 bits) or double precision (64 bits). Single precision uses 9 bits for the exponent and 22 bits for the mantissa. The IEEE standard also defines a short (32 bits) and a long (64 bits) format, and further defines a 128-bit format called a 'quad real'. The IEEE format defines a single precision number to contain 8 bits for the exponent and 23 bits for the mantissa.

While the difference is small, it affects the size of the numbers that can be stored. Further, the IEEE standard defines the way error, exception, and trap handling is to be done to a very exact level. The HP 3000 format does not, and the exception handling is defined by the microcode which performs the various floating point operations. On MPE XL, all IEEE floating point operations are performed by the floating point coprocessor. If one does not exist, the hardware traps to software routines, which simulate the execution of this piece of hardware. MPE XL uses software to perform HP 3000 format floating point operations.

The floating point format can be a problem in migration if the format is used extensively in disc files and databases. Two options exist for converting floating point code:

☐ Write programs which will convert the floating point numbers from the HP 3000 format to the new IEEE format. This is accomplished by writing a program which reads the data files/databases and calls the HP-supplied intrinsic HPFPCONVERT, which allows full conversion among all the floating point formats.

☐ Use the compiler option HP 3000_REALS in either Pascal or FORTRAN. This option causes the compiler to treat all reals as HP 3000 format reals, but because no hardware support exists for this format, calculations and manipulations are handled entirely in software. This reduces the performance of the code doing the numerical calculations.

If an application being migrated uses floating point heavily, you should convert the data if at all possible. TurboIMAGE and QUERY assume all real numbers are in HP 3000 floating point format. This must be taken into account if NM languages are to access data bases.

VPLUS

VPLUS is the only HP-supplied forms package for the HP 3000 line and, as such, is widely used. It provides access to routines that manipulate HP terminals in block mode.

VPLUS operates the same under MPE V and MPE XL. Compatibility is maintained by the communications area (comarea) and other parameter areas assuming 16-bit addressability. This means that in HP Pascal/XL, all integer references in the comarea must be of type SHORTINT. Since data packing is handled the same as it is on MPE V-based systems, Pascal programs must specify HP 3000_16 packing for the comarea and for other variables passed to VPLUS.

Because of the mixed-mode environment, VPLUS has changed: The Native Mode switch stubs now do additional parameter checking; programs that call VPLUS routines with the wrong number of parameters no longer work in Native Mode; and the COBOL compiler now assumes (for VPLUS and IMAGE calls) a CALL mode using the intrinsic mechanism. If the CALL INTRINSIC syntax is used on MPE V, a warning is issued and the VPLUS intrinsics probably don't work correctly. This is because the VPLUS intrinsics do parameter address manipulation (very easily done in SPL under MPE V) depending upon the language ID field in the comarea. If the CALL INTRINSIC mechanism is used in MPE V, the default calling conventions of COBOL (word address by reference), are overridden by the intrinsic mechanism, and VPLUS manipulates the address incorrectly. One clever way others have used to get around this problem is to rewrite any COBOL program to be migrated to Native Mode to pass a language ID of 5 (Pascal) and use the CALL INTRINSIC mechanism. This 'fools' VPLUS into using the correct addressing scheme and maintains forward compatibility when the application is running in full Native Mode.

VPLUS also has new functionality. Many applications manipulate the terminal explicitly with escape sequences. For example, when output is to be printed on a slaved printer, the application must turn off block mode, reset some firmware straps on the terminal, and do I/O to the terminal with escape sequences. This type of environment usually results in a very specific application that will run on just one type of terminal with just one type of terminal controller.

In an attempt to provide a more device-independent method to attain this functionality, several intrinsics have been added to VPLUS. VTURNON and VTURNOFF perform the same functions as VOPENTERM and VCLOSETERM, but do not clear the form from the screen when they execute. With these intrinsics, the application can turn off block mode and re-strap the terminal for the necessary operations.

Two other intrinsics, VBLOCKREAD and VBLOCKWRITE, allow the application direct block mode access to the terminal, independent of any forms definition, as is the case with VREADFIELDS and VSHOWFORM. These intrinsics allow direct communication between the application data buffer and the actual terminal screen -- without the intermediate manipulation of VPLUS's internal buffer.

Several additional intrinsics are now provided to handle the IEEE floating point formats. By default, the VGETREAL, VGETLONG, VPUTREAL, and VPUTLONG intrinsics assume normal HP 3000 floating point formats. The new intrinsics VGETIEEREAL, VGETIEEELONG, VPUTIEEREAL, and VPUTIEEELONG are provided for access to the Native Mode floating point formats on HPPA. If a VPLUS application is migrated to Native Mode and any floating point fields in the data files are converted with HPFPCONVERT, these VPLUS intrinsics must also be converted at the same time to maintain compatibility with the newly converted application.

For many years, a debate has existed in the HP community as to the relative merits of VPLUS and other block mode communications compared to character mode operations. This debate will not be solved here, but one fact about block mode under MPE XL must be mentioned: The Distributed Terminal Controller (DTC) used with the MPE XL system is very much optimized for block mode communications. Using the DTC for character mode operations is simply not as efficient as using block mode. For this reason, VPLUS and other block mode packages should do well on the new machines.

What's Missing?

Hewlett-Packard has done an excellent job in anticipating the needs of migration to HPPA. The effort it has put into Compatibility Mode and the other MPE V-based HP 3000 environments has paid off. There are a few areas, however, where no migration path has been given.

Probably the largest segment of the user community with few easy alternatives to migration are those using FORTRAN 66/V instead of the newer HP FORTRAN 77/XL. No Native Mode FORTRAN 66/V compiler exists under MPE XL. The two languages, while both FORTRAN, are quite different: HP FORTRAN 77/XL conforms to the ANSI standards for FORTRAN, while FORTRAN 66/V does not. Because of this, FORTRAN 66/V performs many functions (such as bit extractions) very differently than HP FORTRAN 77/XL. A translation tool exists to detect and modify the source code when the differences in the standards are found. However, this tool translates only 85 to 90 percent of the code. For some shops, this might be adequate. But for shops with thousands of lines of code, the hand conversion of the remaining 10 to 15 percent can be very expensive.

Another language not adequately provided for is BASIC/V. For users of BASIC, HP provides a form of BASIC, called 'HP Business BASIC/V'. This particular implementation of the language was designed to provide a growth path for HP 250/260 users. This language will be provided on the HPPA systems, and thus HP Business BASIC/V users have an excellent migration path to the new MPE XL-based machines.

As a dialect of the BASIC language, HP Business BASIC/V is an excellent implementation. However, the older BASIC/V compiler is not compatible with the HP Business BASIC/V compiler. BASIC/V is closer to the original Dartmouth BASIC than to the newer implementations. Because of BASIC/V's age, HP has essentially dropped all support (i.e., new development) on it. Thus, with no Native

Mode version of this language planned by HP, users with large investments in BASIC/V are faced with a costly conversion to HP Business BASIC/V in order to achieve the full benefit of the new MPE XL machines.

While not a language, another environment lacking in MPE XL is the traditional implementation of Distributed Systems/3000 (DS). Part of the DS environment is a facility which allows a master program on one CPU to run and communicate with a process on another machine. This facility is called 'PTOP' (Process-TO-Process) communication. While other facilities exist that can accomplish the same functionality in Network Services (NS) software, the exact intrinsics for PTOP, such as GET, SEND, etc., do not exist. Users who require these routines for the functioning of their software will have to rewrite those portions using PTOP to use Socket I/O in NS.

HP apparently felt that these segments of their user base were too small to warrant the effort needed to smoothly migrate their code. So these users will have to be content with translated object code or, in the case of PTOP, a forced conversion to provide the migration path to MPE XL.

19

Language
Considerations

This chapter outlines migration issues for most of the languages implemented on HPPA computers and suggests ways of dealing with some of the incompatibilities that arise from converting a program from an MPE V-based HP 3000 to an MPE XL-based system.

In the cases where a formal ANSI standard does not exist, the languages have been designed to adhere as closely as possible to some commonly accepted norm for the language. This adherence to standards allows for a great deal of portability among different vendors' systems, which have compilers conforming to these standards.

All the Native Mode compilers are invoked with different commands than was the case under MPE V. Typically, the command name is a three-character abbreviation followed by XL. For example: :FTNXL invokes HP FORTRAN 77/XL; :PASXL invokes HP Pascal/XL; and :COB85XL invokes COBOL II/XL with the COBOL85 entry point.

Just as there were the PREP and GO versions of the compilers under MPE V (SPLGO, BASICPREP), the compiler commands have equivalents. For example, the MPE V command FTNGO now becomes FTNXLGO.

In a majority of the cases, the mechanics of converting a program in a specific language from an MPE V-based HP 3000 for use by the compiler on an HPPA machine involves some compiler control statement changes, plus a recompile.

The COBOL Language

The COBOL compilers running under MPE XL closely conform to the ANSI 1974 and 1985 standards. The Native Mode compiler currently uses most of the same front-end code as the version running on MPE V-based HP 3000s. Entry points in the compiler allow the user to select the 1974 or 1985 standards of the language.

Very little else can be said for compatibility as far as the language itself is concerned. The ANSI standards for COBOL are well-known, documented and accepted by the industry. But much can be said about its conversion from MPE V-based machines to MPE XL-based machines.

The hardware design of the HPPA processors dictate that memory locations must be aligned on particular address boundaries. Word accesses (32 bits) can be done only to addresses that are evenly divisible by 32. Likewise, half-word accesses (16 bits) can only be done only on half-word boundaries, and so on. This hardware requirement can have dire consequences on migration.

Of all the languages, COBOL is perhaps the most affected by this requirement. The strong record structure definition mechanism of COBOL is probably the language's best feature, and this feature is heavily used in production code. To understand why this is a problem for migration, it is necessary to see how some of the COBOL data types are viewed at the lowest level.

All PICTURE definitions specifying USAGE COMP (or BINARY in COBOL '85) translate to integers at the machine level. The standard integer format defined by HPPA is 32 bits, and therefore, the optimum integer definition is PIC S9(09) COMP. Additionally, the default bit-alignment (termed SYNCHRONIZED by COBOL) is to 32 bits. Consider the following:

```
01  RECORD-STRUCT-EXAMPLE.
    03  INTEGER-NUMBER-1          PIC S9(04) COMP SYNC.
    03  INTEGER-NUMBER-2          PIC S9(08) COMP SYNC.
```

In the above example, INTEGER-NUMBER-1 will be aligned on a 32-bit boundary by COBOL II/XL, as will INTEGER-NUMBER-2. The number of bits assigned to each, however, will be the same under both MPE V and MPE XL. The net effect is that COBOL II/XL inserts 2 'slack bytes' between the two integers. If this structure is part of a data file definition, the data file created under the MPE V version of COBOL cannot be read by a program with this exact definition.

Several compiler options directly address these problems. The 16-bit alignment situation is solved by the COBOL II/XL compiler option $CONTROL SYNC16. When this option is included in the source, it instructs the compiler to assume the same word alignment as it would on an MPE V-based HP 3000. A similar compiler directive, $CONTROL INDEX16, applies to data items defined as USAGE IS INDEX. Indexed data items default to 32-bit quantities on HPPA, as this is the most efficient integer size. Again, if the index item is part of a record structure, $CONTROL INDEX16 must be specified to make it compatible with the MPE V version of COBOL.

An interesting side effect is that with the $CONTROL SYNC16 option present, the data item INTEGER-NUMBER-2 will be aligned on a 16-bit (half-word) boundary. The HPPA hardware design specifies that 32-bit quantities loaded into a register (via the LDW instruction) must be stored in memory aligned on a 32-bit boundary. Since INTEGER-NUMBER-2 in the example above is not, manipulation of this data item for any sort of calculation would require 2 half-word loads (via the LDH instruction), followed by a deposit to combine the two halves.

This sequence increases the amount of work required for loads and stores but most of the time it is not a major problem. However, for computation-intensive applications with large amounts of data, this type of alignment could noticeably decrease system performance. This is not an issue on MPE V-based HP 3000s, since double-word variables are required to reside only on 16-bit boundaries. Note that this applies only to COMP SYNC. If a PIC clause specifies COMP without SYNC, then COBOL II/XL will align the data items as it does on MPE V, although the inefficiency in loading and storing INTEGER-NUMBER-2 would still occur.

Alignment becomes an issue when intrinsics are called. On MPE V-based machines, the COBOL compiler has some default rules for passing parameters to procedures named in CALL statements. Essentially, all parameters are passed as 16-bit word addresses by reference. These defaults can be overridden by using the keyword INTRINSIC before the name of the procedure. This causes the compiler to check the system intrinsic declaration file (SPLINTR.PUB.SYS) for the correct calling sequence. If the called procedure is correctly defined in the intrinsic file, COBOL will generate the call correctly. Thus, the default calling rules can be bent, and a procedure (called by a COBOL program) that expects a byte array will be given a byte address instead of the usual word address.

On MPE V-based HP 3000s, data can be aligned only on 8-bit (byte) or 16-bit (word) boundaries. The hardware is very lax on data addressing requirements, and the SPL compiler (the language in which most intrinsics are written) is very loose on type-checking. Thus, very little data type checking is done in the MPE V environment.

Specifying the calling sequence for COBOL in this environment is therefore easy. Even if the procedure is not an intrinsic, it is simple to tell the compiler to override the defaults (to load a byte address, for instance) because there are so few variations on the parameter passing.

On HPPA systems, things get much more complex. Data can be 8-, 16-, 32-, or 64-bit aligned. The alignment and data type of each parameter is strictly enforced by the called procedure. Since virtually all of the procedures are written in Pascal, the strong type checking facets of this language come into play. Thus, not only does the compiler have to worry about alignment of the parameters, but it must also worry about the possible types.

Because of this more complex matrix of alignment and data types, it is impossible to fit all of these options into the syntax of the COBOL II/XL language. It becomes very desirable to have this data defined in an external mechanism that accounts for all the variations. For this reason, the Native Mode intrinsic file, SYSINTR.PUB.SYS, becomes much more important to the COBOL II/XL compilation process than is SPLINTR.PUB.SYS under MPE V.

This seemingly simple requirement of always specifying INTRINSIC can cause problems. In virtually any COBOL program that is useful on a production HP 3000, not all CALL statements specify the INTRINSIC keyword. These programs use CALL to access certain major software packages, including IMAGE and VPLUS. For migration to work correctly, the intrinsic mechanism must be accessed. The brute-force method of accomplishing this is to modify every CALL statement to include this keyword. For a typical shop with tens or hundreds of thousands of lines of code, this could be a major undertaking.

However, another option exists to facilitate this process. The COBOL II/XL compiler has a new compiler directive, $CONTROL CALLINTRINSIC. When placed at the front of the source file, this causes the compiler to automatically search the intrinsic file for a definition of the called procedure, even if the call does not specify the INTRINSIC keyword.

TurboIMAGE and VPLUS are important in the COBOL environment. Because they can be accessed only via the CALL verb in COBOL, the intrinsic mechanism must be accessed as well. To ensure the use of the intrinsic mechanism, the COBOL II/XL compiler has been modified to detect when one of the TurboIMAGE or VPLUS intrinsics is called and assume the CALL intrinsic form of the verb, even if the INTRINSIC keyword and the $CONTROL CALLINTRINSIC directive is not specified. Furthermore, since the VPLUS intrinsics were designed before COBOL knew about intrinsics, they 'break the rules' and modify parameter addresses according to the calling language used. Under MPE XL, the intrinsic mechanism will always be used, and this will force the parameters to be passed in such a way that VPLUS will modify their address incorrectly.

For this reason, HP is recommending that all COBOL programs which call VPLUS be modified to 'fool' VPLUS into thinking that Pascal is the calling language by modifying the language ID parameter of the communications area (comarea). This, combined with the calling sequence dictated by the intrinsic mechanism, will ensure the proper functioning of the VPLUS intrinsics.

The data alignment solution is completed by the $CONTROL CALLALIGNED and LINKALIGNED options. These are used for calling procedures that are not intrinsics, such as COBOL subprograms. The CALLALIGNED option makes sure the procedures passed are aligned on the proper boundaries, while the LINKALIGNED option is used for the linkage section of the called module. Intrinsic calling is not affected by either, and data alignment is dictated by the SYSINTR file.

Several other COBOL features which have less of an impact on migration are either changed or are missing:

□ Segment numbers no longer have meaning. No segmentation is done by these numbers as was the case under MPE V.

□ $CONTROL ANSIPARM, BIGSTACK, and USLINIT are ignored.

□ Multiple nested PERFORM statements which exit from the same point may cause runtime errors.

□ COBOLLOCK and COBOLUNLOCK are not available in Native Mode.

□ COBOL II/XL no longer performs any validation or zero fill on numeric data being transferred via a MOVE statement.

□ Dynamic procedure calling via the CALL identifier is no longer supported.

To summarize, the transition from COBOL on the MPE V-based machines to COBOL II/XL is relatively painless. Specifying the $CONTROL SYNC16, INDEX16, and CALLINTRINSIC options, COBOL II/XL will treat data areas exactly like COBOL II on MPE V systems. If the code being migrated uses none of the missing features listed above, the code should migrate straight across.

In addition, COBOL allows $CONTROL directives to be placed in a global control file (COBCNTL.PUB.SYS). COBOL automatically includes these statements with every compile, removing the need to include them in every source program. This is a very nice features that the other compilers, unfortunately, do not have.

The Pascal Language

Like COBOL, the Pascal language enjoys a well-defined syntax. Pascal was created by Niklaus Wirth as a vehicle for teaching the principles of computer science and good coding habits. It has well-developed record structures, very strong type-checking, and a very elegant orthogonal syntax. Standard Pascal syntax, however, contains very few facilities for I/O and no facilities to access any hardware features. The real usefulness and strength of a Pascal implementation resides in the vendor-provided extensions to the language.

The Pascal that runs under MPE XL, HP Pascal/XL, has extensions added by HP that include a somewhat extensive I/O library, a set of very good string-handling procedures, and several facilities that allow access to the hardware features of HPPA. HP Pascal/XL suffers, however, from the same migration ills that we saw in COBOL. Again, data addressing must be dealt with, as the MPE V addressing model is not treated as the default. The problems are exacerbated because Pascal/V and HP Pascal/XL define some fundamental entities differently hence the migration programmer must make changes to virtually every program.

The pervasive problem of data alignment affects Pascal as well as other languages. Since the natural word length of the machine is 32 bits, the defaults for the integer size is this length. All integers and strings are aligned on 32-bit boundaries in Pascal XL and on 16-bits boundaries in MPE V. This is not of concern unless the program depends upon this, such as when an external data file is accessed.

Just as COBOL is equipped with the $CONTROL SYNC16 option, in HP Pascal/XL, the $HP3000_16$ option enables Pascal/V packing of records. This option must appear before the PROGRAM statement. The program can be temporarily switched into the HP Pascal/XL packing mode with the $HP3000_32$ option. This is useful, for example, if a program is written to convert a data file for use with MPE XL. The following example shows the use of these features:

```
$HP3000_16$
PROGRAM Convert(input,output);

TYPE
  cm_array = ARRAY [1..5] of -32768..32767;
  cm_record = RECORD
                cm1,cm2:char;
                END;


  nm_array =$HP3000_32$ ARRAY [1..5] of -32768..32767;
  nm_record=$HP3000_32$ PACKED RECORD
                nm1,nm2:char;
                END;

VAR
  cm_arr : cm_array;
  nm_arr : nm_array;
  cm_rec : cm_record;
  nm_rec : nm_record;

BEGIN
  nm_arr.nm1 := cm_arr.cm1;
  nm_arr.nm2 := nm_arr.nm2;
  FOR i := 1 to 5 DO nm_array[i] := cm_array[i];
END;
```

The $HP3000_32$ is interspersed with the code and causes the compiler to switch back to the 'natural' data alignment temporarily.

When a program is compiled with the $HP3000_16$ option on, it behaves very much like the Pascal/V version of the program. All data packing (except for file and pointer types) is performed as on an MPE V-based HP 3000. In addition, $HP3000_16$ instructs the compiler to use HP 3000 floating point formats for all floating point (REAL) numbers. Note that you cannot mix the two floating point formats in the same compilation module.

Because file and pointer types are hardware-dependent, they are not treated the same. This is of concern only when these types actually appear in data records. If they are used only within a program, the size is generally of no concern to the programmer. Note, however, that if either of these data types appear in a record definition, this file cannot be used without conversion. Therefore, if a data file contains these types, it is impossible to just recompile the program and run in Native Mode. The file must be converted first, then both the Native Mode version of the program and the converted file placed in production at the same time.

The data alignment incompatibilities are insignificant when compared with some of the other differences between the two Pascal implementations. Foremost among these is the way in which HP Pascal/XL treats subranges. In HP Pascal/XL, any subrange with a negative lower bound is assigned 32 bits of storage by default. Any subrange with a non-negative lower bound is assigned the minimum integral number of bytes that will store the range:

```
TYPE

    s_int    = -32768..32767;  {32 bits}

    l_int    = 0..65535;       {16 bits}
```

In Pascal/V, however, the opposite is true. Logical (non-negative) subranges are treated as if they had a negative lower bound, even though they do not:

```
TYPE  {HP Pascal/XL}
   shortint = -32768..32767; {allocate 16 bits }

   l_int   = 100..33000;            {only needs 16 bits to store,
                                     but allocates 32 bits}
```

In the examples above, 32 bits would be assigned where the programmer so carefully declared 16 bits under Pascal/V. In HP Pascal/XL, the type SHORTINT is predefined, whereas in Pascal/V, the 16-bit integer can be only an subrange. With this aspect of the language, every Pascal/V program to be converted which uses short integers must be modified to allow for short integers correctly.

Another fundamental difference between Pascal/V and HP Pascal/XL is the way in which records are packed. In HP Pascal/XL, the default is to assign 32 bits to every type. For example, consider the following Pascal/V record:

```
examp_rec : PACKED RECORD
               f1: -128..127; {8 bits}
               f2: -128..127;
            END;
```

This record definition would allocate 16 bits of storage with Pascal/V. Under HP Pascal/XL, the same definition would allocate two 32-bit words of storage, for a total of 64 bits. To achieve the same effect, the HP Pascal/XL reserved word CRUNCHED would be used instead of PACKED.

These differences, while minor, can become bothersome if application code must run in Compatibility Mode on MPE V-based machines and in Native Mode on HPPA units. It is virtually impossible to do this without implementing some compiler switches to tell the compiler what constructs to compile. Here's an example of a common implementation:

```
$SET 'cm=true,nm=false'$
   .

   .

examp_rec : $IF 'cm'$ PACKED $ENDIF$
            $IF 'nm'$ CRUNCHED $ENDIF$
              RECORD
                f1: -128..127;
                f2: -128..127;
              END;

   TYPE
$IF 'cm'$
     shortint = -32768..32767;
$ENDIF$
```

In summary, none of these incompatibilities are major, and ways of dealing with them can easily be implemented in the Pascal source code. Specifying the $HP3000_16$ option handles most of the problems.

The FORTRAN Language

The implementation of FORTRAN 77 under MPE V and MPE XL enjoy a great deal of compatibility, probably the most of any language discussed here. The difference between the two compilers are minimal, especially when compared with COBOL and Pascal.

HP FORTRAN 77/XL has the same alignment problems as the other languages. As with Pascal, the method used to make the program behave as it would under MPE V is to specify the $HP3000_16 directive. This will cause all data alignment to be on 16-bit boundaries where appropriate and will use the HP 3000 real number formats, as opposed to the IEEE formats. In essence, specifying the $HP3000_16 format is virtually all that is necessary to convert an MPE V program to Native Mode.

After the new version is running, the site can convert the data files by writing conversion programs, which allows all integers to be converted to 32-bit quantities and aligns all variable on 32-bit boundaries. These two things alone will noticeably increase performance on CPU-intensive applications.

This is not true, however, for the many sites still running under FORTRAN 66/V. When this compiler was written, standards for the language were not yet well-defined. The HP FORTRAN 77/XL compiler conforms well to the existing ANSI standards, but the FORTRAN 66/V compiler shares no such standardization.

Many of the operations performed by FORTRAN 66/V are possible in HPFORTRAN 77/XL, but they are done with very different syntax such as:

□ Bit extraction. Under FORTRAN 66/V, bit extraction is done with subscript-like syntax: i = i[1:7]. FORTRAN 77/XL provides a library routine to perform bit extraction.

□ INTEGERs and LOGICALs are 16 bits in FORTRAN 66/V vs. 32 bits in HP FORTRAN 77/XL.

□ Procedures without parameters must have a null parenthesis pair on HP FORTRAN 77/XL (time = clock()) vs. FORTRAN 66/V (time=clock)

□ Mixed-mode operations are evaluated differently.

□ Predefined files are different in the two languages.

A conversion utility called 'CONVERT' will find many of the source differences and change them. However, it does not convert 5 to 10 percent of the code; that must still be done by hand. There is no getting around the fact that a potentially costly conversion is necessary for this language.

The C Language

The C language is a newcomer to the commercial HP computers. The dialect of C used under MPE XL is essentially the same one used to implement HP-UX, a very successful and solid implementation of the AT&T operating system UNIX. Naturally, the implementation which runs under MPE XL was modified to understand operating system specific features, such as intrinsics.

Although there has never been an HP-supplied version of C for the MPE V-based HP 3000, third party versions do exist, and migration from them to HP C on MPE XL systems is quite straightforward.

C is probably one of the most portable languages that exist. The definitive standard for the language was presented in Kernigan and Richie's book, *The C Programming Language*. Since Kernigan and Richie also originated the language, their standard still stands. Another standard that has emerged is S.C. Johnson's Portable C Compiler (PCC) available on a wide variety of machines. HP C conforms closely to the syntax and semantics of the PCC.

Because of this good standard among C versions, C migrations appear to pose few problems to the site converting to the HPPA-based machines.

The SPL Language

Perhaps the most interesting language migration story involves SPL (Systems Programming Language). The original SPL ran only under MPE V and was implemented with a great deal of dependence upon (and allowed access to) the hardware features of the HP 3000. Early in the development of HPPA, Hewlett-Packard announced that it would not develop an SPL compiler for this new machine. The official word from HP was that SPL could still run in Compatibility Mode, and a Native Mode version of the language would not be forthcoming. The intention was that SPL sites would convert their code to Pascal or C (a costly proposition at best), or translate using the OCT.

For this reason, Software Research Northwest (SRN) decided to create a project to fill this 'hole' in the HPPA migration strategy. Software engineers from Allegro Consultants of Redwood City, California, and Denkart of Kontich, Belgium, joined with their colleagues at the Vashon Island, Washington, Research and Development center of SRN to define and create a Native Mode version of SPL dubbed SPLash!, signifying the resurrection of SPL from the ashes.

SPLash! was designed from the ground up to be as compatible as possible with its MPE V counterpart. Since the language was highly dependent upon the hardware environment of the MPE V-based HP 3000, it was necessary to emulate the addressing modes. For this reason, the stack limitation is present strictly for migration purposes; for new applications, a full 32-bit mode is available. When 32-bit mode is enabled, certain machine-dependent constructs are not usable. Essentially, this mode disallows any construct which assumes a 16-bit word length and implements the stack as 32-bit words instead of 16-bit words.

All constructs supported by SPL/V are supported by SPLash!, including almost all ASSEMBLEs (except those noted below), all stack references (such as TOS and stack decrements), and all other statements. The features not supported fall into three categories:

☐ Privileged operations (including ASSEMBLEs) that do not exist under HPPA, especially ones that are not provided in Compatibility Mode.

☐ Any references to code locations are now 32 bits -- one aspect of the HPPA environment that is impossible to mask by SPLash!. The effect of this is that some features, such as stacked code locations and P-relative branches in ASSEMBLEs, are not supported. Also, whenever a code location is stored to a variable, the receiving variable must be changed to a type DOUBLE.

☐ Features (such as XEQ 0, PCAL 0, and LLBL) which would be very difficult to emulate under HPPA and are highly dependent upon the MPE V-based HP 3000 architecture are not supported.

Using the SPLash! compiler, true Native Mode performance can be obtained from the HPPA machines.

Other Languages

The languages which are not going to be ported to Native Mode by Hewlett-Packard are the previously mentioned SPL/V, FORTRAN 66/V, and BASIC/V. HP's version of RPG (Report Program Generator) will be available only in Compatibility Mode on the first release. The language solutions provided by HP are quite complete and provide for the differences in the machine architectures very well. No matter how well the compilers are written, however, some source code changes may be required to allow programs written for the MPE V operating environment to run under MPE XL.

20

The MPE XL
Migration Process

Many issues are present when considering a migration to MPE XL. This chapter will examine some of these issues by evaluating some common situations through a checklist approach. In addition to MPE migration, this chapter will also focus on the migration to MPE XL from IBM and DEC systems. This large body of machines represents a potential market for Hewlett-Packard, and any discussion of migration would not be complete until some of the issues regarding non-HP migration are discussed.

MPE Migration

The migration process is a cohesive sequence of steps resulting in the successful migration of an MPE V application, or set of applications, to MPE XL. The process is not a trivial one and involves many choices. Many documents have already been written by Hewlett-Packard on this subject of migration. For more detail on the mechanics of the process, refer to the following handbooks:

☐ Introduction to MPE XL for MPE V Programmers

☐ HP FORTRAN 77/XL Migration Guide (31501-90004)

- COBOL II XL Migration Guide (31500-90004)

- HP Pascal XL Migration Guide (31502-90004)

- Introduction to MPE XL for MPE V System Administrators (30367-90003)

- MPE V to MPE XL: Getting Started (30367-90002)

- Switch Programming Guide (32650-90014)

- Migration Process Guide (30367-90007)

To begin with, the proper individuals must be gathered to perform the migration. At most sites, the migration team should consist of personnel from the operations, programming and management staffs. In addition, users of the major applications being migrated should be involved -- or at the very least, trained in the new procedures. Finally, an HP representative (from either the sales or software organization) should coordinate any involvement with Hewlett-Packard. As with any project, a strong leader is needed to ensure that the other team members are productive and able to meet their schedules. This leader should be a senior programmer (or team leader) or a consultant (either from HP or a consulting company) who has experience in migration to MPE XL-based machines.

Like any complex project involving many people, migration cannot be performed all at once. Before a successful migration can even be attempted, the application must first be characterized and analyzed. How difficult will it be to migrate the application? What resources are needed to complete the migration? What incompatibilities might exist as a result of the migration?

Incompatibilities can take many forms. Some are static, such as an application that calls an intrinsic supported in MPE V that does not exist in MPE XL (e.g., FCARD). Others are dynamic, such as an application which calls the COMMAND intrinsic (which *is* supported on MPE XL) but attempts to execute a command that doesn't exist in MPE XL.

Hewlett-Packard provides two tools for the analyzing applications, and they have been packaged together as the Migration Toolset (32428A). The Object Code Analyzer (OCA) looks at program files and the associated system languages for static incompatibilities. The OCA then produces reports in either a short or long form. The short form summarizes the incompatibilities, while the long form provides more detailed information, such as the incompatible code and offset of the code.

Dynamic incompatibilities, such as runtime errors, are detected by the Real Time Monitor (RTM). This tool consists of several parts: An SL which is bound by the loader to programs at runtime; the program, RTMSYS, which serves as a controller; and a report program, RTMREP, which produces a report of the incompatibilities.

RTM traps all incompatibilities, regardless of the source language. It also flags runtime dynamic data, such as return codes that have changed between the two versions of MPE.

The main difference between the Object Code Analyzer and the Real Time Monitor is seen in the code paths taken when a program runs. RTM will detect incompatibilities only if the program actually executes that code path during the monitor run. OCA, on the other hand, analyzes the entire program and points out all incompatibilities -- *even if the program never reaches that part of code.*

It is also necessary to evaluate the application's characteristics to determine the magnitude of the migration job ahead. Source language, number of lines of code, third-party packages, data access methods, interface to other applications, and source code availability all should be considered. This step is crucial, and all relevant aspects of the application must be studied before a decision to migrate is made.

In general, the limitations of the target environment must be considered. If, for example, the application is in BASIC/V and the desired execution mode is Native Mode, migration will be difficult because no Native Mode BASIC/XL compiler exists.

In any event a migration plan should be drawn. In practice, this step will probably happen concurrently with the analysis, but the formal plan will undoubtedly change as more data is accumulated from the analysis. At a minimum, the plan should address the following:

- The purpose and scope of the plan and the migration

- The migration strategy, the migration schedule, and the resource requirements

- The training of users and technicians, and associated documentation

- The applications analysis

- The detailed test plan that ensures proper application function

In the next step of the migration process, preparation, certain tasks can be accomplished on the MPE V-based system that can minimize the conversion time. The following areas of the software environment should be examined:

- **Compilers:** Convert any application code to the standards of the corresponding Native Mode compilers: COBOL/V to COBOL II/V, FORTRAN 66/V to HP FORTRAN 77/V, BASIC/V to HP Business BASIC/V, and SPL to SPLash!.

- **Subsystems:** Convert any incompatible subsystems to those compatible with software running under MPE XL: IMAGE/3000 to TurboIMAGE and DS/3000 to NS/3000.

- **Application:** Examine output from RTM and OCA, and resolve any incompatibilities that will affect the program. Determine areas of the application which must run in switch mode.

- **System:** Prepare the accounting structure and other disc-resident configuration parameters for migration. Check for account dependencies that are used by MPE XL, such as DIAG.SYS and CONFIG.SYS. Use :LISTF to find duplicate files between MPE V and MPE XL. List the logging tables using :LISTLOG. Use :RELLOG to release any logging identifiers that should not be migrated.

- **UDC:** Disable all UDCs that should not be migrated, then run the HP-supplied migration utility GETUDC.PUB.SYS to create a file of UDCs to be migrated.

- **Sysdump:** Create a SYSDUMP tape, specifying '@.@.@' for the file set. Make sure that the file COMMAND.PUB.SYS is *not* on the tape. In addition, delete global RINS that will not be migrated. Define user logging parameters.

- **Hardware:** Ensure that all peripherals not being replaced in the migration are compatible with the new system. These include terminals, printers, disc drives, and tape drives.

The final preparation stage of migration involves installing the new hardware, which is the responsibility of your HP support team. The installation is completed by loading the MPE V SYSDUMP tape into the HP 3000 900 Series. This step is performed by using the HP-supplied tool DIRMIG (DIRectory MIGrate), which uses a SYSDUMP tape as input and can migrate the accounting structure, RINS, user logging information, private volume information, and UDC files. As a final step, DIRMIG will restore the user files from the SYSDUMP tape, completing the migration of the MPE V environment.

While some sites may want to move immediately to Native Mode, many others will probably want to operate initially in Compatibility Mode. (Incompatibilities may exist between MPE V and Compatibility Mode, and 'corrected code' can be tested only on the new machine.)

The functionality of the application should also be verified by using the Object Code Translator (:OCTCOMP command) to compile the Compatibility Mode programs into pseudo Native Mode program files. This step improves performance by eliminating some of the overhead involved in the Compatibility Mode emulator, at the cost of larger program files on disc.

The final step in the process is the jump to Native Mode. Here's how to do that:

- □ **Resolve** any Native Mode incompatibilities -- in data alignment, for example. Remember that the various compiler options ($HP3000_16$, $CONTROL SYNC16, etc.) affect the entire program, and take care to ensure individual data structures are compiled with the proper alignment option.

- □ **Recompile** the application: Invoke compilers with the proper MPE XL compiler commands, and invoke the LinkEditor rather than the SEGMENTER.

- □ **Validate** the program: Execute the test plan to ensure the application works properly.

- □ **Optimize** the program: After testing, recompile using the proper compiler directive to enable optimization, such as $OPTIMIZE ON$ in Pascal. This step ensures the best performance from the compilers.

- □ **Take advantage** of other performance gains: Use the 32-bit address space and other architectural advances of the HPPA like mapped files and a large memory addressing area, such as that employed by the Pascal Heap.

If the planning was good, your application should now be operating in Native Mode.

IBM Migration

The process outlined for MPE migration has merit in the IBM environment as well. However, unlike migrating from an MPE V-based HP 3000, the incompatibilities are more varied and complex. Very basic issues need to be addressed, such as choosing a data base management system, or changing Job Control Language. Unlike the IBM environment, choosing an operating system will not be an issue, since HP offers only MPE for the 3000 family of computers. Terminal connectivity will also not be an issue in the HP environment, since connectivity is an integral part of MPE.

Migration from some of the smaller IBM machines (System 32, 34, 36, System 3) poses fewer problems than migration from the larger mainframes. Hewlett-Packard and independent software houses have fielded very good migration tools, such as TRANSFORM/3000 and RPG conversion products, that help sites move from these small IBM machines. The RPG/V compiler is very similar to the RPGII compiler and Native Mode RPG/XL will be available at a future release.

Conversion of batch programs from Disc Operating System (DOS) and Operating System (OS) should be fairly straightforward, especially if the applications were written in COBOL. The indexed file structure verbs as standardized in the ANSI '74 version of COBOL are virtually identical on the IBM and the HP. Therefore, programs written to this standard should be easily transportable.

The IBM MVS operating system offers two options for terminal connection: Time Sharing Option (TSO for program development, and CICS for production application terminals. Migration from TSO will require retraining programmers and technicians for the MPE XL command language and environment. Migration of the application code calling CICS will probably prove more difficult. The comparable environment under MPE XL is VPLUS, and moving from CICS to VPLUS would require completely rewriting the application program. Under MVS, a pre-processor exists which generates the proper interface to CICS. In VPLUS, the programmer must make use of the CALL statement to access the VPLUS procedures.

For data base systems, HP offers software that is functionally similar to the IBM alternatives. If TurboIMAGE is chosen as the data base system, then considerable work will be needed in rewriting the application software due to the change in the CALL structure. For conversion from the IBM relational data base, HP's SQL product was designed to be very similar to DBII. The programmatic interface and query language are virtually identical, thereby facilitating conversion from IBM to HP.

In summary, shops still running primarily in batch on the older 370 series machines under DOS or OS will find a very viable migration path to the HP 3000 900 Series machines. The addressing scheme and similarities in application software will make for a relatively painless transition, although some work would be involved in migration of JCL. For IBM shops running heavy online environments, migration of software will be a much bigger job, requiring a rewrite of at least the online portion, and possibly the batch portion of the application.

DEC Migration

Unlike IBM, Digital Equipment Corporation has placed heavy emphasis on standardizing on one architecture and operating system with its VAX line of computers and VMS operating system.

The DEC VMS operating system is similar to Hewlett-Packard's MPE XL in that they both provide a standard command line interface to access the commands of the system. One major difference, and a possible stumbling block in the migration process, is the accounting structure. Where VMS provides a true hierarchical directory structure, MPE XL has a three-level account, group, and file structure. Migration planning would have to include considerable attention to the account structure, file management, and security.

Another area for consideration by the migration planning team is the VMS command files used as batch jobs. Under MPE, a batch job must have a job card at the beginning of the file and all VMS command files used for background processing would need to modified.

The degree of difficulty associated with migrating applications software from DEC to HP will depend largely on the file structures, languages, and data base systems used. COBOL applications that use the ANSI '74 indexed file access methodologies can be easily ported from the DEC FMS structure to the HP KSAM structure. Conversion from the DEC RDB data base management system to any of the HP data base products would require a substantial rewrite of the application. Conversion from certain other data base systems that run on DEC would not be as difficult. For example, the Cincom TOTAL data base system is very similar to TurboIMAGE and would be a relatively straightforward migration situation. Other third-party data base solutions, such as Oracle, would be an even easier port since Oracle expects to make its product available for HP 3000 computers sometime in 1988. Any SQL data base management system is likely to be a relatively easy conversion to HP SQL.

The migration of applications written using the COGNOS Powerhouse package (QUIZ, QUICK, QTP) is extremely easy since both the VAX and HPPA machines run similar versions of this software. Conversion of COGNOS applications will require attention to the file structure but little work on the actual routines.

Forms design using the DEC FMS system differs radically from the HP VPLUS system. FMS has a character mode orientation and does not take advantage of the terminal's forms buffering capabilities. VPLUS has a block mode orientation and allows use of forms caching. Therefore, migration from FMS to VPLUS would be quite a bit of work.

For users of VAX systems under UNIX, or any of the UNIX derivatives available for DEC machines, migration to the HP 9000 Series of HPPA based machines should be an extremely cost-effective and viable migration path. Migration from VMS or UNIX to MPE XL would not, in general, be an easy migration. Such a conversion should be carefully planned and given a timeframe that will allow for the attention to detail that the process will require.

Appendices

Appendix A

The Instruction Set

All HP Precision Architecture processors use the same instruction set, which this appendix briefly discusses. For more detailed information, refer to Hewlett-Packard's *Precision Architecture and Instruction Reference Manual* (Manual Part Number 09740-90014).

Addressing Techniques

All memory references, both real and virtual, are accomplished using byte addressing (relative to zero). Some machine instructions demand that the supplied byte addresses be divisible by two or four.

Most memory reference instructions can address both the real memory and virtual memory. This is governed by the D bit in the processor status word (PSW). Instructions can be fetched from real memory or via virtual addressing. This is governed by the C bit in the PSW.

Three instructions always address real memory, disregarding the value of the D bit in the PSW: STWAS, LDWAS and LDWAX. They may only be accessed by privileged users.

All standard language compilers generate code to address virtual memory only. It is the responsibility of both the hardware and the operating system to map virtual addresses into the real memory.

A virtual address is a 64-bit value which is broken into a 32-bit space identifier and a 32-bit offset. The left 32 bits are the space identifier; the right 32 bits are an offset within that space. Because this is a byte-addressed architecture, a 'space' is limited to 4 gigabytes (2^{32} bytes).

Since all instructions on HPPA computers are 32 bits wide, it is obvious that direct addressing is limited to a single space. An instruction therefore does not contain the address itself, but rather a set of fields that indicate how the address can be built.

The S field, or space register identifier, is a 2-bit field when referencing data, and a 3-bit field when referencing code. If it contains any of the values 1, 2 or 3 then it indicates the space register where the space identifier (left 32 bits) of the virtual address can be found. The value 0 for the S field is a special case and will be considered separately.

The B field, or base register identifier, is 5 bits wide and can thus have a value between 0 and 31. This field refers to one of the 32 general purpose registers. The contents of that register are used to form the base of the offset (right 32 bits) of a virtual address. A displacement can be applied to this base to create the full offset.

The D field, or displacement, is 14 bits wide and can thus have values between -8192 and +8191. The immediate value of the D field is added to the contents of the base register to compose the offset of a virtual address.

Some instructions don't have 14 bits to spare for a displacement and will use a 5-bit field short displacement field. The field will be called the I field in this document to differentiate it from the D field.

Alternatively to a displacement, indexing can be used. This is achieved by using the X field, or index register indicator. This field is 5 bits wide and indicates any of the 32 general purpose registers. The contents of that register is added to the base, to compose the offset of a virtual address.

When indexing is used, byte indexing or true element indexing is used, depending on the value of the U field, a 1-bit field.

The three notations for a virtual address are:

```
d(s,b)
i(s,b)
x(s,b)
```

Let us now consider the case where the value of the S field is 0.

The offset of the virtual address is calculated exactly as described above, using the B, D, I and X fields. The space identifier is taken from one of the space registers SR4, SR5, SR6 or SR7, depending on the value of the two most significant bits of the offset. Adding the value 4 to the value of these two bits yields the number of the space register to be used. The two bits considered here are called the Q field, or quadrant identifier.

The Q field serves two purposes: it identifies the space register and it is a part of the offset. Therefore, using this technique, one can only address one quarter of a space -- a quadrant -- through a given space register. SR4 allows addressing the first quadrant of its space, SR5 addresses the second quadrant etc..

The advantage of this technique is that a virtual address can be maintained as a 32-bit value in a program.

Note that space registers 4 through 7 have an architected meaning, and do not change during the execution of a program unit. Space registers 1, 2 and 3 are used as scratch pads.

Some instructions allow the modification of the contents of the base register before or after execution of the instruction. This modification is performed by adding either the signed value of the D or I field or the contents of the index register to the base register.

Delayed Branching and Nullifying

The instruction immediately following a branch instruction is executed before the branch is taken. This is done to save an execution cycle because the branch instruction will incur an additional cycle.

The return point of a 'branch and link register' instruction is thus the second instruction after the branch.

Branch and computational instructions can specify that the next instruction in sequence should be skipped. This is referred to as 'nullification'.

For an unconditional branch instruction, nullification means that the next instruction in line is not executed.

For a conditional branch, nullification means that the next instruction is not executed for a forward branch which is taken or for a backward branch which is not taken. This odd arrangement is introduced to allow optimization of loop constructs in standard programming languages.

Computational instructions conditionally nullify the next instruction. The type of condition differs with the instruction type.

Conditions for branching or nullifying are indicated by the C field. This field is 3 bits wide and, depending on the instruction, is taken from one of the following sets. The value for the C field and its meaning are given below.

The notation 'result{n..m}' means bits n through m of result. Bits are counted from left to right, starting with 0. Some instructions allow the use of the negation of a condition.

Three sets of conditions exist to be used for testing: arithmetic and logical, unit, and extract and deposit.

Nullification and Branch Conditions

Descriptions for arithmetic and logical conditions follow below, with the value of the C field shown to the left of the colon (:), and the condition description to the right.

```
0 : never
1 : result{0..31} = 0
2 : result{0} = 1 xor signed overflow
3 : result{0..31} = 0 or (result{0} = 1 xor signed overflow)
4 : carry = 0 for ADD, borrow = 0 for subtract
5 : result{0..31} = 0  or  (carry = 1 for ADD, borrow = 1 for subtract)
6 : signed overflow
7 : result{31} = 1
```

The interpretation for ADD instructions is as follows:

```
0 : never
1 : operand1 = -operand2
2 : operand1 < -operand2 signed
3 : operand1 <= -operand2 signed
4 : no overflow unsigned
5 : zero or no overflow unsigned
6 : overflow signed
7 : odd
```

The interpretation for SUBTRACT or COMPARE instructions is as follows:

```
0 : never
1 : operand1 = operand2
2 : operand1 < operand2 signed
3 : operand1 <= operand2 signed
4 : operand1 < operand2 unsigned
5 : operand1 <= operand2 unsigned
6 : overflow signed
7 : odd
```

Operand1 can be a register or an immediate value from the instruction. Operand2 is a register value.

For logical instructions (OR, AND...), the condition is set up based only on the result of the operation. Some values of the C field are not defined:

```
0 : never
1 : result{0..31} = 0
2 : result{0} = 1
3 : result{0..31} = 0 or result{0} = 1
7 : result{31} = 1
```

Some instructions allow testing on several fields (bytes, digits) of a value simultaneously. The conditions that can be tested are known as unit conditions:

```
0 : never
2 : some byte zero
3 : some half-word zero
4 : some digit carry
6 : some byte carry
7 : some half-word carry
```

The extract, deposit, shift and move instructions allow testing on certain conditions. The C field is then defined as:

```
0 : never
1 : result{0..31} = 0
2 : result{0} = 1
3 : result{31} = 1
4 : always
5 : result{0..31} <> 0
6 : result{0} = 0
7 : result{31} = 0
```

Branch Addressing

The branch target is the address where program execution continues after a branch is taken.

Branching within the same code space is performed by indicating a word displacement relative to the currently executing instruction. The hardware requires several fields in an instruction to compose the word displacement.

Branching to a different code space (external branching) uses a virtual address to indicate the branch target. The space identifier for this virtual address is referenced by the contents of the Space Register indicated by the SR field in the mnemonic. The offset is composed of the B field and additional word displacement fields. In this case, the SR field is 3-bits long and can indicate any of the 8 space registers. The mnemonic indication is 'wd(sr,b)'. The length of the WD fields is not equal for all branch instructions.

A vectored branch uses a word index relative to a base register to calculate the new program offset. The mnemonic indication is 'x(b)'.

The Instruction Set

Abbreviations used in the instruction descriptions are as follows:

```
b    : base register identification.
be   : begin or end indicator for a byte move.
ca   : arithmetic or logical condition.
```

```
caf    : arithmetic or logical condition or its negation.
cc     : cache control.
ce     : extract or deposit condition.
cop    : coprocessor identifier.
cr     : control register.
cu     : unit condition.
d      : displacement
i      : short displacement.
imm    : immediate value.
i1     : first immediate value.
i2     : second immediate value.
l      : length of bit field.
m      : address modification indicator(yes/no).
ma     : address modification indicator(yes/no and before/after).
n      : directive to nullify the 'next' instruction
n.o.c.: nullify on condition.
op     : operation code.
ovfl   : overflow
p      : bit position (0 through 31).
r      : source register.
r1     : first source register.
r2     : second source register.
s      : space register identification.
sfu    : special function unit.
sr     : space register.
t      : destination register (one of the general purpose regs).
tlb    : translation lookaside buffer.
u      : unit descriptor (bytes or units).
wd     : word displacement.
wx     : word index.
x      : index register.
```

The instruction format is:

```
MNEM,modifiers        operands         comment
```

MNEM is the mnemonic name of the instruction. Modifiers is an optional list of instruction modifiers. They give parameters such as the nullification option and condition type. Options are separated with commas. Operands is an optional list of up to three operands. Source operands are at the left of the list, destination operands are at the right hand side. Operands are separated with commas.

Load and Store Instructions

Load instructions fetch an element from memory and store it in a general purpose register:

```
LDB              d(s,b),t          load byte
LDBS,ma,cc       i(s,b),t          load byte short
LDBX,u,m,cc      x(s,b),t          load byte indexed
LDH              d(s,b),t          load half-word
LDHS,ma,cc       i(s,b),t          load half-word short
LDHX,u,m,cc      x(s,b),t          load half-word indexed
LDW              d(s,b),t          load word
LDWAS,ma,cc      i(b),t            load word absolute short
LDWAX,u,m,cc     x(b),t            load word absolute indexed
LDWM             d(s,b),t          load word and modify b
LDWS,ma,cc       i(s,b),t          load word short
LDWX,u,m,cc      x(s,b),t          load word indexed
```

The 'load and clear' instructions fetch a word from memory, store it in a general purpose register and then set the value in memory to 0:

```
LDCWS,ma,cc      i(s,b),t          load and clear word short
LDCWX,u,m,cc     x(s,b),t          load and clear word indexed
```

The LDIL instruction takes the 21-bit immediate value, pads it to the right with 11 zero bits and stores the resulting value in a general purpose register:

```
LDIL             imm,t             load immediate left
```

The LDO instruction loads the offset of a virtual address into a general purpose register (by setting the B field to 0, an immediate value - the D field - can be loaded):

```
LDO              d(b),t            load offset
```

Store instructions store the contents of a general purpose register into memory:

```
STB              r,d(s,b)          store byte
STBS,ma,cc       r,i(s,b)          store byte short
STH              r,d(s,b)          store half-word
STHS,ma,cc       r,i(s,b)          store half-word short
STW              r,d(s,b)          store word
STWAS,ma,cc      r,i(b)            store word absolute short
STWM             r,d(s,b)          store word and modify b
STWS,ma,cc       r,i(s,b)          store word short
```

The STBYS instruction allows the storing of from one to 4 bytes from either side of a general register into memory.

```
STBYS,be,m,cc    r,i(s,b)          store bytes short
```

Arithmetic and Logical Instructions

Note: The instructions ADDBF, ADDBT, ADDIBF and ADDIBT are classified as branch instructions although they perform an addition as well.

The instructions COMBF, COMBT, COMIBF and COMIBT are classified as branch instructions although they perform a comparison as well.

Add instructions add the contents of two general purpose registers, or a register and an immediate value, and store the result into a general purpose register. Nullification of the next instruction can be made dependent on the arithmetic conditions applied to the result:

```
ADD,caf          r1,r2,t           add and n.o.c.
ADDC,caf         r1,r2,t           add with carry and n.o.c.
ADDCO,caf        r1,r2,t           add with carry, trap on ovfl
                                   and n.o.c.
ADDI,caf         imm,r,t           add to immediate and n.o.c.
ADDIO,caf        imm,r,t           add to immediate, trap on ovfl
                                   and n.o.c.
ADDIT,caf        imm,r,t           add to imm and trap on condition
```

ADDITO,caf	imm,r,t	add to imm and trap on condition or ovfl
ADDL,caf	r1,r2,t	add logical and n.o.c.
ADDO,caf	r1,r2,t	add, trap on ovfl and n.o.c.

The ADDIL instruction takes the 21 bit immediate value, pads it to the right with 11 zero bits and adds the resulting value to the contents of a general purpose register; the resulting value is stored into general purpose register 1:

ADDIL	imm,t	add immediate left

Subtract instructions subtract the contents of two general purpose registers (r1-r2), or an immediate value and a general purpose register (imm-r), and store the result into a general purpose register. Nullification of the next instruction can be made dependent on the arithmetic conditions applied to the result:

SUB,caf	r1,r2,t	subtract and n.o.c.
SUBB,caf	r1,r2,t	subtract with borrow and n.o.c.
SUBBO,caf	r1,r2,t	subtract with borrow, trap on ovfl and n.o.c.
SUBI,caf	imm,r,t	subtract from imm and n.o.c.
SUBIO,caf	imm,r,t	subtract from imm, trap on ovfl and n.o.c.
SUBO,caf	r1,r2,t	subtract, trap on ovfl and n.o.c.
SUBT,caf	r1,r2,t	subtract and trap on condition
SUBTO,caf	r1,r2,t	subtract and trap on condition or ovfl

The logical instructions perform a logical AND, OR or exclusive OR on two general purpose registers and store the result into a general purpose register (if complementing is indicated, then r2 is complemented before the logical operation is performed):

AND,caf	r1,r2,t	and and n.o.c.
ANDCM,caf	r1,r2,t	and complement and n.o.c.
OR,caf	r1,r2,t	inclusive or and n.o.c.
XOR,caf	r1,r2,t	exclusive or and n.o.c.

The 'compare and clear' instructions compare a general purpose register to an immediate value or to a general purpose register, while a general purpose register is cleared:

COMCLR,caf	r1,r2,t	compare, clear and n.o.c.
COMICLR,caf	imm,r,t	compare imm, clear and n.o.c.

The 'decimal correct' instructions performs an intermediate correction after an add or subtract instruction as a step in adding or subtracting BCD coded numbers:

DCOR,caf	r,t	decimal correct and n.o.c.
IDCOR,caf	r,t	intermediate decimal correct and n.o.c.

The Divide Step instruction provides a primitive step to create integer division. It calculates one bit of the quotient r1/r2 and leaves the partial quotient in a general purpose register:

DS,caf	r1,r2,t	divide step and n.o.c.

The 'shift and add' instructions are the basic instructions to build integer multiplication. The first operand is shifted left and added to the second operand; the result is stored in the destination register:

SH1ADD,caf	r1,r2,t	shift one, add and n.o.c.
SH1ADDL,caf	r1,r2,t	shift one, add logical and n.o.c.
SH1ADDO,caf	r1,r2,t	shift one, add, trap on ovfl and n.o.c.
SH2ADD,caf	r1,r2,t	shift two, add and n.o.c.
SH2ADDL,caf	r1,r2,t	shift two, add logical and n.o.c.
SH2ADDO,caf	r1,r2,t	shift two, add, trap on ovfl and n.o.c.
SH3ADD,caf	r1,r2,t	shift three, add and n.o.c.
SH3ADDL,caf	r1,r2,t	shift three, add logical and n.o.c.
SH3ADDO,caf	r1,r2,t	shift three, add, trap on ovfl

The unit instructions are steps in decimal operations:

UADDCM,caf	r1,r2,t	unit add complement and n.o.c.
UADDCMT,caf	r1,r2,t	unit add complement and trap on condition
UXOR,caf	r1,r2,t	unit exclusive or and n.o.c.

Branch Instructions

The 'add and branch' instructions add the contents of a general purpose register to a general purpose register or to an immediate value, and branch depending on the arithmetic conditions applied to the result:

```
ADDBF,ca,n        r,t,wd          add and branch if false
ADDBT,ca,n        r,t,wd          add and branch if true
ADDIBF,ca,n       imm,t,wd        add imm and branch if false
ADDIBT,ca,n       imm,t,wd        add imm and branch if true
```

The 'branch on bit' instructions test a bit with a fixed or variable position and branch depending on the extract conditions applied to the result:

```
BB,ce,n           r,p,wd          branch on bit
BVB,ce,n          r,wd            branch on variable bit
```

The simple branch instructions transfer execution to other instructions in the same or another programming unit:

```
BE,n              wd(sr,b)        branch external
BL,n              wd,t            branch and link
BLE,n             wd(sr,b)        branch and link external
BLR,n             x,t             branch and link register
BV,n              wx(b)           branch vectored
```

The 'compare and branch' instructions compare two general purpose registers, or an immediate value with a register, and branch depending on the logical conditions applied to the comparison:

```
COMBF,ca,n        r1,r2,wd        compare and branch if false
COMBT,ca,n        r1,r2,wd        compare and branch if true
COMIBF,ca,n       imm,r,wd        compare imm and branch if false
COMIBT,ca,n       imm,r,wd        compare imm and branch if true
```

The GATE instruction allows a branch while the execution privilege level is changed:

```
GATE,n              wd,t            gateway
```

The 'move and branch' instructions move an immediate value or the contents of a general purpose register to a general purpose register and branch conditionaly depending on the extract conditions applied to the value moved:

```
MOVB,ce,n           r,t,wd          move and branch
MOVIB,ce,n          imm,t,wd        move imm and branch
```

Shift, Extract and Deposit Instructions

Note: Variable bit positions or shift amounts are taken from the shift amount register (SAR or control register 11).

Deposit instructions move an immediate value or the contents of a general purpose register to a bit field in a general purpose register at a given bit position:

```
DEP,ce              r,p,l,t         deposit and n.o.c.
DEPI,ce             imm,p,l,t       deposit imm and n.o.c.
VDEP,ce             r,l,t           variable deposit and n.o.c.
VDEPI,ce            imm,l,t         variable deposit imm and n.o.c.
```

The 'zero and deposit' instructions clear a general purpose register and deposit an immediate value or the contents of a general purpose register into a bit field:

```
ZDEP,ce             r,p,l,t         zero, deposit and n.o.c.
ZDEPI,ce            imm,p,l,t       zero, deposit imm and n.o.c.
ZVDEP,ce            r,l,t           zero, variable deposit and n.o.c.
ZVDEPI,ce           imm,l,t         zero, variable deposit imm and n.o.c.
```

Extract instructions extract a bit field from a general purpose register and put the result into a general purpose register. The source register is extended to the left by 32 zeros (unsigned) or 32 bits equaling the left most bit (signed) before the extraction is performed; the resulting field is extended to the left by the same method to fill a 32-bit register:

```
EXTRS,ce        r,p,l,t         extract signed and n.o.c.
EXTRU,ce        r,p,l,t         extract unsigned and n.o.c.
VEXTRS,ce       r,l,t           variable extract signed and n.o.c.
VEXTRU,ce       r,l,t           variable extract unsigned and n.o.c.
```

The 'double shift' instructions concatenate the contents of two general purpose registers, shift the result to the right by a fixed or variable amount and store the result into a general purpose register.

```
SHD,ce          r1,r2,p,t       shift double and n.o.c.
VSHD,ce         r1,r2,t         variable shift double and n.o.c.
```

Space and Control Register Move Instructions

The space and control register move instructions move values between a general purpose register and a space register or a control register:

```
MFCTL           cr,t            move from control register
MFSP            sr,t            move from space register
MTCTL           r,cr            move to control register
MTSP            r,sr            move to space register
```

System Control Instructions

The system control instructions perform a variety of functions to support the implementation of an operating system. They are not normally used by application programmers:

```
BREAK           i1,i2           break
DIAG                            diagnose
FDC,m           x(s,b)          flush data cache
FDCE,m          x(s,b)          flush data cache entry
FIC,m           x(sr,b)         flush instruction cache
FICE,m          x(sr,b)         flush instruction cache entry
```

```
IDTLBA            r(s,b)            insert data tlb address
IDTLBP            r(s,b)            insert data tlb protection
IITLBA            r(sr,b)           insert instruction tlb address
IITLBP            r(sr,b)           insert instruction tlb protection
LDSID             (s,b),t           load space identifier
LHA,m             x(s,b),t          load hash address
LPA,m             x(s,b),t          load physical address
MTSM              r                 move to system mask
PDC,m             x(s,b)            purge data cache
PDTLB,m           x(s,b)            purge data tlb
PDTLBE,m          x(s,b)            purge data tlb entry
PITLB,m           x(sr,b)           purge instruction tlb
PITLBE,m          x(sr,b)           purge instruction tlb entry
PROBER            (s,b),x,t         probe read access
PROBERI           (s,b),imm,t       probe read access immediate
PROBEW            (s,b),x,t         probe write access
PROBEWI           (s,b),imm,t       probe write access immediate
RFI                                 return from interrupt
RSM               imm,t             reset system mask
SSM               imm,t             set system mask
SYNC                                synchronize caches
```

Special Function Unit and Coprocessor Instructions

The special function and coprocessor instructions are used to transfer data to and from external units, and to initiate processing in these units. The exact significance of each field varies between processors:

```
CLDDS,cop,ma,cc      i(s,b),t        coprocessor load double word short
CLDDX,cop,u,m,cc     x(s,b),t        coprocessor load double word indexed
CLDWS,cop,ma,cc      i(s,b),t        coprocessor load word short
CLDWX,cop,u,m,cc     x(s,b),t        coprocessor load word indexed
COPR,cop,op,n                        coprocessor operation
CSTDS,cop,MA,cc      r,i(s,b)        coprocessor store double word short
CSTDX,cop,u,m,cc     r,x(s,b)        coprocessor store double word indexed
CSTWS,cop,MA,cc      r,i(s,b)        coprocessor store word short
CSTWX,cop,u,m,cc     r,x(s,b)        coprocessor store word indexed
SPOP0,sfu,op,n                       special operation zero
SPOP1,sfu,op,n       r               special operation one
SPOP2,sfu,op,n       r               special operation two
SPOP3,sfu,op,n       r1,r2           special operation three
```

Alphabetical List of Instructions

ADD,caf	r1,r2,t	add
ADDBF,ca,n	r,t,wd	add and branch if false
ADDBT,ca,n	r,t,wd	add and branch if true
ADDC,caf	r1,r2,t	add with carry
ADDCO,caf	r1,r2,t	add with carry and trap on ovfl
ADDI,caf	imm,r,t	add to immediate
ADDIBF,ca,n	imm,r,wd	add imm and branch if false
ADDIBT,ca,n	imm,r,wd	add imm and branch if true
ADDIL	imm,t	add immediate left
ADDIO,caf	imm,r,t	add to immediate and trap on ovfl
ADDIT,caf	imm,r,t	add to imm and trap on condition
ADDITO,caf	imm,r,t	add to imm and trap on condition
ADDL,caf	r1,r2,t	add logical
ADDO,caf	r1,r2,t	add and trap on ovfl
AND,caf	r1,r2,t	and
ANDCM,caf	r1,r2,t	and complement
BB,ce,n	r,p,wd	branch on bit
BE,n	wd(sr,b)	branch external
BL,n	wd,t	branch and link
BLE,n	wd(sr,b)	branch and link external
BLR,n	x,t	branch and link register
BREAK	i1,i2	break
BV,n	x(b)	branch vectored
BVB,ce,n	r,wd	branch on variable bit
CLDDS,cop,ma,cc	i(s,b),t	coprocessor load double word short
CLDDX,cop,u,m,cc	x(s,b),t	coprocessor load double word indexed
CLDWS,cop,ma,cc	i(s,b),t	coprocessor load word short
CLDWX,cop,u,m,cc	x(s,b),t	coprocessor load word indexed
COMBF,ca,n	r1,r2,wd	compare and branch if false
COMBT,ca,n	r1,r2,wd	compare and branch if true
COMCLR,caf	r1,r2,t	compare and clear
COMIBF,ca,n	imm,r,wd	compare imm and branch if false
COMIBT,ca,n	imm,r,wd	compare imm and branch if true
COMICLR,caf	imm,r,t	compare imm and clear
COPR,cop,op,n		coprocessor operation
CSTDS,cop,MA,cc	r,i(s,b)	coprocessor store double word short

CSTDX,cop,u,m,cc	r,x(s,b)	coprocessor store double word indexed
CSTWS,cop,MA,cc	r,i(s,b)	coprocessor store word short
CSTWX,cop,u,m,cc	r,x(s,b)	coprocessor store word indexed
DCOR,caf	r,t	decimal correct
DEP,ce	r,p,l,t	deposit
DEPI,ce	imm,p,l,t	deposit imm
DIAG		diagnose
DS,caf	r1,r2,t	divide step
EXTRS,ce	r,p,l,t	extract signed
EXTRU,ce	r,p,l,t	extract unsigned
FDC,m	x(s,b)	flush data cache
FDCE,m	x(s,b)	flush data cache entry
FIC,m	x(sr,b)	flush instruction cache
FICE,m	x(sr,b)	flush instruction cache entry
GATE,n	wd,t	gateway
IDCOR,caf	r,t	intermediate decimal correct
IDTLBA	r(s,b)	insert data tlb address
IDTLBP	r(s,b)	insert data tlb protection
IITLBA	r(sr,b)	insert instruction tlb address
IITLBP	r(sr,b)	insert instruction tlb protection
LDB	d(s,b),t	load byte
LDBS,ma,cc	i(s,b),t	load byte short
LDBX,u,m,cc	x(s,b),t	load byte indexed
LDCWS,ma,cc	i(s,b),t	load and clear word short
LDCWX,u,m,cc	x(s,b),t	load and clear word indexed
LDH	d(s,b),t	load half-word
LDHS,ma,cc	i(s,b),t	load half-word short
LDHX,u,m,cc	x(s,b),t	load half-word indexed
LDIL	imm,t	load immediate left
LDO	d(b),t	load offset
LDSID	(s,b),t	load space identifier
LDW	d(s,b),t	load word
LDWAS,ma,cc	i(b),t	load word absolute short
LDWAX,u,m,cc	x(b),t	load word absolute indexed
LDWM	d(s,b),t	load word and modify

LDWS,ma,cc	i(s,b),t	load word short
LDWX,u,m,cc	x(s,b),t	load word indexed
LHA,m	x(s,b),t	load hash address
LPA,m	x(s,b),t	load physical address
MFCTL	cr,t	move from control register
MFSP	sr,t	move from space register
MOVB,ce,n	r,t,wd	move and branch
MOVIB,ce,n	imm,t,wd	move imm and branch
MTCTL	r,cr	move to control register
MTSM	r	move to system mask
MTSP	r,sr	move to space register
OR,caf	r1,r2,t	inclusive or
PDC,m	x(s,b)	purge data cache
PDTLB,m	x(s,b)	purge data tlb
PDTLBE,m	x(s,b)	purge data tlb entry
PITLB,m	x(sr,b)	purge instruction tlb
PITLBE,m	x(sr,b)	purge instruction tlb entry
PROBER	(s,b),x,t	probe read access
PROBERI	(s,b),imm,t	probe read access immediate
PROBEW	(s,b),x,t	probe write access
PROBEWI	(s,b),imm,t	probe write access immediate
RFI		return from interrupt
RSM	imm,t	reset system mask
SH1ADD,caf	r1,r2,t	shift one and add
SH1ADDL,caf	r1,r2,t	shift one and add logical
SH1ADDO,caf	r1,r2,t	shift one, add and trap on ovfl
SH2ADD,caf	r1,r2,t	shift two and add
SH2ADDL,caf	r1,r2,t	shift two and add logical
SH2ADDO,caf	r1,r2,t	shift two, add and trap on ovfl
SH3ADD,caf	r1,r2,t	shift three and add
SH3ADDL,caf	r1,r2,t	shift three and add logical
SH3ADDO,caf	r1,r2,t	shift three, add and trap on ovfl
SHD,ce	r1,r2,p,t	shift double
SPOP0,sfu,op,n		special operation zero
SPOP1,sfu,op,n	r	special operation one
SPOP2,sfu,op,n	r	special operation two

SPOP3,sfu,op,n	r1,r2	special operation three
SSM	imm,t	set system mask
STB	r,d(s,b)	store byte
STBS,ma,cc	r,i(s,b)	store byte short
STBYS,be,m,cc	r,i(s,b)	store bytes short
STH	r,d(s,b)	store half-word
STHS,ma,cc	r,i(s,b)	store half-word short
STW	r,d(s,b)	store word
STWAS,ma,cc	r,i(b)	store word absolute short
STWM	r,d(s,b)	store word and modify
STWS,ma,cc	r,i(s,b)	store word short
SUB,caf	r1,r2,t	subtract
SUBB,caf	r1,r2,t	subtract with borrow
SUBBO,caf	r1,r2,t	subtract with borrow and trap on ovfl
SUBI,caf	imm,r,t	subtract from imm
SUBIO,caf	imm,r,t	subtract from imm and trap on ovfl
SUBO,caf	r1,r2,t	subtract and trap on ovfl
SUBT,caf	r1,r2,t	subtract and trap on condition
SUBTO,caf	r1,r2,t	subtract and trap on condition or ovfl
SYNC		synchronize caches
UADDCM,caf	r1,r2,t	unit add complement
UADDCMT,caf	r1,r2,t	unit add complement and trap on condition
UXOR,caf	r1,r2,t	unit exclusive or
VDEP,ce	r,l,t	variable deposit
VDEPI,ce	imm,l,t	variable deposit imm
VEXTRS,ce	r,l,t	variable extract signed
VEXTRU,ce	r,l,t	variable extract unsigned
VSHD,ce	r1,r2,t	variable shift double
XOR,caf	r1,r2,t	exclusive or
ZDEP,ce	r,p,l,t	zero and deposit
ZDEPI,ce	imm,p,l,t	zero and deposit imm
ZVDEP,ce	r,l,t	zero and variable deposit
ZVDEPI,ce	imm,l,t	zero and variable deposit imm

Appendix B

MPE XL Debug

This appendix discusses DEBUG, the powerful system level debugging tool of MPE XL that allows you to examine and correct programs as they run on the system. The MPE XL version of DEBUG contains some significant improvements over its MPE V predecessor. To see this, let us first examine the capabilities a typical debugging facility will have:

- [ ] the ability to display and modify data areas

- [ ] the ability to stop the execution of the program at a pre-determined location, called a 'breakpoint'

- [ ] the ability to do calculations so that the user can do such tasks as calculate an address or verify a calculation the program is doing

- [ ] the ability to format data in record-style format

- [ ] the ability to retrieve information about symbols, such as procedure names, from the code structures

Debug on MPE V

The debugging facility that operates under MPE V was originally developed as an internal lab tool to debug MPE during its development. In this role it was not required to have an operating environment or style that would be immediately clear to a new user. Its commands were terse and its error messages could be quite cryptic to the uninitiated. To some extent, these qualities still remain in MPE V DEBUG.

The MPE V debugging facility is invoked one of four ways:

☐   By calling the DEBUG intrinsic from within the program.

☐   By running a program with the ;DEBUG option on the :RUN command.

☐   By hitting a previously set breakpoint.

☐   By typing the :DEBUG command. (This applies only to users with Privileged Mode capability.)

The commands in this debugging facility are all one or two letters long. The two most commonly used commands are D (Display) and M (Modify). These allow the user to display and modify data and to display code.

Each of these commands further requires that a base be entered to instruct the debugging facility what is to be displayed or modified. Several modes can be specified:

DB   Use the current value of the DB register as
        the base.

Q   Use the current value of the Q register as
        the base.

P   Use the current value of the P register as
        base. (Displays code.)

After this, the address is entered. For example, if a variable is known (from the compiler listing) to be stored at DB+22, the command to display this would be:

```
?D DB+22
000032
?
```

The above number is in octal. To display it in decimal:

```
?D DB+22,I
+0026
?
```

The ',I' indicates base 10, or decimal. Other modes are H for Hex, and C for Assembly mnemonics. For example, to display the current machine instruction and the next four in assembly mnemonic format:

```
?D P+0,5,C
021004    LDI 4
171004    LRA DB+4
000600    ZERO,NOP
041012    LOAD DB+10
031003    PCAL STT 3
?
```

To modify the variable at DB+22 in the display command above, the following would be entered:

```
?M DB+22
000032 := 000031
?D DB+22
000031
?
```

Other modes for displaying and modifying data exist for users with Privileged Mode capability. These modes allow access to any part of the system:

A   Absolute. Specifies a word in bank 0.

DA   Data Segment. Specifies an address within a
        particular data segment.

CO   Code Segment. Specifies an address within a
        particular code segment.

EA   Extended Address. Specifies an address using
        a bank number and an offset within the bank.

SY   Sysglob. Specifies an address in bank 0
        relative to Sysglob, which is address %1000.

Using these Privileged display and modify modes, it is possible to examine and modify any data within the system, even that maintained by MPE itself. Using this facility, a systems programmer can examine what is occurring in the entire system That same programmer can also damage the system so that MPE fails. Thus, using PM debug carries both great power and great responsibility.

Debug on MPE XL

The debugging facility contained within MPE XL does more than just expand the concepts used in the MPE V debugging facility so that they will work with HPPA. It also adds a much friendlier user interface to the debugging facility.

Invocation of DEBUG is exactly as described before for MPE V. In fact, the MPE XL DEBUG is a direct replacement of the MPE V DEBUG. Even Compatibility Mode programs use the new debugging facility. The MPE V debugging facility does not exist at all on MPE XL. MPE XL DEBUG determines the mode in which the program is running, and adjusts its displays accordingly.

DEBUG on MPE XL can be run in two different modes. The first will be called line mode for lack of a better term. This mode is the same as the MPE V debugging facility. An example of this is:

```
$ nmdebug> DV DP+8,10
```

This mode allows the programmer to interrogate the computer just as is done on MPE V, and allows the programmer familiar with MPE V to quickly start debugging programs.

The second mode of operation is called window mode. An HP terminal (one that responds to HP cursor address and display enhancement escape sequences) or equivalent is required to run in this mode. DEBUG separates the screen into different portions, or windows, and places data from a specific area of the machine on the screen. Each of the windows is given a name. For example, the 32 general registers are displayed in the General Register window. Program machine instruction information is placed in the P window, etc.

Figure B.1 shows an example of how the screen looks with windows enabled in Native Mode. The top window shows the General Registers, the next window down is the P window. The next window is a virtual window showing the area of memory above the DP registers for 16 words. The last window is the command window. This area of the screen is used for entering commands and displaying their results. It is possible to have windows turned on and still use all of the line mode commands to display and modify data.

Window mode in DEBUG has several interesting features. The most useful is that the debugging facility will always update the screen to show the current state of the machine. This update is done whenever a breakpoint is hit, when control returns to the debugging facility. All data areas (e.g., the registers) are updated and any values that have changed are displayed against an inverse background. This makes it easy to spot what has occured since the last time the debugging facility was in control.

```
GR$   ipsw=0006000f=jthlnxbCVmrQPDI  priv=3  pc=000000e8.000461c0  pin=0000001e
r0  00000000 83c00000 0004606f 00000000 r4  00000000 00000000 00000000 00000000
r8  00000000 00000000 00000000 00000000 r12 00000000 00000000 00000000 00000000
r16 00000000 00000000 00000000 00000000 r20 00000000 0000000a 83c00000 4005299c
r24 40050008 00046067 000000e8 40050008 r28 00000000 00000001 40052790 00000003

P $   PROG e8.461b8  DBUG1Y.PUB.SPELJMG/_start+$134                 Level  0,0
000461b8:        _start+$134        e280e000  BE    0(7,20)
000461bc:        _start+$138        000024b5  MFSP  4,21
000461c0:      > PROGRAM            6bc23fd9  STW   2,-20(0,30)
000461c4:        _start+$4          37de00b0  LDO   88(30),30
000461c8:        _start+$8          6bc03ff9  STW   0,-4(0,30)
000461cc:        _start+$c          e85f1f5d  BL    _start+$fc,2
000461d0:        _start+$10         08000240  OR    0,0,0

VO$ st         SID=ed      HOME=ed.40050020              Values in $
40050008:00000000 00000000 00000000 00000000 00000000 00000000 00000000 00000000
40050028:00000000 00000000 00000000 00000000 00000000 00000000 00000000 00000000

Commands
```

Figure B.1

Another useful feature of the MPE XL debugging facility is that it possesses a very powerful macro facility. Some commands allow repetitive execution, as well as compound statements. Variables can be defined for string or numeric data. These features allow the user to define powerful macros that perform a great deal of work with a very few keystrokes. Examples of this facility will be shown later.

The basic commands used by the MPE XL debugging facility are similar to those used by MPE V. What follows is not intended to be an exhaustive list of commands nor a tutorial, but rather a brief outline of the differences between the two debugging facilities. Commands are shown in all capitals for clarity only. Commands in DEBUG are case insensitive, but some command parameters *are* case sensitive.

DEBUG differentiates between Compatibility Mode and Native Mode programs. The basic commands, such as Display and Modify, have options which relate to the current execution mode. For example the Display command allows data to be displayed either by virtual address (the DV command) or by using the Compatibility Mode DB Register.

Address indirection is indicated by square brackets ([ ]). Thus, the expression 'DP+8' would normally be interpreted by the debugging facility as the value of DP (GR27) plus 8. The expression '[DP+8]' would be interpreted as the area of memory whose address is the value of DP plus 8.

As mentioned above, data display and modification commands are similar between MPE XL and MPE V:

```
DA    Display Absolute (same as MPE V)
DDB   Display using DB as base (CM)
DS    Display using S as base (CM)
DC    Display using Code segment as base (CM)
DV    Display using Virtual Memory address
DZ    Display using real address.
```

A corresponding set of commands exist for the Modify command. For example, to modify the value at DP+8c, the following would be entered:

```
nmdebug> MV DP+8c      (indirection is implied)
00004444      :=       (enter new value)
```

Breakpoints are set using various commands, each indicating the addressing base of the code being considered:

```
B  call_proc+4         (break in program)
BA                     (break in absolute address)
BG                     (break in group NL)
BP                     (break in public NL)
BS                     (break in system NL)
BU libname address     (user library)
```

Since MPE XL supports runtime searching of arbitrary library paths in addition to Group, Pub, and System, the last form allows a breakpoint to be set in any library currently loaded. Breakpoints are listed using the BL command, and deleted using the BD command.

HP Precision Architecture supports traps when a particular page is modified. Using this feature, the MPE XL debugging facility allows a feature new to the HP 3000 called data breakpoints. This allows the program to stop if an area of memory is modified. For example, assume the variable 'i' (located at DP+144) is being modified when it is not supposed to be, and it is necessary to find out where the modification is occurring:

```
$ nmdebug > DATAB DP+144,4   (break if DP+144 or any of the next three
                              bytes are modified)
```

Data breakpoints are deleted and listed with the DATABD and DATABL commands, respectively.

Variables can be defined with the VAR command. The variable is created and set to an initial value. It can then be used within a subsequent expression:

```
$ nmdebug > VAR pc_x = pc      (set pc_x to the value of PC)
$ nmdebug > PJ [!pc_x + 144]   (jump program window to the value
                                of pc_x+144)
```

The exclamation mark '!' is used to explicitly instruct the debugging facility to interpret the symbol following as a variable, and substitute its value into the command.

Arithmetic can be done on variables as well:

```
$ nmdebug > VAR pc_x = pc_x + 4
```

Macros are defined with the MACRO command. The macro is given a name and a definition. Macros can be given a type (to be used in an expression), and can have parameters. The macro in the following example shows all of these properties:

```
$ nmdebug > MACRO double:INT (p1:INT) {RETURN p1*2}
$ nmdebug > VAR pc_x = double(pc)
```

Reserved words are shown in all-capital letters. The above macro is used as a function in a VAR statement. The RETURN reserved word indicates what value is to be returned.

The calculator command is similar to MPE V. An equals sign command (=) is used to indicate a calculation is to occur. A macro or built-in function can be used within the expression:

```
$ nmdebug > = double(pc) + [pc+144]
```

This expression tells the computer to double 'pc', add to this result the contents of 'pc+144', then display the result.

Window Commands

The commands used to manipulate the windows deserve some special attention. Windows are enabled by using the WON (Windows On) command. When this command is entered, the screen is cleared and several windows are drawn (see Figure B.1). Window commands can then be used to manipulate one window at a time, to enable or disable it, or to change its size or other properties.

With windows enabled, the line mode commands are available in the bottom window. This bottom window is effectively a command window that can be used to accept and display the results of line mode commands. DEBUG permits commands and their results to scroll up under the other windows. The terminal's scroll keys allow you to review this record.

When a window command is entered, the window display is updated immediately to reflect the change. Just as line mode commands are available when windows are on, the window commands are also available when the windows are turned off. Window commands entered in line mode will take effect as soon as windows are enabled.

In general, the commands are one or two letters with a prefix or suffix used to indicate which window is to be affected. For example, 'PE' means "program enable" and 'GE' means "group enable". The notation for this command would be 'wE', where 'w' is to be substituted for the letter for the correct window.

In addition to WON and WOFF (Windows off), two commands allow specific windows to be turned on or off. The wD and wE commands allow windows to be Disabled or Enabled. Similarly, the wK command allows a window to be killed. It works by setting the number of lines to zero. The wD command merely sets a toggle to display the window or not. The wK command in effect eliminates the window from existence. For example:

```
$ nmdebug > GK;SRE;GRD;WON
```

This sequence kills the Group window, enables the Special Registers window, disables the General Registers window, then turns windows on. The display would consist of the Special Registers window, then the Program window, then the Command window.

One special type of window allowed by the debugging facility is a 'Group window', which is applied to a group of user-defined windows. Each user window can display a different area of memory. It is possible to define up to three Group windows, each with a maximum of 10 user windows. This facility is handy for displaying areas of memory that are disparate in location but related in function.

The window commands are summarized below:

```
wB    Backwards - Scroll the window backwards.
wC    Current - Mark the window as the Current window.
wD    Disable - Turn off the window.
wE    Enable - Turn on the window.
wF    Forward - Scroll the window forwards.
wH    Home - Reset the window to its current location
wJ    Jump - Aim the window to a particular address.
wK    Kill - Remove the window.
wL    Lines - Set the number of lines.
wN    Name - Give the window a name.
wR    Radix - Set the display radix.
wW    Window - Create a window, and aim it
      at a specified address.
```

The abbreviations for the various windows are:

```
R     CM Registers
GR    NM Registers
SR    NM Special Registers
P     NM or CM program
CMP   CM program window (used from NM)
NMP   NM program window (used from CM)
Q     CM Q stack frame
S     CM S stack frame
G     Group window
U     User-defined window (contained within a group window)
V     Virtual address window
Z     Real address window.
```

Certain combinations of a command and a window are not valid. For example, 'GRB' is not valid because it makes no sense to scroll the General Registers back. Similarly, 'SRL' is invalid because the special registers always take up a specific number of lines on the screen.

An Example

The following description and figures show an example of how to debug a program. The program used is shown in Figure B.2. Figures B.3 through B.14 show a sequence of screen displays that illustrate the use of the debugging facility, utilizing the variable and macro facilities, as well as DEBUG's ability to set breakpoints and modify data.

The program is written in standard HP PASCAL XL. The listing in Figure B.2 shows the source, along with the symbol table map and the locations of all the statements. Statement numbers generated by the compiler are in the first column, line numbers assigned by the editor are in the second. The compiler command is shown in Figure B.2. This command (PASXL) is actually a command file that is executed by the MPE XL command interpreter.

The program adds two numbers together, 'i' and 'j', then executes a case statement based upon the value of the sum. A literal is moved to the variable 'st' in the case statement, and then a writeln is done to display this literal. In the example below, the values of 'i' and 'j' will be modified so that a different branch of the case statement is taken than would be if the program were allowed to run with no intervention.

In Figures B.3 through B.14, a screen image is presented. In the command window, a command is entered, and the screen image resulting from that command sequence is shown in the next figure. Under each figure, a description of each command and its effects are given.

```
:PASXL DEBUGIV


    0    1.000   0    $STANDARD LEVEL 'OS_FEATURES'$
    0    2.000   0    $TABLES ON, CODE OFFSETS ON$
    0    3.000   0    {   This program is for use in demonstrating MPE XL DEBUG
   **    4.000   0
    0    5.000   0    }
    0    6.000   0    PROGRAM show debug(input,output);
    0    7.000   0    VAR
    0    8.000   0       i,j,k              : integer;   {integer math is simple to show}
    3    9.000   0       st                 : string[10];
    4   10.000   1    BEGIN
    4   11.000   1       st := '';           {initialize string}
    5   12.000   1       i := 2;
    6   13.000   1       j := 10;
    7   14.000   1       k := j + 1;
    8   15.000   1
    8   16.000   1       CASE k OF
    9   17.000   1
    9   18.000   1         0..20    : st := '0..20';
   10   19.000   1         21..100  : st := '0..100';
   11   20.000   1         101..1000: st := '0..1000';
   12   21.000   1
   12   22.000   1       END; { of case }
   12   23.000   1
   12   24.000   1       writeln (st);
   13   25.000   1    END.
```

```
                        I D E N T I F I E R   M A P

          IDENTIFIER         CLASS         TYPE        ADDRESS/VALUE

          I                  VARIABLE      INTEGER     DP+  10.0 (4.0)
          INPUT              PARAMETER     FILE        MB+   0.0 (248.0)
          J                  VARIABLE      INTEGER     DP+   C.0 (4.0)
          K                  VARIABLE      INTEGER     DP+   8.0 (4.0)
          OUTPUT             PARAMETER     FILE        MB+   0.0 (248.0)
          ST                 VARIABLE      STRING      DP+  18.0 (10.0)

          GLOBAL STORAGE USED = 0.0      TEMPORARY STORAGE USED = 0.0
          PARAMETER STORAGE USED = 0.0   CONSTANT STORAGE USED = 0.0


                        C O D E   O F F S E T S


                                 PROGRAM

        STMT  OFFSET   STMT  OFFSET   STMT  OFFSET   STMT  OFFSET   STMT  OFFSET
           4      CC      5      D4      6      E0      7      EC      8     100
           9     128     10     150     11     178     12     1B0


          NUMBER OF ERRORS =   0    NUMBER OF WARNINGS =  0
          PROCESSOR TIME 0: 0: 6    ELAPSED TIME 0: 0:18
          NUMBER OF LINES =   25    LINES/MINUTE =   250.0
          NUMBER OF NOTES =    0


  END OF PROGRAM

    :
```

Figure B.2 Sample Program

```
:SHOWME
USER: #S12,MGR.SPELJMG,PUB      (NOT IN BREAK)
MPE VERSION: HP32033A.B0.01.  (BASE ).
CURRENT: THU, DEC 18, 1986,  9:43 AM
LOGON:   THU, DEC 18, 1986,  9:08 AM
CPU SECONDS: 33          CONNECT MINUTES: 35
$STDIN LDEV: 23          $STDLIST LDEV: 23
:RUN DBUG1Y;DEBUG


Break at:    [0] PROG e8.00046064 PROGRAM
$1 ($1e) nmdebug > WON
```

Figure B.3

Figure B.3 illustrates the environment in which the program runs and the invocation of the program. The standard :RUN command parameter ;DEBUG is used. The debugging facility displays where the entry point of the program is, and gives the debug prompt. The command WON is entered, which enables window mode debugging.

```
GR$   ipsw=0006000f=jth1nxbCVmrQPDI  priv=3  pc=000000e8.00046064  pin=0000001e
r0   00000000 83c00000 002f8ae4 00000000 r4   00000000 00000000 00000000 00000000
r8   00000000 00000000 00000000 00000000 r12  00000000 00000000 00000000 00000000
r16  00000000 00000000 00000000 00000000 r20  00000000 0000000a 83c00000 4005299c
r24  40050008 00046067 000000e8 40050008 r28  00000000 00000001 40052790 00000003

 P $   PROG e8.4605c  DBUG1Y.PUB.SPELJMG/$START$+$14                    Level  0,0
 0004605c:           $START$+$14            00000000  BREAK    (rdb)
 00046060:           $START$+$18            000004a0  MFSP     0,0
 00046064:         > PROGRAM                e84002a8  BL       PROGRAM,2
 00046068:           PROGRAM+$4             d45f0c1e  DEP      31,31,2,2
 0004606c:           PROGRAM+$8             4bd53fc9  LDW      -28(0,30),21
 00046070:           PROGRAM+$c             4bc23fd1  LDW      -24(0,30),2
 00046074:           PROGRAM+$10            00153820  MTSP     21,4

 Commands

 $5 ($1e) nmdebug > use macs
 $c ($1e) nmdebug > maclist
 MACRO stmtfno : ANY/U16 = $0000
 MACRO mi      : ANY/U16 = $0000
 MACRO init    : ANY/U16 = $0000
 MACRO execf   : ANY/U16 = $0000
 MACRO stmtf   : ANY/U16 = $0000
 MACRO mj      : ANY/U16 = $0000
 $d ($1e) nmdebug > s;s
```

Figure B.4

Figure B.4 shows the starting environment of the program. The entry stub PROGRAM is the current location of the PC register (denoted by a '>' symbols in the P window between the first and second columns). The commands entered set the environment for the macros that will be used as an aid to debugging. The 'use' command informs the debugging facility to execute the file MACS as if it contained debug commands. The 'maclist' command lists the macro names and types. The 's;s' command single steps through the first two instructions, a DEPosit and a (delayed) Branch and Link. This effectively places the machine instruction pointer at the beginning of the program's first source language.

```
mac init {var pcx=pc}
mac stmtf {var pcx=pcx+4;while [pcx]>>10 <> $2000 do var pcx=pcx+4;&
       pj !pcx}
mac mi {WP 'Current Value of i=';=[dp+10];mv dp+10}
mac mj {WP 'Current Value of j=';=[dp+c]; mv dp+c}
mac execf {ss;while (([pc]>>#16) <> $2000) do ss}
mac stmtfno (stmt) {var pcx=pcx+4;while (([pcx]>>10 <> $2000) AND &
       (([pcx] BAND $0000FFFF) <> !stmt)) do var pcx=pcx+4; pj !pcx}
```

Figure B.5

Figure B.5 shows a listing of the macros used. These macros are:

init   Initializes the variable 'pcx' to be equal to the pc register.

stmtf   Used to move forward (without execution) to the next statement
        number, then move the program window to that location via a
        program jump (pj) command. Statement numbers are imbedded in
        the code by the compiler. The instruction LDIL (Load Immediate
        Left) is used with a target register of zero, which is an effective
        NOP instruction. The debugging facility looks for this sequence
        and interprets it as a statement number. The macro 'stmtf' finds
        these instructions by shifting the instruction pointed to by 'pcf'
        right $10 (16) bits ([pcx]>>10) and comparing it to the literal
        $2000, the bit pattern of an LDIL 0 instruction.

mi   Modify variable i. Displays the current value of 'i', then executes
        an MV command to modify its contents.

mj   Same as above, with variable 'j'.

execf   Same as 'stmtf' except the machine is single stepped to the point.
        The 'stmtf' macro acts to preview the code, the 'execf' actually
        executes it.

stmtfno Similar to 'stmtf', but this allows a specific statement number to be
        entered. The debugging facility will search until the specific
        statement is located, then pj to that location.

```
GR$   ipsw=0006000f=jthlnxbCVmrQPDI  priv=3  pc=000000e8.000461c0  pin=0000001e
r0   00000000 83c00000 0004606f 00000000 r4   00000000 00000000 00000000 00000000
r8   00000000 00000000 00000000 00000000 r12 00000000 00000000 00000000 00000000
r16 00000000 00000000 00000000 00000000 r20 00000000 0000000a 83c00000 4005299c
r24 40050008 00046067 000000e8 40050008 r28 00000000 00000001 40052790 00000003

P $    PROG e8.461b8  DBUG1Y.PUB.SPELJMG/_start+$134              Level  0,0
000461b8:          _start+$134          e280e000  BE    0(7,20)
000461bc:          _start+$138          000024b5  MFSP  4,21
000461c0:        > PROGRAM              6bc23fd9  STW   2,-20(0,30)
000461c4:          _start+$4            37de00b0  LDO   88(30),30
000461c8:          _start+$8            6bc03ff9  STW   0,-4(0,30)
000461cc:          _start+$c            e85f1f5d  BL    _start+$fc,2
000461d0:          _start+$10           08000240  OR    0,0,0

Commands




$f ($1e) nmdebug > init
$10 ($1e) nmdebug > stmtfno (4)
```

Figure B.6

Figure B.6 shows the result of the two single step instructions at the bottom of Figure B.4. The commands show the 'pcx' variable initialized by the 'init' macro, and the 'stmtfno' macro is used to find statement number 4.

```
GR$   ipsw=0006000f=jthlnxbCVmrQPDI  priv=3  pc=000000e8.000461c4  pin=0000001e
r0   00000000 83c00000 0004606f 00000000 r4   00000000 00000000 00000000 00000000
r8   00000000 00000000 00000000 00000000 r12  00000000 00000000 00000000 00000000
r16  00000000 00000000 00000000 00000000 r20  00000000 0000000a 83c00000 4005299c
r24  40050008 00046067 000000e8 40050008 r28  00000000 00000001 40052790 00000003

P $    PROG e8.4628c  DBUG1Y.PUB.SPELJMG/_start+$cc                  Level   0,0
00046 28c:           _start+$cc           20000004  ** Stmt  4
00046290:            _start+$d0           6b600030  STW      0,24(0,27)
00046294:            _start+$d4           20000005  ** Stmt  5
00046298:            _start+$d8           34150004  LDO      2(0),21
0004629c:            _start+$dc           6b750020  STW      21,16(0,27)
000462a0:            _start+$e0           20000006  ** Stmt  6
000462a4:            _start+$e4           34160014  LDO      10(0),22

Commands




$15 ($1e) nmdebug > b _start+cc;c
```

Figure B.7

In Figure B.7, the program window has now jumped to statement number 4. Note that the program is still stopped at the beginning of the program. A breakpoint is set at the location '_start+cc'. The same breakpoint could have been set by entering 'b 4628c'. The program is continued with the 'c' command.

```
GR$    ipsw=0006010f=jthlnxbCVmrQPDI  priv=3  pc=000000e8.0004628c  pin=0000001e
r0   00000000 000000a5 0004628f 00000000 r4   00000000 00000000 00000000 00000000
r8   00000000 00000000 00000000 00000000 r12  00000000 00000000 00000000 00000000
r16  00000000 00000000 00000000 000000a1 r20  40050284 000000e8 40050284 0000ffff
r24  00002f02 000000a1 40050278 40050008 r28  83c00000 40050030 400527e8 00000001


P $   PROG e8.4628c  DBUG1Y.PUB.SPELJMG/_start+$cc                    Level  0,0
0004628c:   [1]> _start+$cc          20000004  ** Stmt  4
00046290:        _start+$d0          6b600030  STW     0,24(0,27)
00046294:        _start+$d4          20000005  ** Stmt  5
00046298:        _start+$d8          34150004  LDO     2(0),21
0004629c:        _start+$dc          6b750020  STW     21,16(0,27)
000462a0:        _start+$e0          20000006  ** Stmt  6
000462a4:        _start+$e4          34160014  LDO     10(0),22

Commands




$1d ($1e) nmdebug > execf;execf;execf
```

Figure B.8

In Figure B.8, the breakpoint has been hit, as indicated by the breakpoint indicator
'[1]' and the pc indicator '>' being at the same line. Three 'execf' commands are
entered to execute forward through three statement numbers.

```
GR$    ipsw=0006010f=jthlnxbCVmrQPDI   priv=3  pc=000000e8.000462ac  pin=0000001f
r0   00000000 000000a5 0004628f 00000000 r4   00000000 00000000 00000000 00000000
r8   00000000 00000000 00000000 00000000 r12  00000000 00000000 00000000 00000000
r16  00000000 00000000 00000000 000000ed r20  40050284 00000002 0000000a 0000ffff
r24  00002f02 000000ed 40050278 40050008 r28  83c60000 40050030 400527e8 00000001


P $    PROG e8.462a0  DBUG1Y.PUB.SPELJMG/_start+$e0                 Level   0,0
000462a0:         _start+$e0           20000006  ** Stmt  6
000462a4:         _start+$e4           34160014  LDO       10(0),22
000462a8:         _start+$e8           6b760018  STW       22,12(0,27)
000462ac:      >  _start+$ec           20000007  ** Stmt  7
000462b0:         _start+$f0           4b610018  LDW       12(0,27),1
000462b4:         _start+$f4           4b7f0020  LDW       16(0,27),31
000462b8:         _start+$f8           0be10e13  ADDO      1,31,19

Commands




$20 ($1f) nmdebug > uwv dp+10 i;uwv dp+c j;gl#3;vw dp+18 st
```

Figure B.9

In Figure B.9, statement seven is the one that adds the two numbers 'j' and 'i' together. This sum is then used by the case statement to determine which writeln is executed. At this point, we wish to set up the debugging facility to view i and j, modify them, and view the resultant output. This is done by a rather lengthy sequence. The 'uwv' command sets a virtual user window to dp+10 (the location of i) and names it 'i'. The next 'uwv' does the same with j, which is located at dp+c. Then the group window is enabled and given a length of three screen lines, which encompasses the two user windows just defined, plus the line defining the top of the window. A virtual window is defined at dp+18 for the string array 'st', and given that name.

```
GR$    ipsw=0006010f=jthlnxbCVmrQPDI   priv=3  pc=000000e8.000462ac  pin=0000001f
r0   00000000 000000a5 0004628f 00000000 r4   00000000 00000000 00000000 00000000
r8   00000000 00000000 00000000 00000000 r12  00000000 00000000 00000000 00000000
r16  00000000 00000000 00000000 000000ed r20  40050284 00000002 0000000a 0000ffff
r24  00002f02 000000ed 40050278 40050008 r28  c6200000 40050030 400527e8 00000001


P $    PROG e8.462a0  DBUG1Y.PUB.SPELJMG/_start+$e0                       Level  0,0
000462a0:         _start+$e0            20000006  ** Stmt  6
000462a4:         _start+$e4            34160014  LDO      10(0),22
000462a8:         _start+$e8            6b760018  STW      22,12(0,27)
000462ac:       > _start+$ec            20000007  ** Stmt  7
000462b0:         _start+$f0            4b610018  LDW      12(0,27),1
000462b4:         _start+$f4            4b7f0020  LDW      16(0,27),31
000462b8:         _start+$f8            0be10e13  ADDO     1,31,19

VO$ st           SID=ed       HOME=ed.40050020              Values in $
40050020:00000000 00000000 00000000 00000000 00000000 00000000 00000000 00000000
40050040:00000000 00000000 00000000 00000000 00000000 00000000 00000000 00000000

Group:1      $  Virt/Real addr in $
U1   i       000000ed.40050018 $ 00000002    00000000    00000000    00000000
U2  *j       000000ed.40050014 $ 0000000a    00000002    00000000    00000000

Commands
$1d ($1f) nmdebug > mi;mj
Current Value of i=$00000002
$ VIRT ed.40050018 = "...."  $2        := 100
```

Figure B.10

Figure B.10 shows the effect of defining all the windows. The virtual window zero (V0) is below the P window, and the group 1 window is below that. The command window shows the two macros 'mi' and 'mj' being executed. The effect of 'mi' is shown. For clarity, 'mj' is not shown. The figure further shows variable 'i' being changed from its value of 2 to $100.

```
GR$    ipsw=0006010f=jthlnxbCVmrQPDI  priv=3  pc=000000e8.000462ac  pin=0000001f
r0  00000000 000000a5 0004628f 00000000 r4  00000000 00000000 00000000 00000000
r8  00000000 00000000 00000000 00000000 r12 00000000 00000000 00000000 00000000
r16 00000000 00000000 00000000 000000ed r20 40050284 00000002 0000000a 0000ffff
r24 00002f02 000000ed 40050278 40050008 r28 c6200000 40050030 400527e8 00000001


P $   PROG e8.462a0  DBUG1Y.PUB.SPELJMG/_start+$e0                 Level   0,0
000462a0:         _start+$e0        20000006  ** Stmt  6
000462a4:         _start+$e4        34160014  LDO      10(0),22
000462a8:         _start+$e8        6b760018  STW      22,12(0,27)
000462ac:      >  _start+$ec        20000007  ** Stmt  7
000462b0:         _start+$f0        4b610018  LDW      12(0,27),1
000462b4:         _start+$f4        4b7f0020  LDW      16(0,27),31
000462b8:         _start+$f8        0be10e13  ADDO     1,31,19

V0$ st          SID=ed     HOME=ed.40050020              Values in $
40050020:00000000 00000000 00000000 00000000 00000000 00000000 00000000 00000000
40050040:00000000 00000000 00000000 00000000 00000000 00000000 00000000 00000000


Group:1       $ Virt/Real addr in $
U1  i         000000ed.40050018 $ 00000100    00000000    00000000    00000000
U2 *j         000000ed.40050014 $ 00000150    00000100    00000000    00000000

Commands

$21 ($1f) nmdebug >
```

Figure B.11

Figure B.11 shows the results of the two modifications. The variable 'j' has been modified to $150, and both areas of memory are shown enhanced, indicating they changed. The program window was then advanced to statement 12, and a breakpoint set at '_start+$1b0'. (These steps not shown).

```
GR$    ipsw=0006000f=jthlnxbCVmrQPDI  priv=3  pc=000000e8.00046370  pin=0000001f
r0   00000000 00046000 0004628f 00000000 r4   00000000 00000000 00000000 00000000
r8   00000000 00000000 00000000 00000000 r12 00000000 00000000 00000000 00000000
r16 00000000 00000000 00000000 302e2e31 r20 30303000 40050028 00000007 0000ffff
r24 00002f02 000000ed 40050278 40050008 r28 c6200000 40050030 400527e8 00046020

P $    PROG e8.46368  DBUG1Y.PUB.SPELJMG/_start+$1a8              Level   0,0
00046368:           _start+$1a8          e85f1be5  BL      _start+$dc,2
0004636c:           _start+$1ac          341904da  LDO     621(0),25
00046370:    [2]> _start+$1b0            2000000c  ** Stmt 12
00046374:           _start+$1b4          341a0008  LDO     4(0),26
00046378:           _start+$1b8          2b600000  ADDIL   $0,27,1
0004637c:           _start+$1bc          34380050  LDO     40(1),24
00046380:           _start+$1c0          030010b7  LDSID   (0,24),23

VO$ st             SID=ed      HOME=ed.40050020              Values in $
40050020:00000007 302e2e31 30303000 00000000 00000000 00000000 00000000 00000000
40050040:00000000 00000000 00000000 00000000 00000000 00000000 00000000 00000000

Group:1       $  Virt/Real addr in $
U1  i         000000ed.40050018 $ 00000100    00000000    00000007    302e2e31
U2 *j         000000ed.40050014 $ 00000150    00000100    00000000    00000007

Commands


$24 ($1f) nmdebug > vr a
```

Figure B.12

In Figure B.12, the program is now stopped at statement 12. This is after the case statement which moves the literal to the variable 'st'. The virtual window shows the string has been changed. By changing the radix to ascii (a), it is possible to view the string as we expect it.

```
GR$    ipsw=0006000f=jthlnxbCVmrQPDI  priv=3  pc=000000e8.00046370  pin=0000001f
r0   00000000 00046000 0004628f 00000000 r4  00000000 00000000 00000000 00000000
r8   00000000 00000000 00000000 00000000 r12 00000000 00000000 00000000 00000000
r16  00000000 00000000 00000000 302e2e31 r20 30303000 40050028 00000007 0000ffff
r24  00002f02 000000ed 40050278 40050008 r28 c6200000 40050030 400527e8 00046020

P $    PROG e8.46368  DBUG1Y.PUB.SPELJMG/_start+$1a8                    Level  0,0
00046368:         _start+$1a8          e85f1be5  BL      _start+$dc,2
0004636c:         _start+$1ac          341904da  LDO     621(0),25
00046370:    [2]> _start+$1b0          2000000c  ** Stmt 12
00046374:         _start+$1b4          341a0008  LDO     4(0),26
00046378:         _start+$1b8          2b600000  ADDIL   $0,27,1
0004637c:         _start+$1bc          34380050  LDO     40(1),24
00046380:         _start+$1c0          030010b7  LDSID   (0,24),23

V0$ st         SID=ed     HOME=ed.40050020              Values in A
40050020:  "...." "0..1" "000." "...." "...." "...." "...." "...."
40050040:  "...." "...." "...." "...." "...." "...." "...." "...."

G   Group:1       $  Virt/Real addr in $
U1  i        000000ed.40050018 $ 00000100   00000000   00000007   302e2e31
U2 *j        000000ed.40050014 $ 00000150   00000100   00000000   00000007

Commands


$26 ($1f) nmdebug > woff
```

Figure B.13

In Figure B.13, the literal '0..1000' is seen in the 2nd and 3rd words of the string. The first word is the string length. Looking back at Figure B.12 shows that the length is seven. At this point, windows are turned off with the 'woff' command.

```
$17 ($1f) nmdebug > continue
0..1000

END OF PROGRAM
:
```

Figure B.14

Finally, in Figure B.14, the program is continued, and the literal '0..1000' is displayed to the screen.

Glossary

ADCC

The Asynchronous Data Communications Controller replaced the ATC as the terminal controller for the HP 3000. The ADCC was capable of higher speeds (9600 baud) and handled parity in a different style than the ATC.

Address

An address in HPPA is a 64-bit quantity that specifies a particular byte in memory. The high-order 32 bits are a 'space number', and the low-order 32 bits are a byte offset within the space. A 64-bit address is often referred to as a 'long address', because HPPA provides a method of using 32-bit 'short addresses' as a performance aid. Hardware automatically translates short addresses to long addresses by using their high-order 2 bits to select a 32-bit space register, thus resulting in a long address.

Alignment

Addresses in HPPA are byte-oriented. However, instructions that work with 16- or 32-bit chunks of data require that their data addresses be 'aligned'. Alignment means that the byte addresses are a multiple of the unit the instruction manipulates. For example, the LDW instruction, which loads 32 bits of data from memory, requires byte addresses that are multiples of 4 bytes (32 bits). The LDH instruction, which loads 16 bits of data from memory, requires addresses that are multiples of 2 bytes (16 bits). If LDW or LDH is executed with a non-aligned address, a 'data alignment' trap results, interrupting the program execution.

ATC

The Asynchronous Terminal Controller. In the early days of the HP 3000, it was the only data communications controller for asynchronous terminals and other devices. The ATC ran at a top speed of 2400 baud and supported both block and character mode operation.

ATP

The Advanced Terminal Controller replaced the ADDC as the terminal controller of choice for the HP 3000. It supports higher speeds (19200 baud) than either the ADCC or the ATC.

Block Mode

A method of terminal input flow control that allows a user to edit information on a CRT screen locally without interaction with the HP 3000. Hitting the 'Enter' key causes the terminal to send the screen data to the HP3000. Block mode uses DC1/DC2/DC1 handshaking to control the actual flow of characters.

BNF	Backus-Naur Form is a notational style that is used to rigorously define grammar for languages.
Branch	Logic branches in software are decision points where the program may take alternate paths depending upon some set of circumstances. In HPPA, a branch instruction will be executed in two clock cycles. The instruction that follows the branch instruction in the code stream is executed *before* the branch takes effect. This concept is called 'delayed branching'. By doing a delayed branch, rather than having extra hardware that would pre-fetch the instruction at the branch target address, the cost and complexity of the CPU is kept down.
Byte	The smallest unit addressable by HPPA. A byte consists of eight bits. Under MPE V, a word is composed of two bytes (16 bits). Under MPE XL, a word is composed of four bytes (32 bits), and a half-word is composed of two bytes (16 bits).
Chain	In the TurboIMAGE data base management system, a chain is a list of records in a data set that are 'connected' by having a common key value. Chains are implemented as doubly linked lists. TurboIMAGE allows chainheads and chaintails (the first and last records of a chain) to be located by specifying the key value. Chains may be traversed forwards or backwards.
CISC	Prior to Reduced Instruction Set Computing, most computers employed a scheme which relied on a large number of instructions, termed Complex Instruction Set Computing.
Collision	Hewlett-Packard's Local Area Network (LAN) observes the carrier-sense, multiple-access / collision-detect (CSMA / CD) protocol to control transmission throughout the communications medium. In essence, each node on the LAN attempts to transmit its message whenever it is ready. A collision is an attempt by two nodes to transmit at the same instant. A collision will result in both nodes 'backing off' for a random interval before retransmission.
Command Interpreter	The CI is the program that processes the 175 commands that a user can execute under MPE XL. Commands may be entered directly by typing them to the CI (interactively or batch), or programmatically via an intrinsic called COMMAND.

Compatibility Mode	CM allows programs written for MPE V-based HP 3000 computers to execute under MPE XL on the 900 Series without recompilation.
Control Register	HPPA relies on 25 control registers to provide interruption control, memory access protection, and processor state control.
CPU	The Central Processing Unit of a computer is that portion of the system that fetches and execute instructions.
CPU Cache	Under HPPA, there is a 'layer' of high-speed memory between regular memory and the CPU that acts as a fast retrieval resource for fetching recently used data or instructions.
Dynamic RAM	Dynamic Random Access Memory is a form of memory that must be refreshed every few milliseconds in order to retain the value it holds. The overhead of refreshing the memory is offset by the relatively low cost of this type of RAM.
ERISC	Early Reduced Set Computing is a term coined to describe the computing methods of early computers. At that time, computers had very few instructions.
Extents	Under MPE V, an extent is a contiguous area of disc that is a multiple of 256 bytes long. Disc files are composed of 1 to 32 extents. In a given file, all extents except the last are of the same size. The last extent may be smaller than the rest. Extents of a single file need not be contiguous, or even on the same disc drive.
File	A disc file is a set of logically related records stored on disc. On MPE V, the basic unit of file storage is a sector consisting of 256 bytes. On MPE XL, the basic unit of file storage is the page, which consists of 4096 bytes. All files are created with a particular organization, which is remembered and used for all accesses to a file.
Half-word	A half-word is two bytes (16 bits). Instructions accessing half-words require their addresses to be 16-bit aligned (i.e.: divisible by 2). See also: alignment.

HPPA   Hewlett-Packard Precision Architecture is the name given the new RISC-based approach to computing incorporated into current HP computer design.

HP-UX   The Hewlett-Packard implementation of UNIX is called HP-UX.

ILR   Intrinsic Level Recovery is a mechanism provided by TurboIMAGE for recovering a database from a system interruption. With ILR enabled, every call to DBPUT or DBDELETE causes a copy of data to be written to a special file for later use if recovery is needed. After a system crash which interrupts DBPUT or DBDELETE, ILR will either undo the intrinsic or redo it. In either case, neither intrinsic will be left partially done. Thus, ILR guarantees the integrity of a TurboIMAGE database at the level of an intrinsic. This guarantee is required for the implementation of Transaction Rollback.

Intrinsics   MPE provides a large library of documented procedures for use by programmers. These procedures are referred to as 'intrinsics'. Intrinsics written in CM languages reside in the file SL.PUB.SYS, and are described (in a manner readable by compilers) in the file SPLINTR.PUB.SYS. Intrinsics written in NM languages reside in the file XL.PUB.SYS, and are described (for compilers) in the file SYSINTR.PUB.SYS. On MPE XL, an effort is being made to restrict the definition of an intrinsic to only those procedures that are described in the SYSINTR or SPLINTR file. On MPE V, the word 'intrinsic' was often loosely applied to any procedure found in SL.PUB.SYS, even if it were undocumented and did not have an entry in SPLINTR.PUB.SYS.

LAN   A Local Area Network (LAN) is a method of connecting large numbers of terminals to a computer without having a large number of connectors plugged into the computer. On MPE XL, all terminals other than the system console are connected by a LAN, which is controlled by a Distributed Terminal Controller (DTC).

Lexical Analysis Lexical analysis is the process of converting a stream of input characters into a stream of tokens. Compilers use this to simplify the process of compiling a program into machine code.

Linker	The linker program takes as input one (or more) object modules and produces a single executable program file.
Long Pointer	The long pointer (64 bits) is one of two pointer types allowed under HPPA. See also: address.
Mapped Files	MPE XL provides the ability to access a disc file as though it were one large array, even though it might not be stored in contiguous areas of disc. The concept of associating a virtual memory address with a named disc file is referred to as 'mapping' the file onto virtual memory. Mapped files are one of the major new features of MPE XL.
Microcode	Modern CISC computers generally do not have every instruction executed by dedicated hardware. Instead, they are typically implemented as computers with a simpler (and faster) instruction set. A program is written for this simple instruction set which emulates the desired CISC instruction set. This program is usually stored in very fast ROMs. The program's code is referred to as microcode. Some computers have writable microcode, which means that their microcode is stored in RAM and a mechanism exists to replace it with a new version. HPPA computers have no microcode. Instead, their instruction set is implemented directly in hardware. The stack-based HP3000 computers are microcoded. Some (Series 37, 68, 70, and Micro/3000) have writable microcode.
MPE	MPE (Multi Programming Executive) is the generic name for the HP3000 operating system. MPE has undergone a number of evolutionary changes since the it first appeared with the HP3000 Series I. MPE V and MPE XL are the most recent versions of MPE.
Native Mode	The instruction set of the HPPA computers is referred to as Native Mode. Compatibility Mode is an emulated and/or translated stack-based HP3000 instruction set.
NMOS III	NMOS (Negative Metal Oxide Semiconductor) III is a technology used in integrated circuit (IC) design. Compared to other technologies, NMOS ICs are rated as 'high speed', and 'medium power'. NMOS ICs are slightly faster than CMOS (Complementary Metal Oxide Semiconductor). The HP 3000/930 and HP 3000/950 both utilize primary NMOS ICs.

OCT	The Object Code Translator (OCT) is a program under MPE XL which translates CM programs (those using the stack-based HP3000 instruction set) into a blend of native mode and emulated instructions, resulting in performance gains over strictly emulated programs.
Packet	Data transmitted from one node to another on a LAN is sent as a 'packet'. A packet is a collection of data with an address, user data, and error detection/correction information. The minimum packet size of the Distributed Terminal Controller is 64 bytes.
Pages	A page is 2048 bytes. The HPPA hardware segments memory into pages. MPE XL uses both the hardware page size of 2048, and a software page size of 4096 bytes, for keeping track of data in memory and on disc.
Path Length	The number of instructions executed between two points in a program is referred to as the 'path length'. The path length is a useful metric for determining the performance of system software. For example, consider the HPFOPEN intrinsic, which is used to open a disc file. If tuning the operating system were to reduce the number of instructions executed by HPFOPEN from, say, 100,000 to 50,000, then the path length was cut by a factor of two.
Pipelining	The pre-fetching of instructions to execute by the HPPA hardware before the program gets to the point of executing them is called pipelining. The pipeline in HPPA is shallow, holding only one extra instruction.
Roll-Back Recovery	In TurboIMAGE, database recovery can be initiated after a system failure using roll-back recovery, but only if both transaction logging and ILR have been enabled. In this situation, ILR restores the structural consistency of the database, while roll-back recovery mechanisms 'back out' incomplete transactions.
Roll-Forward Recovery	In TurboIMAGE, database recovery can be initiated after a system failure using roll-forward recovery if transaction logging has been enabled *and* a backup copy of the database exists. Once the backup copy has been restored after a failure, roll-forward recovery mechanisms 'reapply' logical transactions.

Root File	In TurboIMAGE, the root file is the translated version of the schema file, which defines the structure of the database. It is in a binary format, and is directly used by the TurboIMAGE intrinsics.
Schema	A schema is a high level specification of the structure of a database. In the case of TurboIMAGE, a schema is stored in an ASCII data file, and is read by the program DBSCHEMA, which 'compiles' the schema into a database root file.
Segmenter	The segmenter is the program responsible for maintaining libraries of compiled CM code, and for binding one (or more) USLs into a CM program file.
Short Pointer	The short pointer (32 bits) is one of two pointer types allowed under HPPA. See also: address.
SLLIC	Spectrum Low-Level Intermediate Code is normally produced by the UCODE package, but can be generated by a compiler directly. It represents an interface to describe the individual HPPA instructions in a consistent manner. The SLLIC package is responsible for creating SOM (Spectrum Object Module) files.
SOM	The Native Mode object file used by the linker and the loader is called a Spectrum Object Module (SOM) file. It contains both relocatable and executable object code. It is analogous to MPE V's USL (User Subroutine Library) file.
Stack	The stack model is used to access data, with data queued in a 'Last-In-First-Out' fashion; that is, data is placed on top of the stack and then removed from the top. The MPE V based HP3000s are almost completely stack oriented, with few instructions that can address data without also referencing the stack. These machines have special purpose hardware to aid in manipulating the stack. The HPPA machines do not have a stack implemented in hardware, but as in all modern computers, a stack exists. In HPPA, the stack is manipulated explicitly with software instructions to 'push' and 'pop' data from it.
Static RAM	Static RAM (Random Access Memory) is a form of memory that will remember its data even when power is turned off. Static RAMs are typically less dense, faster, and more expensive than dynamic RAMs.

Switch Stub	The SWITCH facility permits transfer between Compatibility Mode to Native Mode. Switch stubs are small procedures that accept parameters from calling programs and format the information to call the desired procedure in the opposite execution mode.
TLB	The Translation Lookaside Buffer in an HPPA computer is used to calculate the real (physical) address corresponding to a particular virtual address. The HPPA design forbids having more than one virtual address map to the same real address.
Transaction Logging	TurboIMAGE's Transaction logging is the process of writing a record of every transaction in a database to a separate log file. The data in the log file can be used after a system crash to back-out (undo) incomplete transactions.
Translated Code	The result of the OCT (Object Code Translator) is a program file that contains the original CM code *and* the native mode equivalent of the CM code. This NM code is referred to as translated code.
UCODE	This is a language that represents a 'generic' 32-bit stack-based machine, and is generated by most native mode compilers under MPE XL. UCODE is converted by the UCODE package into SLLIC, which is then directly converted to HPPA instructions stored in a SOM file.
UNIX	Originally developed in 1969 at Bell Labs, UNIX was designed to be a simple, powerful, easily extensible operating system of software development that could be ported to any hardware system.
USL	The User Subroutine Library contains files used by the segmenter under MPE V, and is analogous to the SOM file used by linker under MPE XL. USL's only contain relocatable code and must be :PREPed before execution.
Word	Under MPE XL, a word is four bytes (32 bits) and a half-word is 2 bytes (16 bits). Under MPE V, a word is two bytes (16 bits).

The Authors

Reprinted by permission: Tribune Media Services, Inc.

Each of the authors is an experienced software engineer, and all have spent time 'in the labs' at Hewlett-Packard's Information Technology Group as consultants to the Spectrum Program. This includes an aggregate total of 91 months in the MPE XL Reliability Project, the TurboIMAGE/XL Testing Project, and the MPE XL Destructive Testing Project.

Photo Credits: Black & White Photo of Palo Alto, Daniels Photography, Gebhardt Productions, and David Herberg.

Steven M. Cooper

is well-known within the HP 3000 community as a specialist on MPE performance and database management systems. Active with the HP 3000 since 1977, he developed the Environment/3000 product for American Management Systems. In particular, he designs and consults on large applications for diverse clients, such as the Banco del Exportacion de Guatemala and Harvard University. He is a member of the Adager Research and Development Laboratory.

A long-time member of INTEREX, he is active in the Bay Area Regional User Group, the Southern California Regional User Group, and the Northwest Regional User Group. He is the past Chairman of SIGIMAGE, the INTEREX special interest group for IMAGE.

He received a B.A. degree, with high honors, in Applied Physics and Information Science from the University of California at San Diego in 1975; in 1977, he received an M.B.A. with concentration in Computers and Information Systems from the University of California at Los Angeles.

He is a Senior Consultant for Allegro Consultants Inc. of Redwood City, California.

Jason M. Goertz

has been involved with the HP 3000 community since 1978. A frequent speaker at seminars and conferences, he is an expert on data communications, MPE performance, and operating system internals. He began his career at Whitman College as a technical programmer, and became an SE for HP's Northwest Region in 1980. He was the MPE Field Software Coordinator when he left HP to become Vice-President for MIS at Generra Sportswear in 1984. Now an independent consultant, he provides technical training, system performance analysis, and applications design services for major clients.

He has been active in the Northwest Regional User Group and INTEREX since 1979. He has been honored twice by INTEREX: Publications Achievement (1980) and Outstanding Library Contributor (1983). Hewlett-Packard named him as the SE Consultant of the Year for the Northwest Region in 1982.

He received a B.A. degree in Chemistry from Whitman College in 1978. He is President of Mattedor Computer Services of Bellevue, Washington.

Wayne E. Holt

has been actively involved with the computer industry since 1966 in a variety of hardware environments. He has been involved with the HP 3000 since 1977, and is a noted author and consultant on site management, computer center design, and data communications. He has held positions with Maricopa County of Arizona, Computer Science Corporation, Whitman College, and Union College of New York.

In 1978, as the first Chairman of the INTEREX Library Committee, he established the HP 3000 Contributed Software Library as a student project at Whitman College in Walla Walla, Washington. His involvement with User Groups includes founding the Columbia Basin Regional User Group (1977) and the Adirondack Area Regional User Group (1982) of INTEREX, and the Eastern New York Chapter of DECUS (1984). He served on the INTEREX Board of Directors as Vice-Chairman between 1980 and 1981, and is a long-time member of the Northwest Regional User Group.

He has been honored by the community on several occasions: Outstanding Contributor, Denver Conference (1978); Publications Achievement (1980); Best International Conference Paper (1981); and INTEREX Hall of Fame (1982).

He received a B.A degree in Mathematics from Whitman College in 1972. He is currently the Director of Research & Development at Software Research Northwest Inc. of Vashon Island, Washington.

Scott E. Levine

began his HP 3000 experience as a system manager at Bendix Field Engineering Corporation in 1982. He has an extensive background in data communications, systems programming, graphics, and laser technologies. His positions at Union College of New York, and the Group Health Association of Washington D.C. emphasized multi-vendor, multi-operating system environments. He has particular expertise with Local Area Networks, and participates in network planning for major clients.

He received B.S. and M.S. degrees in Computer Science from Union College of New York in 1982. He is a Senior Software Engineer at Software Research Northwest Inc. of Vashon Island, Washington.

Joanna L. Mosher

has been a member of the HP 3000 community since 1984. She is a specialist in data base management systems, particularly TurboIMAGE, HP IMAGE (HP-UX and MPE), and HP SQL. As the system manager for Union College of New York, she was responsible for administering a network that linked multiple HP 3000's with multiple Digital VAX computers for campus-wide information exchange.

She received a B.S. degree in Management and Industrial Engineering from Rensselaer Polytechnic Institute in 1983. She is currently a Software Engineer at Software Research Northwest Inc. of Vashon Island, Washington.

Stanley R. Sieler, Jr.

began his career in 1972 as a programmer, and is well-known in the HP 3000 community as an author and frequent contributor to the INTEREX Software Library. A systems programmer for Burroughs Corporation until 1978, he joined Hewlett-Packard in 1979 as an engineer in the MPE Lab. His list of accomplishments in the lab is extensive: writing Q-MIT STORE, designing MPE V/E RESTORE, Intrinsic Level Recovery for IMAGE/3000, and On-Line Backup for IMAGE/3000, as well as designing and developing Process Management for MPE XL.

He is now a consultant, and he specializes in operating system performance issues. He is also a member of the Adager Research and Development Laboratory.

He has been honored several times for his contributions to the community: in 1985, as INTEREX Author of the Year, and in 1986, as Outstanding Contributor to the Software Library.

He graduated from the University of California at San Diego in 1974 with a B.A. degree in Computer Science. He is currently a Senior Consultant with Allegro Consultants Inc. of Redwood City, California.

Jacques Van Damme

was an early contributor to the INTEREX Software Library, with the routines COBGEN, ADM-RTE, and CALC. He is an MPE performance specialist and a well-known instructor in the field of systems internals. He joined Hewlett-Packard in 1973 as a Systems Engineer in Belgium, and was the SEO manager when he left the company in 1981 to form Sydes N.V.

As the systems designer at Sydes, he created FSEDIT, METRO, SYDAID, and MAKEUP. Now with Denkart N.V., he is a frequent speaker at European User Group meetings.

He graduated as a Civil Electronics Engineer from the University of Leuven in Belgium in 1972. He is currently the Director of Research and Development for Denkart N.V. of Kontich, Belgium.

A Chronological
Authors' Bibliography

December, 1986   Goertz, Jason M. "Beyond RISC - A Technical Evaluation of HP Precision Architecture", *SuperGroup*, Vol. 6, No. 12 & Vol. 7, No. 1, SuperGroup Association.

Jan.-Dec. 1986   Holt, Wayne E. and Goertz, Jason M. "The Neophyte", Column in *The HP Chronicle, 12 issues,* Wilson Publications.

October, 1986   Goertz, Jason M. "A Brief Guide to Privileged Mode Programming", *Proceedings of the INTEREX Conference/Detroit.*

October, 1986   Holt, Wayne E. & Barnett, Donald M. "Meeting the Challenge: An Inside Look at the Spectrum Testing Environment", *Proceedings of the INTEREX Conference/Detroit.*

October, 1986   Sieler, Stanley R., Jr. "A Comparison of C Compilers for the HP 3000", *Proceedings of the INTEREX Conference/Detroit.*

September, 1986   Holt, Wayne E. "Choice Not Chance - A Manager's Overview of HP 3000 Datacom Solutions", *Interact*, Vol. 6, No. 9, INTEREX Association.

August, 1986   Holt, Wayne E. "The Local Area Network - A Guided Tour", *SuperGroup*, Vol. 6, No. 8, SuperGroup Association.

July, 1986   Sieler, Stanley R., Jr. "Software Review: Advancelink and Reflection", *Interact*, Vol. 6, No. 7, INTEREX Association.

May, 1986   Sieler, Stanley R., Jr. "How to Speed Up Your HP 150: A New Chip", *The HP Chronicle*, Vol. 3, No. 6, Wilson Publications.

April, 1986   Sieler, Stanley R., Jr. "What I Wish I Knew Before I Bought My HP 3000", *Interact*, Vol. 6, No. 4, INTEREX Association.

February, 1986   Holt, Wayne E. "The RJ-11 Modular Jack", *Interact*, Vol. 6, No. 2, INTEREX Association.

January, 1986	Goertz, Jason M. "Managing a Large HP 3000 Shop", *Interact*, Vol. 6, No. 1, INTEREX Association.
November, 1985	Sieler, Stanley R., Jr. "RISC Paper Reveals Clues on Spectrum", *The HP Chronicle*, Vol. 2, No. 12, Wilson Publications.
September, 1985	Holt, Wayne E. "Ethernet: Communicating in a Mixed-Vendor Environment", *Proceedings of the INTEREX Conference/Washington, D.C.*
September, 1985	Sieler, Stanley R., Jr. "HP 150 and IBM PC Emulators", *Interact*, Vol. 5, No. 9, INTEREX Association.
August, 1985	Goertz, Jason M. "MPE Internals for Beginners", *Paper presented at INTEREX Technical Seminar.*
July, 1985	Sieler, Stanley R., Jr. "The Impact of Detpack on System Performance and Vice Versa", *SuperGroup*, Vol.5, No. 4, SuperGroup Association.
June, 1985	Goertz, Jason M. "Internal Structures of MPE V", *Interact*, Vol.5, No. 6, INTEREX Association.
June, 1985	Holt, Wayne E. and Levine, Scott E. "To Build A Bridge: Linking the HP 3000 with VAX", *SuperGroup*, Vol. 5, No. 3, SuperGroup Association.
May, 1985	Cooper, Steven M. "Variations on a Tune: Another Look at the Never-Ending Struggle Towards Optimal Performance", *Proceedings of the NOWRUG Conference/1984.*
April, 1985	Cooper, Steven M. "Tuning Large Systems for Optimal Performance", *Interact*, Vol. 5, No. 4, INTEREX Association.
February, 1985	Sieler, Stanley R., Jr. "Software Review: Personal Tax Planner", *Interact*, Vol. 5, No.2, INTEREX Association.
February, 1984	Goertz, Jason M. "CAP=PM: Privileged Mode Demystified", *Proceedings of the INTEREX Conference/Anaheim.*

July, 1984	Sieler, Stanley R., Jr. "Debugging Using Debug and Decomp", *Proceedings of the U.K. HP Users 1st Joint Confrence/Exeter.*
July, 1984	Cooper, Steven M. "Where, Oh Where Have my DST's Gone?", *Proceedings of the U.K. HP Users 1st Joint Confrence/Exeter.*
April, 1983	Goertz, Jason M. "The MPE Memory Dump or How to Make a Statue of an Elephant", *Proceedings of the INTEREX Conference/Montreal.*
October, 1982	Holt, Wayne E. "Low-Budget Site Renovation", *Proceedings of the INTEREX Conference/Copenhagen.*
July, 1982	Goertz, Jason M. "System Disaster Recovery", *Interact*, Vol. 2, No. 4, INTEREX Association.
March, 1982	Holt, Wayne E. & Galpin, Amy J. "System Resource Accounting: An Overview of Available Software", *Proceedings of the INTEREX Conference/San Antonio.*
April, 1981	Holt, Wayne E. & Payne, Delores R. "Programming Standards: A Tool for Increased Programmer Productivity", *Proceedings of the INTEREX Conference/Orlando.*
September, 1980	Holt, Wayne E. "The Hardcopy Console: A Tool for Installation Management", *Proceedings of the INTEREX Conference/Montreux.*
February, 1980	Holt, Wayne E. "The HPGSUG Contributed Software Library: How to Utilize It in Your Shop", *Proceedings of the INTEREX Conference/San Jose.*
November, 1978	Holt, Wayne E. "BEACON & GUARDIAN: Installation Management Solutions in Search of Problems", *Proceedings of the INTEREX Conference/Denver.*
April, 1978	Goertz, Jason M. "Standalone HP 7221A Plotter Operation", *Journal of HP General Systems Users Group.*

Index

A

Addition 52
Address 24-25, 33-34, 38, 40-44,
    55-64, 68, 70, 73, 77-80, 84
Address access locality 58
Address alignment 226
Address mode 37-38, 40, 56
Address space 56-57, 59-60, 65,
    73, 104-105
ALGOL 9, 10, 36, 98, 140
ALGOL 60 214, 218
Alignment 240-247, 255
ANSI 214-217, 239-240, 248,
    256-257
Argument list area 75
Argument registers 71
Arguments 227
Arithmetic 18-19, 24-25, 226
Arithmetic circuitry 22-23
ASCII 118, 126-127, 132-133, 156
Assembler 59, 80, 86-87, 103
Assembler languages 23
Asynchronous 97, 111, 113-116,
    118

B

Bandwidths 97
BASIC 174, 216, 237
BASIC/3000 210
BASIC/V 216, 219, 237-238,
    253-254
BASIC/XL 253
Benchmark 98
Binary pattern 21, 24-25, 27, 140
Binary transfer 120
Binary tree (B-Tree) 125, 127,
    129, 140, 142, 156

B

Binding 73, 206-207
BISYNC 115, 118
Block-structured language 214
BNF (Backus-Naur Form) 81
Boundary 43, 30, 149, 151, 226,
    240-241
Branches 25, 74-75, 78-79, 89
Branching 63, 70, 75
Buffers 35, 113-114, 118-119,
    147, 199, 236
Burroughs 9, 33, 36, 140
Byte-aligned operation 226
Byte-orientation 131

C

Cache 27, 30
Cache memory 58-59
CALLALIGNED option 243
Chain 172, 177, 180-185
Cheapernet 116
CISC 24, 26-29, 31-32, 48, 50,
    71, 79, 226
COBOL 31, 36, 44-45, 81, 83, 85,
    174, 198, 208-209, 215,
    217, 227-228, 232, 235,
    236, 240-244, 247, 256
COBOL II 217, 244, 254
COBOL II/V 216, 254
COBOL II/XL 208, 209, 216,
    220, 239-244
COBOL/3000 210, 217
COBOL/V 254
COBOLLOCK 243
COBOLUNLOCK 243
Code path 77, 253
Comarea 235-236
Compatibility Mode 13, 72,
    105-106, 225, 228-231, 233, 237

Condition code   41, 229-230
Control store   24-25
Coprocessor   95, 97, 101
CPU   23-25, 27, 33-35, 55, 58,
    61, 98-100
CPU cache   58
CPU registers   53, 55
CSMA/CD   116

D

D-cache   58, 63, 96
Data storage   32, 37, 40
Database management   163-167
DBSCHEMA   174
DBUTIL   173-174, 181
Deadlock   200
DEBUG   106
DEC   29, 117-118, 251, 257-258
DECserver   117-118
Delimit   33-34, 38, 42, 71, 81,
    83-84, 196
Demand-paged memory   105
Directory   110, 125, 127, 130,
    132-134, 257
Disc address   134
DMA (Direct Memory Access)   97
Double-precision calculations
    97-98, 100-101
Data storage   32, 37, 40
Double-word variables   241
DS (Distributed Systems)
    118, 238
Dynamic RAM   23, 27
Dynamic procedure calling   243

E

Echo   117, 121

Efficiency   22, 35-36, 60-61, 79,
    130, 208, 210, 237, 241
Emulation   13, 98, 105, 210, 212,
    228
ENIAC   20
ESPOL   9
Exponentiation   24, 51, 233-234
Extent   125, 129, 133

F

FCONTROL   121, 144, 154
FCOPY   35, 173
Fetch   21, 23-26, 29, 58, 62
Filename   126-127, 134-135
Firmware   9, 11, 140, 229, 236
Fixed-length records   130, 147,
    153
Flat file   153, 156, 159
Floating-point calculation   97, 98
FOPEN   121, 126, 131, 132, 140,
    143, 145, 154, 156, 159
Foreground processing   110-111
FORTRAN   23, 24, 80, 147, 174,
    235
FORTRAN 66   217
FORTRAN 77   217, 247
Function   40, 50, 63-64
FWRITE   154, 156
FWRITEDIR   154

G

Gallium Arsenide   101
Generic key   156
Global database locks   179

H

Half-word 51, 63, 131, 226
Half-word accesses 240
Hashing 182, 184
Hewlett, Bill 1, 2, 5
Hewlett-Packard Company 2, 5
Hierarchical data base 165
Hollerith, Herman 19
HP Business BASIC/V 254
HP FORTRAN 66/V 217, 237,
    248, 250, 254
HP FORTRAN 77/XL 144, 217,
    220, 237, 239, 247
HP FORTRAN 77/V 217
HP Pascal/XL 144, 149, 151,
    208, 214, 215, 229, 232, 235,
    239, 244
HP SQL 187, 257
HP Standard Pascal 214
HP-UX 13, 100, 109, 248
HPCICOMMAND 231, 232
HPFOPEN 126, 127, 131, 133,
    139, 143, 145,
HPPA 13, 17, 29, 47-52, 54-56,
    58, 63, 67, 69-71, 73, 75, 80,
    85-87, 89, 91

I

IBM 19-21, 23, 25, 29, 48, 80,
    115, 118-119, 217-218, 256
IEEE Standards 51, 97, 115, 118,
    233-236,
ILR (Intrinsic Level Recovery)
    180-181
IMAGE 156-157, 165
IMB (InterModule Bus) 11

Incompatibilities in migration
    239, 246, 247, 252-256
Increment 40, 42-43, 52, 75
Indexes in HP SQL 189, 192, 201
ININ (Internal Interrupt) 44
Integer variables 37, 40, 51-52,
    215, 219, 240-241, 244,
    246, 248
Interface 66, 86
Interface, UCODE 86
Interlanguage calls 213, 215, 221
Interpreter 25, 110
InterSOM/IntraSOM access 74
Interspace/Intraspace 74, 77, 78
Intrinsics 86, 105, 107, 121,
    126-127, 131-134, 139,
    142-143, 154-158,206-207,
    212, 215-217, 228-232,
    235-236, 238, 241-243,
    249, 252
INP (Intelligent Network
    Processor) 115
ISO (International Standards
    Organization) 214

J

JCWs (Job Control Words) 107

K

KEYINFO 157
Keywords for SQL 198
KSAM file 134, 155-157, 217

L

LAN (Local Area Network) 97,
  116-118
Lexical analysis 83-85
Link-time 221
LINKALIGNED option 243
Linkedit 205, 207-208
Linker 72-74, 80, 86
LISP 81
LISTDIR5 command 108,
  135-137
LISTREDO command 107
Loader 68, 72, 74, 78, 80, 86, 155,
  206, 212, 221, 231
Logfile 181, 192, 200
Long-mapped file 142, 143, 145
Long-pointer 142-145

M

Macro 106, 216, 218
Mapped file 104, 127, 132,
  139-140, 142-149, 226, 229
Marker 68, 229
Micro-fetcher 25
Micro-stepper 25
Microcode 9, 11-12, 24, 31-35, 43,
  50, 52, 67-68, 71, 80
Microinstruction 24
Migration 111, 166, 185, 213,
  217-218, 225-226, 228,
  230, 232-233, 235,237-239
Modem 100, 113, 115, 117
MPE 10-13
MPE II 12
MPE V 114, 119, 125, 130, 207
MPE XL 103-108, 116, 119,
  139-140, 142, 146, 205

Multiplication 63

N

Network 115-118
Network database 167
NMOS III VLSI 22, 98
NMPRG 207-208, 229
NMPROG 231
NOP-type 55

O

Object Code 253
OCA (Object Code Analyzer) 252
OCT (Object Code Translator)
  106, 210, 249, 255
Opcodes (Operational Codes)
  21, 140
Operand 41-42
Operator 82, 84, 86, 108, 119,
  196
Optimization 84, 88, 208, 255

P

Packard, Dave 1, 2, 5
Packed array 150
Packed decimal 31, 53, 215
Packet 116, 118
Page 34, 56, 65, 105, 125, 129,
  140, 146, 148, 192, 201
Parity 96, 113, 115, 119
Parser 84-85
Partition 76, 129

Partition-based 50
Pascal 35, 51, 54, 59, 79, 82, 85,
     149, 198, 214, 232,
     243-244
Pascal/V 35, 214, 244
Path 96-99, 208
Path length 98
PID 146
PLABEL 68, 80
Pipeline 26, 29, 61-62
Port 115, 118, 121
Privilege level 55, 65, 106, 133
Privileged Mode 13, 41, 106, 121,
     134
Privileged files 173
Process-Dispatch Latency 111
Processor Status Word (PSW) 56
Processor 10, 49-50, 96
Protocol 115, 117

Q

Quadrant 60, 73, 142

R

RAM 11, 57-58, 67, 71
Record 130, 132
Recovery 97, 157, 164, 167,
     180, 200
Register 21, 26, 34, 42, 52, 70,
     71, 146, 241
Relational 165, 167, 256
Relational database 187
Remote 115-118
RISC 29, 33, 48, 50, 64, 67,
     79-80, 85, 87, 91, 208, 219

RJE 115, 118
RL file 205-206
ROM 11, 24, 67, 71
RS-232 117
RTM (Real Time Monitor)
     253-254

S

SEGMENTER 221, 255
Segmenter 68, 72, 205
SET ECHO 117
Shell 110
Short-mapped file 142, 145
Short-pointer 142
SHORTINT 51, 246
Shortint 215, 220
Single-precision 98, 100-101
SL 72, 208, 212, 253
SL file 206-207
SLLIC 86, 89, 208
SNA 118
SOM (Spectrum Object Module)
     72
SOM file 72-73, 86, 207-209
Spectrum 5
SPL 10, 36, 52, 54, 83, 87, 89,
     140, 147, 170, 174, 210, 218,
     220, 249, 254
SPL/3000 140, 210-211
SPL/V 140, 250
SPLINTR.PUB.SYS 241-242
SPLash! 144, 174, 209, 218-219,
     249-250, 254
Stack 9, 32, 34, 52-54, 59, 68-71,
     146, 211, 218-219, 226, 228,
     229, 249-250
Stack marker 40, 70, 79, 231
Stack operations (stackops) 41

Epilogue

Cartoon by Gail Terzi